In the Shadow of a Prophet

MERCER UNIVERSITY

MERCER UNIVERSITY PRESS

Endowed by

TOM WATSON BROWN

and

THE WATSON-BROWN FOUNDATION, INC.

IN THE SHADOW OF A PROPHET

The Legacy of Walter Rauschenbusch

Edited by

William H. Brackney

and

David P. Gushee

Foreword by Paul B. Raushenbush

MERCER UNIVERSITY PRESS
WITH
ACADIA CENTRE FOR BAPTIST AND ANABAPTIST STUDIES
2020

MUP/ P605

Published by Mercer University Press
1501 Mercer University Drive
Macon, Georgia 31207

30 29 28 27 26 25 24 23 22 21 9 8 7 6 5 4 3 2 1

Books published by Mercer University Press are printed on acid-free paper that meets the requirements of the American National Standard for Information Sciences—Permanence of Paper for Printed Library Materials.

Printed and bound in the United States.

This book is set in Adobe Garamond Pro.

Cover/jacket design by Burt&Burt.

ISBN 978-0-88146-746-8
Cataloging-in-Publication Data is available from the Library of Congress

Contents

Foreword

Paul B. Raushenbush

I bring you greetings from two Walters—my father, Walter Brandeis Raushenbush, and my son, Walter Gooch-Raushenbush. As you can already imagine, my life is surrounded by a cloud of Walters.

Just to situate myself to begin, I am the great-grandson of Walter and Pauline and the grandson of Paul, who was the third of five children. Obviously, I'm only representing my perspective. My cousins and siblings would give a different yet equally engaging talk.

So, with that in mind, I want to start with some lines from a letter written by my grandfather, Paul Raushenbush, when he was nineteen and a student at Amherst. He sent the letter to Walter on July 24th, 1918. "But I look forward still, father, to our walking and talking and working together sometime in the not too distant future, when the world steadies to its keel again. It has listed far to port for a time, but life is still worth living, and there is better time ahead, when the off-shore gust has been safely weathered."

There is tenderness and intimacy to this passage that strikes me even now as I read it. My grandfather, by the time I met him, was a powerful, intimidating, somewhat grouchy figure. Yet as a young man he reached out to his father, who was very sick with cancer, using boating metaphors—thus tapping into the shared love of the outdoors that was a hallmark of Walter's life, and would be a consistent part of my grandfather's life as well.

This short passage evokes my great-grandfather's love of the wilderness that he passed along to his children and which is infused within his prayers and writing. With these words, I am transported to the family summer home in Canada, where the sensorial experiences of the cool water on the skin, the physicality of hiking, and the challenge of boating offered an antidote to the struggle of alienation of their father, who was deaf and unable to fully communicate. The letter my grandfather sent to his father displays both a personal yearning and a social hope, joined to paint a future of possibility, to be arrived at together.

Unfortunately, Walter never read the letter from my grandfather. He died before it arrived. On July 25th, 1918, Walter's wife, Pauline, sent Walter's secretary, Dores R. Sharpe, a telegraph that read: "Walter fell asleep quietly today, his warfare is ended."

Walter was just three years older than I am now when he died. He did not have a chance to see what his children would become or to know any of his grandchildren, and certainly not his great-grandchildren. It is only recently that I considered how much his early death impacted both the public and personal legacy of Walter Rauschenbusch. We are left to imagine how his thought might have adapted to new realities after World War I, the Great Depression, and the rise of Nazi Germany, and how he might have further evolved on race and gender. We must guess how a longer life might have impacted the church and the world. Closer to home, I also wonder how another twenty or thirty years might have affected the continued emotional, intellectual, and spiritual growth of his children, who were in their teens and early twenties when he died.

Recently I discovered a small manila envelope that contained several lapel pins from my grandfather's youth, including a debating pin from Rochester East High School, a fraternity pin from Amherst, and a Phi Beta Kappa key from 1920. There is also a pin from Grandpa Paul's brief domestic military service in WWI, plus an Intercollegiate Socialist Society pin. Noticeably absent from this collection or any other memorabilia from my grandfather is an acknowledgement of religion.

After seven generations of preachers, my grandfather and his siblings broke with tradition and failed to provide a family member to the clergy profession, and all their children followed suit. Not only did they not provide professional Christian leadership, most of them displayed little to no interest in the church.

What can you say? Typical preacher kids. Yet the religious break of Rauschenbusch's descendants invites an important question. Might we consider the path my grandfather's and father's generation took as a parallel track that leads to the same location as their father? Or, because they did not adopt the Christian worldview and language, are they to be viewed as veering irredeemably out of the fold?

For better or worse, the religious choices my Grandpa Paul made were part of a wider effort to winnow his life down to essential concerns. Not only did he shed his father's faith, but he also, along with his two brothers, dropped the "c's" from the family name. As his older brother, Hilmar, changed his name to Steve, Paul changed his middle name from August, the name of his grandfather, to Arthur, and then to the singular initial "A." Which seems a bit like Madonna or Cher—which I kind of love.

Still, Grandpa Paul's professional career, and the career of his siblings, could be viewed as a continuation of Walter's work. After Amherst, Paul entered graduate school in the economics department at the University of Wisconsin, which was known for the Wisconsin Idea—UW became one of the great progressive laboratories for how a university might become a conduit of a better life for citizens. There he studied with the great economist John R. Commons, who wrote a book called *Social Reform and the Church* in 1894, well before Rauschenbusch's major contributions. Also at Wisconsin was Richard Ely, who wrote the book *The Social Aspects of Christianity* and was founding secretary of both the Christian Social Union and the American Economics Association. Ely was a major influence on Walter Rauschenbusch.

At Wisconsin, my grandfather met Elizabeth Brandeis, the daughter of Supreme Court Justice Louis Brandeis. Elizabeth had come to Wisconsin to study law and economics and the couple met in a Torts class. They married and for their honeymoon spent a month paddling in the boundary waters of Canada, not far from where Walter's family had spent the summers. In Wisconsin, my Grandma E. B. and Grandpa Paul created the nation's first unemployment compensation law, one of the most important pieces of economic legislation of the twentieth century, which saved millions of people from poverty during periods of unemployment.

Surrounded by visionaries at Wisconsin who had their roots in Christian social policy, Walter's son, my grandfather, moved society just one step closer to what Social Gospelers might call the kingdom of God on earth. Did he view it in those terms? Assuredly not. But when we Christians intone "thy kingdom come on earth" and we believe that the building blocks of the new heaven on earth are justice, equity, and love, might we be open to the idea that the foundations of that new world might be constructed by unlikely sources?

One other notable feature of Walter's children is that two of them, my grandfather Paul and Carl, the youngest, married Jewish women. Carl, who was also an economist, married Esther, who, as Esther Raushenbush, went on to become the first woman president of Sarah Lawrence College and a pioneer in education. It feels to me that this is also part of Walter's legacy. For all of his writings about Christianizing the social order, I feel absolutely certain that anti-Semitism was not a feature of Walter's household, and my grandmother was always loved and accepted by her mother-in-law.

My father was raised by an interfaith couple, neither of whom were interested in the tenets or rituals of their respective faiths, although perhaps they were influenced by the moral imperatives within their traditions. The Unitarian Church in Madison had attracted both of them with its focus on spirituality and justice, and when it came time to offer religious instruction for their child, they did what many interfaith couples did and shipped their kid off to the Unitarian Church. Yet that didn't stick with my dad.

Which brings me back to the fact of Walter Rauschenbusch's early death. My father spent summers for most of his boyhood with his maternal grandfather, Louis Brandeis, at a family summer home in Chatham, Massachusetts. While my father did visit his grandmother—Walter's widow, Pauline—he has no sense of his grandfather Walter. My dad sat around the table listening and learning from Louis Brandeis. For this reason, I was sure that Walter was much older than Louis, when in fact he was younger. Yet my father had no exposure to him, and I can't help but think that might have made a difference in the family's perspective on Walter.

I once asked my father if he had ever had a personal religious experience, and he said that when he saw my mother standing under the Eiffel Tower in Paris on their third date he knew he wanted to marry her. And he did. My mother, who was a committed Presbyterian at that time, brought us up in the church. So, my religious development is not because of my father's family, but because of my mother. I certainly was aware of Walter Rauschenbusch growing up, but my understanding of him was limited, and my exposure was largely to his prayers that we occasionally read as grace at the table.

That's not to say that my father, like his father, did not have the progressive fire in him. As a law professor, he delivered a speech at churches in Madison in 1960 called "Dare We Be Christian," in which he argued for the rightness of fair housing legislation. Yet when I asked my father recently if he viewed his life's work under the lens of the Social Gospel, he demurred.

I was brought up in the church, and while not a pious young man—I'm pretty sure I am the only person in the history of the Presbyterian church to fail confirmation—I was interested in religion. I ended up majoring in religion in college, primarily so that I would not be expected to have a job after I graduated.

I spent the years after college as a DJ and starting a record company in Barcelona, Spain. I came back to the States and admitted to myself that I had an addiction problem. I spent a year in treatment—first in a hospital, then in a halfway house in Boston. It was in recovery that I began to pray again, and the main prayer used in recovery is the Lord's Prayer, so several times a day I would pray "thy kingdom come, thy will be done, on Earth as in heaven."

I had the kind of spiritual awakening that echoes the experience of my great-grandfather as a young man. I had always known there was a social ethic within the faith, but in recovery I was awakened to the personal Gospel and a sense of an intimate relationship with God. When I moved to New York, I was invited by one of Stephen's sons, Carl Baldwin, and his wife, Mary Ellen, to attend Judson Memorial Church in the Village, where I began to attend church of my own volition for the first time in my life. (The moral of that story is that it is okay to invite people to your church.) Further inquiry led me to seminary, which is where I read Rauschenbusch's major works for the first time.

It was a powerful feeling of recognition. I felt and continue to feel a kinship. His writings resonated with me, in the humor, the passion, the illustration, and the vision of justice that seared my imagination. And I appreciated his critique of that which turned him off from religion in his time, much of which continues to this day. At seminary, I served a small Baptist church that welcomed the poor and the outcast and the foreigner, and I felt called to give my life to this vocation, the first family member to enter the ministry since my great-grandfather.

When my ordination ceremony was being planned, I sent invitations to every member of the small Rauschenbusch clan, which included my father's first cousin Richard (Dick) Rorty, a well-known philosopher who was by then teaching at Stanford. Rorty had been very close to my grandparents, often visiting them in Madison when he was a student at Chicago. But while my father and Dick had spent time together as kids, they were not close. Dick was somewhat famous for his secular humanism. I sent him the invitation but figured he probably didn't make it a habit to attend ordinations, and I did not expect a response. But one day, he called to offer me an ordination gift—Walter Rauschenbusch's couch and chair that had been passed down to him through his mother, Winifred. Winifred was Walter's eldest daughter. She was a sociologist, writer, and activist, whose remarkable story will have to be saved for another time.

A couple months after my ordination I went to pick up the furniture and struck up a friendship with Dick, who much to my delight agreed to write the afterword to the hundredth anniversary edition of *Christianity and the Social Crisis* that I edited in 2008. I called him at one point to check on his progress and he informed me that he had cancer with just a few months to live. Yet he did write the afterword and told me how much he appreciated the opportunity to revisit his grandfather Walter's work.

The afterword was one of the last things Rorty wrote, and in it he wistfully wonders what our world would have been like had the church decided to follow Walter Rauschenbusch's vision set out in *Christianity and the Social Crisis*, lamenting our bad luck that on the whole, it had not.

Our luck may have been bad, but nothing has been lost. Instead of locking Walter Rauschenbusch into an academic, social, or ecclesial framework, I prefer to think of him as one spark in a divine fire that burns for justice, equality, and peace, and that shows up in all kinds of messengers, none of them perfect. Some, like me, continue to find resonance in the Christian faith that Walter Rauschenbusch practiced and share much of the spiritual experience and the language of the vision he laid before us. Others, including my own siblings and cousins, are working towards a vision of the kingdom of God, or Beloved Community, or reign of peace, but are using other language for this destination, finding inspiration from other sources.

As we consider the legacy of Walter Rauschenbusch, one question I ask is whether my siblings and I belong to one another. Do my Jewish cousins, who are doing powerful work for good, fit into the underlying hope of Rauschenbusch's Social Gospel? And what about me—a gay, married man with a child named after my father and great-grandfather. I am not, perhaps, what my great-grandfather had in mind when he considered the future of his familial or Christian legacy. But can my life, my family, be seen as a some kind of expression of his vision?

In any case, here I am. After serving at the Riverside Church, the Princeton University Chapel, and as founding religion editor at *The Huffington Post*, I now serve as senior vice president at Auburn Seminary, where we are helping to build the multi-faith movement for justice. We work with people of all different faith traditions and with people with no formal religion but who have a shared spiritual imperative towards justice. I personally understand our work as an iteration of the Social Gospel, which, as Rauschenbusch insisted, was simply the Gospel. Yet I certainly don't expect my colleagues from the multi-faith movement, or my siblings, or anyone, to define themselves and their work using my terms or the terms of my great-grandfather.

Yet I proudly claim Walter Rauschenbusch, flaws and all, as my ancestor, and I commend him to all of you and any who would keep his memory alive.

In speaking with my father recently I learned a piece of parental advice that Walter Rauschenbusch gave to my Grandpa Paul, who then passed it down to my father. It was a simple phrase, an admonition to develop a "focus of mind."

This seems to me a very Germanic gift from one generation to the next, and indeed all my father's and grandfather's generations did exercise a focus of mind.

The best way I know to honor Walter Rauschenbusch is to extend a radical invitation to as wide a group as possible to have a focus of mind, a focus of heart, and a focus of spirit on the urgent needs of our time, which are crying out for witness and remedy. Let us focus our hearts so that they might break open and repent of oppressions that continue to plague our nation, particularly the sin of white supremacism and systematic racism. Let us focus our minds to envision a world of collective justice, governed by an economy of generosity. Let us focus our spirits so that we might be enlivened by an eternal ethic of love, experienced even now with a song and a dance of joy.

Let us participate in the great collective work of our time the way my great-grandfather did, as best he could, in his time. As he reminded us once: "In a few years all our restless and angry hearts will be quiet in death, but those who come after us will live in the world which our sins have blighted or which our love of right has redeemed."

Introduction

William H. Brackney and David P. Gushee

This volume contains the papers presented at an international conference, "The Legacy of Walter Rauschenbusch," held at Mercer University, April 9–11, 2018. The conference marked the centenary of the death of Walter Rauschenbusch in July 1918 and his enduring contribution to many fields and thinkers. Fifteen international scholars interacted with well over a hundred attendees in a rich environment of hospitality on the Cecil B. Day Campus in Atlanta, Georgia. The conference was convened by the Mercer University Center for Theology and Public Life, the American Baptist Historical Society, and the Acadia University Centre for Baptist and Anabaptist Studies.

Our intent was to plumb anew the depths of Rauschenbusch's multifaceted contribution to social ethics, historical theology, economics and political theory, and social activism. In his era, he upended established canons of biblical interpretation, theological orthodoxy, and prevailing theories of social structure and class. He was influenced by German, Italian, English, Scottish, French, Canadian, and American writers. His work—in his generation and later—reached Europe, Africa, Asia, and the Americas. Macroeconomic and social policies were developed on the basis of his contributions, and he became an iconic figure among social theorists and theologians of all stripes, especially in Germany, Canada, and the United States.

We include here four sections of essays, in this order:

OVERALL ASPECTS OF THE RAUSCHENBUSCH LEGACY

In the context of his own pilgrimage, Gary Dorrien, in "Walter Rauschenbusch as I See Him," traces the development of the Black Social Gospel as a major outcome of Rauschenbusch's work. Dorrien presents a balanced assessment of both Walter Rauschenbusch and the Social Gospel. In "Walter Rauschenbusch: The Soul of the Social Gospel," Christopher Evans again revisits his assessment of Rauschenbusch and suggests that Rauschenbusch's role as a pastor was critical, opening insights into Walter's personality. In the end, Evans believes Walter Rauschenbusch has been vindicated among his critics.

THE EXTENT OF THE RAUSCHENBUSCH LEGACY

The influence of Rauschenbusch extended very widely. Andrea Strübind, in "The Reality of Hope: Walter Rauschenbusch's Theology in German Context," explores the numerous German thinkers and institutions that Walter interacted with, without which he cannot be properly understood. She points out his full adoption of higher critical scholarship and his heavy dependence upon Adolf von Harnack. Adam Bond rediscovers, in his essay "Everybody Is God's Somebody: Samuel Dewitt Proctor and the Black Social Gospel," a major second-generation thinker in the Black Social Gospel tradition, Samuel Dewitt Proctor, and demonstrates Proctor's affinities with Rauschenbusch. Roger Prentice, in "The Impact of Walter Rauschenbusch in Canada," details the significant influence of Rauschenbusch from the growth of Social Gospel consciousness in institutions to the work of Tommy Douglas, the political creator of National Health Care in Canada. Chakravarthy Zadda, in his essay "The Social Gospel in the Orient: The Story of the Telugu Church," informs us of the Rauschenbusch legacy in India, where his sister Emma and spouse, John E. Clough, brought about a new understanding of mission by applying principles of the Social Gospel.

SPECIFIC ASPECTS OF THE RAUSCHENBUSCH LEGACY

Wendy Deichmann's "Walter Rauschenbusch, Gender, Family, and the Social Gospel" examines Rauschenbusch's understanding of the changing role of women in society, giving attention to Rauschenbusch's own family situation and how a dichotomy opened between his public views and his family relations. Darryl Trimiew, in "The Significance of Walter Rauschenbusch to the Black Churches," suggests that Rauschenbusch did not have a noticeable direct impact on black churches. Rather, Trimiew points out that Martin Luther King Jr., who was influenced by Rauschenbusch, was highly influential in the black community in emphasizing the struggle for a "Beloved Community." In "Walter Rauschenbusch's Theology of the Cross: A Postcolonial Reflection," Dominik Gautier, a German theologian, offers a careful examination of Rauschenbusch's precise the theology of cross and considers it in a postcolonial German context. And Christina Littlefield, in her study "Sowing Seeds: How Walter Rauschenbusch's Failed Newspaper *For the Right* Germinated His Later Muckraking Work," takes on Rauschenbusch in the Progressive Era role of a "muckraker," carefully analyzing his work in journalism and particularly the newspaper he helped to start.

THE LARGENESS OF THE RAUSCHENBUSCH LEGACY

Heath Carter's essay, "'Social Christianity's Greatest Prophet'? Walter Rauschenbusch's Place in History," recovers Rauschenbusch's overall rise and fall among American historians, along with the rise and fall of attention to the Social Gospel. Carter concludes that Rauschenbusch's emphasis upon love has profoundly influenced the response to contemporary social questions. David Gushee offers an insightful assessment of Rauschenbusch's ethics, bringing Rauschenbusch into dialogue with Miguel De La Torre. In the end, Gushee points out the difficulties that a kingdom of God ethics presents. William Brackney underscores Rauschenbusch's contribution to his own tradition, citing his education and formation, his literary and theological contributions as a Baptist, his creation of a "basileic theology," and his ongoing and broadening reception in the Baptist communities, liberal and evangelical alike.

A capstone of our conference experience was the autobiographical reflection of Paul B. Raushenbush, Walter's great-grandson, included here as a foreword.

Overall, our assessment is that Walter Rauschenbusch very much continues to be a thinker worth contemporary engagement. While some of his constructs and illustrations feel archaic, clearly captive to the particular spirit of the early decades of the twentieth century, the following contributions are among those that endure:

- Modeling close and detailed Christian attention to economic injustice and the quest for economic democracy
- Making Christian social justice concerns a central part of Christian mission and discipleship
- Laying the foundations for the modern discipline of Christian social ethics
- Demonstrating the personal courage to speak against structural and systemic evils
- Codifying a theological foundation for the Social Gospel
- Integrating social justice commitments with personal piety and devotion
- Personifying, like none other, the soul of the Social Gospel

As Reinhold Niebuhr put it, "Rauschenbusch was, after all, the real founder of social Christianity in this country, and its most brilliant and general satisfying exponent."

We are grateful to the family of Glen H. Stassen and to the Acadia Divinity College for generous grants that underwrote the expenses of the conference. Likewise, Dr. Marc Jolley of Mercer University Press has been a supportive editor for both the three-volume set, *Walter Rauschenbusch: Published Works and Selected Writings* (2018), and this volume.

William H. Brackney
David P. Gushee

Part I

Overall Aspects of the Rauschenbusch Legacy

Chapter 1

How I See Walter Rauschenbusch

Gary Dorrien

I am grateful for the invitation to this conference and for phrasing my topic in such a personal fashion, because I don't know who I would be without Martin Luther King Jr. and Walter Rauschenbusch. I believe that the Black Social Gospel has the greatest legacy of any religious tradition in US American history, the White Social Gospel is not far behind it, and both of these traditions at their best were Christian democratic socialist as exemplified by King and Rauschenbusch.

I grew up in a poor, semi-rural, nominally Catholic family in mid-Michigan, Bay County. My parents moved there after growing up in similarly poor areas of Michigan's Upper Peninsula, where my father took abuse for his Cree heritage. At the age of twenty he acquired passably white status by moving to mid-Michigan. When he looked in the mirror, he saw an inferior caste, so the most loving thing he could imagine as a parent was to claim for his children all the white privilege he could get. Today my father is proudly, even aggressively, Native American, and I appreciate the changes in American society that made it possible for him to reclaim his racial identity. It would not have happened without the civil rights movement. But I am a child of the white working class, having never experienced or claimed any other racial identity, and this nation has never had a breakthrough for racial justice that did not set off a mighty backlash from my group. We are in one now.

In my youth, I got to church occasionally, sometimes hitching a ride with neighbors—just enough to be caught by the figure of the crucified Jesus. This God-figure, who responded to evil with self-sacrificing love, provided a religious ideal, a sign of transcendence that broke through my everyday horizon of lower-class culture and the next game. Then the stunning witness of the civil rights movement similarly broke through, eventually melding in my thought and feeling with the cross of Christ.

I came of age in the climactic years of the movement. The Selma demonstration made a searing impression on me. My teachers described America as the world's greatest nation in every way that mattered and the greatest ever, but the civil rights movement taught a very different lesson. King became the formative figure for me before I understood much of anything about politics or religion. Then King was assassinated, and he became not merely the leader of a justice movement, but also a martyred leader. He was a Jesus figure who died for us, the exemplar of the peacemaking and justice-making way of Jesus.

At Alma College, I had four professors who indulged and guided my autodidactic temperament. Philosopher Wesley Dykstra inspired me to study Aristotle and Kant; physicist Louis Toller persuaded me that nothing on earth is more wondrous than light theory; sociologist Dave Lemmon launched me on social theory and political economics; and theologian Ronald Massanari introduced me to Karl Barth and Paul Tillich. Ron was fresh out of graduate school and taking leave of Christianity. He said that Barth was the towering "neoorthodox" theologian who destroyed the previously dominant liberal theology, and Tillich was part of the anti-liberal ascendancy that took over theology in the 1920s, which was confusing, since Tillich seemed robustly liberal to me.

Liberal theology, according to my religion professors and everyone I read, was long dead and refuted. Adolf von Harnack was the quintessential liberal theologian and readily dismissed. The last significant liberal theologian was Rauschenbusch, who died in 1918 and only mattered because of his social activism, not his theology. It would be hard to exaggerate the force of these conventions when I began reading theologians. The canon consisted of the so-called "neoorthodox" titans who killed liberal theology: Barth, Tillich, Emil Brunner, Rudolf Bultmann, and Reinhold Niebuhr. Their protégés held the prestige chairs in theology, and it was hard to say where theology was going. Young Jürgen Moltmann and young Johannes Metz made an early breakthrough by calling for a political theology of hope and eschatology. The founding texts of black, feminist, and Latin American liberation theology were published during my college years, and I read all of them, believing that liberation theology was the next great movement in theology.

The new theologies were emphatically political, radiating convictions about justice and liberation. But two questions gnawed at me: Would liberation theology ever get a hearing in the churches? And if the new theologies were about justice, why were they so vague and thin about economics? Meanwhile, neoorthodox theologians said almost nothing about economic justice. I was soaked in Karl Polanyi, Karl Marx, and Gunnar Myrdal—political economists who were not vague or thin. The contrast made me skittish about theology. I didn't belong to a church, so there was nothing holding me to theology, except Jesus crucified and the influence of King. I might have lost my way in this ambivalence had it not been for one book: *Christianity and the Social Crisis* by Walter Rauschenbusch.

Rauschenbusch described the teaching of Jesus as a message of radical social transformation. He argued that Christianity obscured the revolutionary spirit of the Gospel, but it was not too late for the church to adopt the way and spirit of Jesus. The church is supposed to be a new kind of community that transforms the world by the power of Christ's kingdom-bringing spirit. The idea of the indwelling and growing commonwealth of God is not merely part of Christianity; it's the central thing holding everything else together. Christianity is a kingdom movement that carries God into everything you do. In a chapter titled "What to Do," Rauschenbusch made a scintillating case for democratic Socialism.

Rauschenbusch's Gospel-centered liberal theology and radical politics were equally compelling to me. I turned the pages exclaiming that this was what Christianity should sound like. For years I had felt that King laid hold of something in Christianity that the rest of the church somehow missed—something that inspired movement idealism and a real surge for social change. Rauschenbusch explained what was missing, and he expressed brilliantly the vision of a socially regenerative Christianity.

The books that I read about the Social Gospel said it was an idealistic understanding of Christianity that briefly influenced liberal Protestantism before it was discredited by the neoorthodox reaction, especially Barth and Niebuhr. Reading Rauschenbusch, I could see various problems. He loved idealistic rhetoric, said almost nothing about racism, and was proudly, stridently, vehemently anti-Catholic. But for grasping and expressing the prophetic core of the Gospel, Rauschenbusch soared above everyone except King. I read all his books in succession, treasuring all of them. One of them surpassed all the others in my view—*Christianizing the Social Order*, a brilliant, passionate, detailed argument for economic democracy published in the bellwether year of 1912.

I was caught by the story of Rauschenbusch's struggle with his father, August Rauschenbusch, a powerful, accomplished, headstrong educator and former German Lutheran missionary who converted to the Baptist faith in the US. August Rauschenbusch bullied his young wife and wounded his children during his long career as head of the German Department at Rochester Seminary. Walter Rauschenbusch admired his father, but Walter was sensitive, kindly, and loving. My introduction to the Progressive Era occurred through Rauschenbusch: the rising prestige of democracy as a social ideal; the struggles over Darwinism and biblical criticism in American Protestant churches; the variety of Socialist and reform ideologies within the Progressive movement; a major character named Henry George; and the founding of the ecumenical movement.

The Social Gospel happened for a confluence of reasons that impacted each other. In white churches, it grew out of the abolitionist movement, the home missions movement, the Progressive reform movements of the Gilded Age, the labor movement, and the example of Christian Socialism in England. In black churches, it grew out of the abolitionist movement, the crisis and abandonment of Reconstruction, and the necessity of a terrible question: What is abolitionism now? Now that the fourteenth and fifteenth amendments are being scuttled and a plague of white terrorism has descended upon black Americans, what should a "new abolitionism" be?[1]

One factor, above all others, caused Washington Gladden and Richard Ely to found the original Social Gospel organizations. Labor leaders condemned the churches for doing nothing for poor and working-class people. The founders of the American Social Gospel realized that this accusation was true. It was pointless to defend Christianity if the churches took an indefensible attitude toward the poor and vulnerable. In Germany, the established churches were alien to the working class, social democracy was the enemy, and most of the unions were Socialist. In the United States, the gap between the churches and the working class was not as steep; at least, Gladden and Ely thought so. In the American Social Gospel, society became a subject of redemption. Social justice became intrinsic to salvation. If there was such a thing as social structure, redemption had to be reconceptualized to take account of it; salvation had to be personal *and* social to be saving.[2]

---

[1] On the Black Social Gospel, see Gary Dorrien, *The New Abolition: W. E. B. Du Bois and the Black Social Gospel* (New Haven, CT: Yale University Press, 2015); Dorrien, *Breaking White Supremacy: Martin Luther King Jr. and the Black Social Gospel* (New Haven, CT: Yale University Press, 2018).

[2] For detailed renderings of these arguments, see Gary Dorrien, *Soul in Society: The Making of American Social Christianity* (Minneapolis, MN: Fortress Press, 1993); Dorrien, *The Making of American Liberal Theology: Imagining Progressive Religion, 1805–1900* (Louisville, KY: Westminster John Knox Press, 2001); Dorrien, *The Making of American Liberal Theology: Idealism, Realism, and Modernity, 1900–1950* (Louisville, KY: Westminster John Knox Press, 2003); and Dorrien,

I loved the story of Rauschenbusch beginning his ministry in Hell's Kitchen in New York City, confronting the social problem in his hurting immigrant congregation, and joining Henry George's mayoral campaign of 1886. In England, the Social Gospel was called Christian Socialism, it was predominantly Anglican and theologically Anglo-Catholic, it had only a tiny smattering of liberal Protestants, and trade unionism was a non-factor until the mid-1890s. In the United States, the founders were liberal Protestant ministers allied with the movement for liberal theology—something that made no sense at all to the leaders of British Christian Socialism. Three things that these movements had in common, however, were a defining commitment to producer and consumer cooperatives, a vague aspiration to support a fledgling labor movement, and the Henry George phenomenon.

Henry George was a high school dropout who had a Damascus-road conversion at the age of thirty. Walking the streets of New York in 1869, he was overwhelmed by the contrast between the wealth of the rich and the degradation of the poor. He vowed to devote his life to reforming the system that produced such extremes of wealth and poverty. Ten years later, in *Progress and Poverty,* he argued that land ownership is the root of all social evil. As long as land values increase, those who work the land are forced to pay more for the right to work.

George had nothing against neoclassical economics. He accepted that economics is a deductive science expounding laws of nature, and he regarded David Ricardo's law of rent as a divine law of nature. George was against monopoly, not capitalism. He argued that the value of land varies with demand and that charging rent for the mere possession of land—something that cannot be reproduced—is unjust. Deriving earnings from the application of labor or capital is legitimate, but extracting wealth as rent is not. Rent unjustly charges producers for the right to produce. It is a toll levied by monopoly, expropriating wealth for mere possession that performs no useful function.

As George saw it, God created the land for everyone, and society creates the increment in the value of land. Therefore, the increment should go to society. George did not want the state to buy the land, since landlords did not deserve any compensation except for whatever capital improvements

---

Social Ethics in the Making: Interpreting an American Tradition (Oxford: Wiley-Blackwell, 2009).

they made. Neither did he want the state to nationalize the land, since he was not a Socialist. The answer was to impose a "single tax" on the increment of land values, appropriating the unearned value. Sufficiently taxing the land was the key to creating a good society. If landowners persisted in calling it their land, let them. What mattered was to confiscate the rent, not to reclaim the land.

Henry George's book electrified an enormous reading public as soon as it was published in the United States in 1879, and in England the following year. In a few years, it sold seven million copies in ten languages, an astounding achievement for a 420-page tome on economics. George implored that abolishing land oppression would change everything. The single tax would free up land held for speculation, stimulate construction, create new housing and jobs, drive down rent, and fund government programs for the needy. In the 1880s he visited Britain six times, conducted extensive lecture tours, and was arrested twice in Ireland for campaigning for land reform. George influenced every Socialist and Christian Socialist leader in Britain, even as they chided him for going halfway, and some confused the public by describing George as an advocate of land nationalization.[3]

His simplicity was crucial to his impact. The single tax did not make heroic demands on the political system or require sweeping transformations of human consciousness. It did not rest on a theory or strategy of class war. All it needed was movement advocacy and a few good electoral outcomes. George said so vibrantly, quoting the Bible on land reform and lifting the yoke. In 1886, that sounded very good to Rauschenbusch, just as Social Gospel leaders began to say that cooperatives and a land tax might not be enough because corporate capitalism was changing the game.

Washington Gladden and Richard Ely spent the entire 1880s urging that profit sharing, worker ownership, and land reform were the answer to the class struggle and the challenge of Social Darwinism. All are commanded to love their neighbors as themselves, so employers and employees should practice cooperation, and society should be organized to serve human welfare. Economics is not a science about an economic state of nature, it should not espouse unchangeable concepts, and a good society manages economic outcomes by safeguarding the common good. Ely and Gladden wrote and

---

[3] On European Socialism and Christian Socialism, see Gary Dorrien, *Imagining Democratic Socialism: Political Theology, Marxism, and Social Democracy* (New Haven, CT: Yale University Press, 2019).

organized with a sense of urgency, imploring that Gilded Age capitalism was a crisis for American Christianity. They founded the American Economic Association in 1885 to oppose Social Darwinism in American society and the emerging social sciences. Social Darwinism justified selfishness, bonded readily with economic orthodoxy, and justified cruel policies of neglect and weeding out, and its growing popularity in American culture was morally toxic for American society. Every Social Gospel organization made this argument, while Ely and Gladden struggled to say exactly where Darwinian science veered into something toxic.

I admire these Social Gospel founders for opposing Herbert Spencer, Ernst Haeckel, William Graham Sumner, and other eminent Social Darwinists despite being outgunned intellectually. The founders knew that nobody on their side had comparable intellectual authority, and this was during the period when they had to persuade the churches not to oppose Darwinian evolution. They insisted that Spencer's commanding mechanistic system must be wrong at some point. They didn't know where to draw the line or how to refute Spencer; they only knew that Social Darwinism was morally a nonstarter. In the 1880s Ely defended the labor movement against a flood of hostility while Gladden stressed his good intentions. In the 1890s Ely wilted from the political battle and Gladden got more radical, explaining that the class struggle was more violent and predatory than ever, so he had no choice. The Social Gospel had to at least defend the labor movement. State Socialism, Gladden said, would be a terrible mistake, but things were so bad for workers that even the bad kind of Socialism was tempting.

Rauschenbusch entered this story just as it turned Socialist and made George Herron briefly famous. Rauschenbusch later recalled that when he came to New York he had no concept of Social Christianity or social anything. His searing encounter with urban poverty, especially the funerals that he performed for children, drove him to social activism. Politics became unavoidable. If people suffer because of politics and economics, the church has to deal with politics and economics. He joined the George campaign, studied Ely's books on political economy, and befriended a local Baptist minister on a similar journey, Leighton Williams. They founded a cheeky, aggressive, sometimes maudlin Christian Socialist newspaper, and Rauschenbusch began to think about writing books.

He later recalled that during his early ministry he had six books in his head: five were scholarly, one was dangerous. Three times he tried to write the dangerous one but had to put it aside, and each time he came back to it, he had outgrown the manuscript and had to start over. Rauschenbusch had turned theologically liberal during seminary—accepting biblical criticism and rejecting forensic atonement theory. In his early ministry, he followed the development of Ritschlian School theology in Germany, reading Albrecht Ritschl and Adolf von Harnack, though his radical Socialism put him far to the left of them. In 1891 Rauschenbusch decided, with deep sadness, that he had to resign from the ministry because he was going deaf. A surf-like roar in his ears made it difficult to do pastoral tasks; he called it "physical loneliness." His father had retired from Rochester, and the seminary invited Walter to come home, but he doubted that teaching would work any better than ministry for a deaf person. Meanwhile, August Rauschenbusch gave himself a retirement present by depositing his wife with Walter, an arrangement that lasted two years. Finally, Rauschenbusch decided to resign from the ministry, go abroad for a year, write the "dangerous" book, and launch a literary career. His congregation insisted, instead, on a paid sabbatical, which he took in England and Germany.

In England, he liked what Christian Socialists were doing but was repulsed by Anglo-Catholicism; thus, he stopped writing nice things about British Christian Socialism. In Germany, he labored on a book titled "Christianity Revolutionary," which argued that Christianity should be essentially revolutionary, in the manner of Jesus. Rauschenbusch later romanticized this part of his story, claiming that he fixed on the kingdom of God only after he had an epiphany in Germany. In truth, he emphasized the kingdom of God before he took his sabbatical, whatever his epiphany may have added to it, and his radically activist idea of the kingdom was emphatically in the mode of the American Social Gospel, not German Ritschlianism. Rauschenbusch was a Ritschlian theologian inasmuch as he absorbed Ritschl and Harnack on the Hellenization of Christian doctrine, the social-ethical character of Christianity, and the challenge of historicism to theology. But he took Ritschlian theology in a direction that no prominent German Ritschlian wanted to go.

The Ritschlian school taught that Christianity is essentially a Jesus movement focused on the kingdom of God, not a structure of Hellenistic doctrine. Christianity is irreducibly historical and social-ethical. Eternal life is the goal of individual existence and the kingdom of God is the goal of humanity. This school of thought dominated German theology for four reasons. It solved the problem of historicism, it accepted the Kantian divide between science and religion, it focused on the person and kingdom language of Jesus, and it provided a theological basis for Culture Protestantism, the civil religion of the German state.

Until Ritschl emerged in the 1870s, every school of modern German theology claimed to reconcile theology with historical criticism, and none of them actually did. Every form of modern theology was a strategy to minimize or circumvent the consequences of historical criticism. Ritschl said this defensive posture was a loser for theology. Theologians needed to make theology explicitly historicist by recovering the historical Jesus and the faith of the early church. At the same time, they needed to be good Germans—patriotic, nationalist, pro-military, supportive of the state church and the German welfare state, and opposed to Social Democracy.

Rauschenbusch was acutely aware of all these factors. On historicism and the social-ethical Jesus, he was fully a Ritschlian, albeit in the fashion of the American Social Gospel. In Germany, the Ritschlian school emphasized Luther's doctrine of justification by faith, applied it to every theological topic, and stressed that faith is an insider perspective; you have to be Christian to understand Christianity. The Americans that adopted Ritschlian theology played down the Lutheran tropes. William Adams Brown and Arthur C. McGiffert got their Ritschlian theology straight from Harnack at Berlin, brought it to Union Theological Seminary, and fashioned the Social Gospel as an alternative to insider insularity. The American Social Gospel was pragmatic, activist, and ecumenical, with a Socialist flank that Rauschenbusch joined.

Writing "Christianity Revolutionary," Rauschenbusch vowed to fix on one thing, the kingdom of God, in the manner of Jesus. Jesus proclaimed a postmillennial idea of the coming reign of God, and the church is supposed to transform the world by the power of Christ's spirit. Rauschenbusch later recalled: "Here was a religious conception that embraced it all. Here was something so big that absolutely nothing that interested me was excluded from it.... It carries God into everything that you do." The kingdom of God includes the heavenly realm, the presence of God in the soul, the church as the body of Christ, the divine commonwealth on earth, and the promise of an eschatological end of history. Rauschenbusch stressed that this idea is beautiful, comprehensive, filled with justice-making ethical content, *and* evangelical: "You have the authority of the Lord Jesus in it."[4]

---

[4] Walter Rauschenbusch, "The Kingdom of God," Cleveland YMCA Lecture, 1913, in *The Social Gospel in America: 1870–1920*, ed. Robert T. Handy (New

But the book never quite came together, Rauschenbusch returned to his congregation in New York, and he married a schoolteacher, Pauline, who helped him cope with his worsening deafness. They made pastoral calls together, expressions of love and affection passed easily between them, and their marriage was a sustained love affair, one that pulled him out of his depressive spiral. The next time that Rochester Seminary called, in 1897, Rauschenbusch felt he was ready for an academic career, carrying on his father's work, which he did for five years, teaching English and American literature, physiology, physics, civil government, political economy, astronomy, zoology, and New Testament, all in German, in addition to raising money for the German Department.

Too many books on Rauschenbusch have rushed past the Germany factor, sometimes in embarrassment. The cliché about Rauschenbusch is that he was hopelessly idealistic. Yet he did not find his courage against racism and militarism until his later life; he could never conceive his beloved American nation as an empire; he gave special permission to German nationalism; and his feminism was tepid, late Victorian, and highly selective.

On imperialism and cultural racism, Rauschenbusch knew what the real thing looked like, because he knew the British Christian Socialists. They were staunchly anti-imperialist and anti-racist. England had Fabian Socialists who sang for nationalism, imperialism, and even eugenics, but Christian Socialist leaders were adamantly opposed, including Charles Marson, Stewart Headlam, Thomas Hancock, Scott Holland, Charles Gore, Maurice Reckett, John Clifford, S. G. Hobson, many others. In Rauschenbusch's early career, he opposed racism and immigration restrictions and he believed that anti-imperialism in England was a very good thing. But he made allowances for the two nations that he loved. American imperialism was not imperialist, Germany should not be blamed for catching up to England, and America needed more Germans.

In 1895, two years before he returned to Rochester, he wrote a racist fundraising letter for the German Department: "Are the whites of this continent so sure of their possession against the blacks of the South and the seething yellow flocks beyond the Pacific that they need no reinforcement

---

York: Oxford University Press, 1966) 267; Rauschenbusch, *The Righteousness of the Kingdom*, ed. Max L. Stackhouse (Lewiston, NY: Edwin Mellen Press, 1999) 79–116; Rauschenbusch, "A Conquering Idea," (1892), in *Walter Rauschenbusch: Selected Writings*, ed. Winthrop S. Hudson (New York: Paulist Press, 1984), 71–74.

of men of their own blood while yet it is time?" Two years later he wrote a similar letter, now as a faculty colleague, and in 1902 Rauschenbusch stood before a commencement assembly and said it aggressively: Germans were first cousins of the British Anglo-Saxons, they helped to build modern democracy, and they deserved to be included in Manifest Destiny. It was shortsighted to give British Anglo-Saxons exclusive credit for civilization. Modern democracy was created by a single Teutonic racial stock, an achievement imperiled by what he called "alien strains" arriving from places like France, Spain, the Slavic lands, Bohemia, Poland, and the Russian Jewish territories.[5]

That was a frightening spectacle to the conscience of American Protestantism. For five years Rauschenbusch poured himself out for a German-American community that was utterly hostile to the Social Gospel. In 1898 there was a flank of the Social Gospel that opposed the Spanish-American War and America's imperial frenzy in Puerto Rico and the Philippines, but Rauschenbusch cheered for all of it as a triumph for Protestant civilization and democracy. Finally, in 1902, the seminary's position in church history opened up, which is why the greatest works of the Social Gospel have a strong historical bent.

He still wanted to write that big, dangerous book, so he went back to his sprawling manuscript to see what he could salvage from it. He found a few things, especially the starting point: Jesus and his kingdom. That was the basis for *Christianity and the Social Crisis.* His previous manuscript had patches of labored writing and clumsy connections, but all was smooth and sparkling in *Christianity and the Social Crisis.* The book enthralled a huge audience with its flowing style and charming metaphors. Rauschenbusch knew about the recent apocalyptic turn in German scholarship, and he did *not* oppose it outright. He reasoned that Jesus undoubtedly shared some of the apocalyptic consciousness of a conquered people, just as he shared the usual belief in devils. But the claim that Jesus was a deluded apocalypticist depended on a handful of "coming Son of Man sayings" that were over-

---

[5] Walter Rauschenbusch (unsigned), "What Shall We Do with the Germans?"; "are the whites," (Pamphlet, 1895, Box 47, Rauschenbusch Family Collections, American Baptist Historical Society, Atlanta, Georgia; hereinafter ABHS); Rauschenbusch (unsigned), "The German Seminary in Rochester" (Pamphlet, 1897, Box 47, ABHS); Rauschenbusch, Commencement Address, "The Contribution of Germany to the National Life of America," 1902, "alien," Box 92, ABHS).

whelmingly outnumbered by social-ethical sayings, and Rauschenbusch judged that the apocalypse of Mark 13 sounded more like the early church than like Jesus.

To Rauschenbusch, the rise of corporate capitalism marked a crisis for American civilization, but also an opportunity to recover the lost kingdom ideal of Jesus. If production could be organized on a cooperative basis, if distribution could be organized by principles of justice, if workers could be treated as valuable ends and not as dispensable means to a commercial end, if parasitic wealth and predatory commerce could be abolished.... His fantasy of "ifs" went on for a half-page. If all these things could be accomplished, it might be possible to organize society on Christian principles.

The book was rocket fuel for the entire Social Gospel movement during its glory phase, making him famous. A third awakening was occurring in American life. In 1908 the newly founded Federal Council of Churches, representing thirty-two denominations, issued a Social Creed of the Churches that was straight out of the Social Gospel, calling for equal rights and universal justice, the abolition of child labor, and a living wage in every industry.

Then came *Christianizing the Social Order* in the heyday year that four presidential candidates competed for the progressive vote. It brimmed with progressive optimism and idealism. Rauschenbusch urged that the crucial thing is the spirit and direction of the religion of Jesus, not the dogmas he retained from his background. The Reformation recovered Pauline doctrine, but not the spirit of Jesus. Theologically, Luther and Calvin were authoritarians who had little feeling for the kingdom and precious little democratic spirit. It took modern social idealism and historical criticism to recover Jesus and his kingdom. The Reformation worked back to Paul; modern theology worked back to Jesus *and* adopted the master concept of modern thought—evolution—which helped Christians understand the world as the reign of God toward which all creation is moving. In 1912, before the Great War savaged his optimism, Rauschenbusch stressed that history is God's workshop, the unfolding of an immanent divine purpose that works toward the commonwealth of spiritual freedom and righteousness.

Even at the high tide of the Social Gospel, *Christianizing the Social Order* was a provocative title. Rauschenbusch tried to be assuring. The Social Gospel was not about putting Christ's name in the Constitution or breaching the American wall between church and state. It wanted social and cultural transformation, not a state religion. To Christianize society was to bring it into harmony with the ethical values of Christ. These values are not exclusive to Christ or Christianity, he said. They are universal, shared by all people of good will, defining the content of good will: freedom, sacrificial love, compassion, community, justice, equality.

So why insist on the language of "Christianizing"? Rauschenbusch had two reasons. One, Jesus should be recognized as epitomizing these ethical values. Two, the church has no spiritual power when it forsakes the name of Christ. Rauschenbusch used "Christianize," "moralize," "humanize," and "democratize" as interchangeable terms. A bad society makes good people do bad things; a good society compels even bad people to be cooperative and democratic. Until the modern age, he said, most families and churches were decidedly bad, being reactionary and coercive. Both were despotic in ways that reinforced each other, condemning women to subservience. But the democratizing spirit of the modern age changed this picture. The churches lost their temporal power, they learned that coercion has the same relation to true religion that rape has to love, and feminism had begun to abolish patriarchy. The churches did not welcome their salvation. They had to be converted against their will, and many of them were still determined to oppress women.

Like many Social Gospelers, Rauschenbusch was a good enough Victorian to be conflicted about women's rights, because he wanted wives and mothers to stay home and take care of their families. Constantly he implored his audiences not to erode the (late Victorian) ideal of family life in the name of individual progress for women. What made the middle-class family *ideal* was precisely that it allowed women not to work outside the home. He could be florid on this subject, warning that capitalism emptied the home of its nurturing wives and mothers. Christian Socialism was the wholesome alternative. It lifted women to the equality they deserved while supporting the family as the key to a healthy society.

America's economic system, by contrast, was completely unregenerate. To Rauschenbusch, the root of the problem was systemic. It was the predatory logic of capitalism, which is inimical to Christianity. Theologians timidly avoided this subject, especially Protestant theologians. In Catholicism, the dominant power was the dogmatic mythology of a priestly class; in Protestantism, it was the financial and cultural power of a ruling capitalist class. To Rauschenbusch, the tests of Christian morality applied to every sphere, including economics: Does a given system reward cooperation and the common good or selfishness and will to power? Does it call people to the good or tempt them downward?

Rauschenbusch insisted that capitalism is essentially corrupting, sapping its own foundations by degrading the cultural capital on which American society depends. Capitalism commodifies everything it touches, turning citizens into small-minded consumers, corrupting the professions, and extending to every sector of society. To commercialize a profession is to corrupt it. The legal profession was the most corrupt of all, because corporations needed lawyers to help them betray the public interest.

Rauschenbusch said the crucial problem is the autocratic power unrestrained by democratic checks that capitalism gives to owners and managers. In the political sphere a worker is a rights-bearing citizen, but in the economic sphere the same worker has no more rights over property than a medieval serf. Workers labor on industrial property that is too expensive for them to own, but which is financed by the savings and labor of working people. The solution is to democratize the process of investment and production: "Political democracy without economic democracy is an uncashed promissory note, a pot without the roast, a form without substance. But in so far as democracy has become effective, it has quickened everything it has touched." Democracy is needed in the economic sphere for the same reasons it is needed everywhere else. It promotes freedom and equality, legitimates the necessary exercise of authority, and serves as a brake on class domination.[6]

This idea of replacing capitalist selfishness and inequality with economic democracy was intrinsic to the Social Gospel. There was an important divide between Social Gospel Socialists such as Rauschenbusch and Social Gospel liberals such as Shailer Mathews and Jane Addams, but the liberals said as plainly as Rauschenbusch that modern democracy had to create an alternative to capitalism. If modernity was a good thing, it had to have a stage beyond capitalism. Social Gospel liberals warned against Marxism and state Socialism, and the radicals replied that Socialism did not have to be atheist, Marxist, or statist. In fact, state Socialism was a latecomer. Christian Socialism existed for nearly fifty years in England before the Fabians founded a state Socialist movement, and Marxism is anti-statist. Rauschenbusch favored decentralized forms of socialization without ruling out state Socialism.

---

[6] Walter Rauschenbusch, *Christianizing the Social Order* (New York: MacMillan Co., 1912), 353.

The American Social Gospel was Socialist in the broad sense that nearly the entire movement supported cooperatives, the nationalization of monopolies, and the rhetoric of economic democracy. It stuck to these positions wherever it sustained vital bonds with the labor movement, and it wavered wherever it tried to get by on middle-class reformism. Heath Carter, in his wonderful book on the Social Gospel in Chicago, picked the best city for documenting the working class origins of the Social Gospel, but this social history story is there to be dug out of every city where Social Christianity existed. Much of this story overlaps the history of subterranean Catholic Socialism in the US and Europe. A type of Catholic Socialism existed wherever Catholics and unions existed, because Catholics surged into the unions, and in Europe the unions were Socialist. But Catholic Socialism did not have clerical leadership or a public profile as such, because Socialism was officially forbidden for Catholic clergy. Among American Catholics prior to 1920, only John Ryan won the kind of attention that the Protestant Social Gospel leaders received, and Ryan zealously guarded his anti-Socialist credentials to stay out of trouble with the Vatican. Sadly, that meant that Rauschenbusch met few people who challenged his anti-Catholicism.[7]

He was emphatically an evangelical liberal, rooted in Protestant pietism, and he epitomized the distinctly American version of liberal theology. All theological liberals accepted the historical critical approach to the Bible, allowed science to explain the world, looked beyond the church for answers to their questions, and refused to establish or compel religious beliefs on the basis of a bare authority claim. What made liberal theology distinct in the United States was its fusion with the Social Gospel. Logically these were two different movements. It was possible to support liberal theology and oppose the Social Gospel, like Borden Parker Bowne, or to support the Social Gospel and oppose liberal theology, like Augustus Strong. But in the United States, these two movements were intertwined from the beginning and soon became synonymous, being led by the same people. Thus, Christopher Evans defines the Social Gospel as "an offshoot of theological liberalism." Gladden, Ely, Rauschenbusch, Mathews, and others accepted biblical criticism *and* committed the churches to social justice, creating the ecumenical movement. They implored the churches to accept Darwinian evolution *and* to reject Social Darwinism. They conceived the liberalizing impulse in

---

[7] Heath W. Carter, *Union Made: Working People and the Rise of Social Christianity in Chicago* (New York: Oxford University Press, 2015).

theology and the social conscience of the Social Gospel as complementary aspects of the same struggle for freedom and progress.[8]

Before World War I, virtually *all* Social Gospelers spoke an optimistic language of progress and social evolution, a third way between predatory capitalism and dictatorial Socialism. Rauschenbusch championed the Socialist version of this argument and Mathews the liberal version. Both of these traditions long outlasted World War I. But the Great Depression yielded a militant Christian radicalism that spoke a binary language of revolution versus barbarism. Reinhold Niebuhr argued throughout the 1930s that there was no third way; there was only the choice between revolutionary state Socialism and reverting to some kind of fascist barbarism. Economic democracy was serious only if it meant outright government control of the economy. Many joined Reinhold Niebuhr in repudiating the Social Gospel and the New Deal. They were finished with third-way appeals to the common good. Wrongly, Niebuhr and his followers equated socialization with nationalization and rejected production for profit. Wrongly, they claimed that state planners could replicate the pricing decisions of markets and that government planners should organize an economy not linked by markets.

In the usual rendering of modern theology, the Social Gospel was naïve and Niebuhr is the hero of the story. I accept this rendering for the period of 1940–1941, but not for the 1930s or the 1950s. In the 1930s the Social Gospel leaders of the Federal Council of Churches called for economic democracy before FDR was elected and later helped him build the New Deal while Niebuhr called them stupid and naïve. They advocated worker ownership, select government ownership, union rights, social security, and public infrastructure projects. In 1932 they issued a new version of the Social Creed calling for public control of the credit and monetary systems, the right to collective bargaining, and equal rights for all people.

On these issues Rauschenbusch and his protégés were much better than the Niebuhrians who ridiculed them. Rauschenbusch advocated mixed forms of worker, community, and state ownership. He contended that democratic control is the heart of the matter and that markets cannot be abolished in a free society. The radical ideologies of the 1930s are long forgotten, but Rauschenbusch's version of economic democracy is as relevant

[8] Christopher H. Evans, *The Social Gospel in American History* (New York: New York University Press, 2017), "an offshoot," 2.

as ever. Moreover, unlike Niebuhr and Paul Tillich, Rauschenbusch did not say that economic democracy is pointless without the pressure of a revolutionary proletariat. Thus, he never quit pressing for it, unlike Niebuhr and Tillich. Rauschenbusch's ethical idealism was his strength, something he had in common with the Black Social Gospel. In some situations, such as the entire 1950s, ethical idealism is the only thing that sustains struggles for social justice. The Social Gospel activists who kept fighting against Jim Crow and American imperialism knew all about that: Mordecai Johnson, Benjamin Mays, Howard Thurman, J. Pius Barbour, James Farmer, Myles Horton, Pauli Murray, Walter Muelder, and Martin Luther King Jr.

Every person that I just named understood that Rauschenbusch was weak and late on racism and American imperialism. Yet they respected him, quoted him, admired him, and related to him as the one who championed Christian Socialism during its heyday. When Europe fell into war in 1914, Rauschenbusch was heartbroken. He believed that imperialism drove Europe into war; he desperately wanted America to stay out of the war, and it galled him when people said he was really pro-Germany, not anti-war. In 1917 he told a friend, "I have been a Christian supporter of the peace idea for some years. During the Spanish-American War I took the average attitude and voiced it effectively. But shortly afterward the peace movement got a strong grip on me." He grieved to another friend that he could not combine Christianity and war and he could not relate to Martin Luther or Oliver Cromwell because they "cheerfully" supported mass killing: "Don't ask me to combine religion and the war spirit. I don't want to lose my religion; it's all I've got."[9]

His last book, *A Theology for the Social Gospel*, had seven chapters on sin, culminating in a powerful chapter on the kingdom of evil. Some liberals wrongly unloaded personal responsibility for sin on society, and orthodoxy did the same thing with Adam, the devil, and predestination. Moreover, the old orthodoxy obsessed over personal foibles while ignoring massive social evils. Following Ritschl, Rauschenbusch said that human beings are bonded to each other in their bondage to sin, but some are more sinful than others, and some traditions are drenched in the blood of victims. Most notably, social cruelty, racism, and ethnic feuds are transmitted through socialization

---

[9] Walter Rauschenbusch to "A Friend," 7 March 1917, "I have been," (Box 32, ABHS); Walter Rauschenbusch to John S. Phillips, 16 May 1917, "don't ask," (Box 32, ABHS).

from one generation to the next: "When negroes are hunted from a Northern city like beasts, or when a Southern city degrades the whole nation by turning the savage inhumanity of a mob into a public festivity, we are continuing to sin because our fathers created the conditions of sin by the African slave trade and by the unearned wealth they gathered from slave labor for generations."[10]

He called the sum of these evils the "kingdom of evil." Evil is not only disjointed events. It is real, powerful, organic, and solidaristic in modern life. All people are bound together in the condition of bearing the yoke of evil and suffering, but only the Social Gospel made sense of this fact. Rauschenbusch urged that God must be democratized, not merely society. If the kingdom of God is democratizing, so must be the God of the divine commonwealth. God is a loving spirit "who strives within our striving, kindles his flame in our intellect, sends the impact of his energy to make our will restless for righteousness, floods our sub-conscious mind with dreams and longings, and always urges the race on toward a higher combination of freedom and solidarity."[11]

He tried to believe that Christianity and economic democracy might break the power of capitalism and nationalism: "Capitalism has overdeveloped the selfish instincts in all of us and left the capacity of devotion to larger ends shrunken and atrophied." He lamented that the habits of cooperation are almost impossible to instill in a selfish culture and that Americans lift themselves to a common purpose only when they go to war. He worried that reformers would settle for liberalism.[12]

Much of the Social Gospel movement was sentimental, moralistic, idealistic, and naïve, exactly as Reinhold Niebuhr charged. It preached a Gospel of cultural optimism and a Jesus of middle-class idealism. It spoke the language of missionary religion and sometimes baptized Manifest Destiny, yielding noxious claims that America invaded and killed only to make the world better. Most Social Gospel leaders opposed World War I right up to the moment that the US intervened, after which they preached about saving the world for democracy. Afterward many of them repented for preaching

---

[10] Walter Rauschenbusch, *A Theology for the Social Gospel* (New York: MacMillan Co., 1917), 79; Albrecht Ritschl, *Die christliche Lehre von der Rechtfertigung und Versöhnung I* (Bonn: A. Marcus und Webers Verlag, 1903), 496, 555–56.

[11] Rauschenbusch, *A Theology for the Social Gospel*, 179.

[12] Rauschenbusch, *Christianizing the Social Order*, 369.

pro-war sermons and converted to pacifism, the drama that started Reinhold Niebuhr on his way.

The greatest failing of the Social Gospel was not what Niebuhr said; that is, that it was too idealistic. It *was* too idealistic, but that was not its greatest failing. Rauschenbusch exemplified the failure by refusing for many years to say *anything* about the racist violence right in front of him. Conservative White Social Gospel leaders such as Josiah Strong and Lyman Abbott advocated black assimilation to an Anglo-Saxon ideal. Left-leaning assimilationists such as Gladden and Henry Morehouse said the same thing with a stronger recognition of the rights of black Americans. The neo-abolitionists such as Herbert Seeley Bigelow, Algernon Crapsey, George Herron, and Harlan Paul Douglass strongly defended the dignity and rights of African Americans, but there were never enough of them.

Occasionally someone got better on this subject. Gladden was a patronizing left-assimilationist for most of his career, but in 1903 he read *The Souls of Black Folk*, met W. E. B. Du Bois, and changed his position. He got an avalanche of hateful letters in reply. Reading his mail, Washington Gladden said it frightened him to see what black Americans were up against. Meanwhile Rauschenbusch said nothing. He knew only a few African Americans personally, he had no moral authority on this subject, and everything that he knew contradicted his claim that Christians were building the kingdom of God. Rauschenbusch waited until his last years to break his silence. In *Christianizing the Social Order* he finally managed to say that the spirit of Jesus "smites race pride and prejudice in the face in the name of humanity." And in his last book he described lynching as the ultimate example of social evil.[13]

These statements came from nowhere, raising a new subject for him. In 1914, he explained why it took him so long to write even a sentence: "For years, the problem of the two races in the South has seemed to me so tragic, so insoluble, that I have never yet ventured to discuss it in public."[14]

If he was to be an agent of hope in racist America, he could not mention racism, a hopelessly depressing topic. The Black Social Gospelers that Rauschenbusch ignored—Reverdy Ransom, Nannie Helen Burroughs, Alexander Walters—knew all about the existential trauma of sustaining hope

---

[13] Ibid., "smites," 60; *A Theology for the Social Gospel*, 79.

[14] Walter Rauschenbusch, "The Belated Races and the Social Problems," *Methodist Review* 40 (April 1914): 258.

in a terrible situation. They dealt with it every day in ministering to people who suffered the tragedy. But to them the response of mute hopelessness was an ethical impossibility. If Christianity had *any* moral meaning in the American context, it had to begin with the evils of racism and hatred that oppressed black Americans.

White Social Gospel idealism, in its heyday, did precious little to dismantle the culture of white supremacy. Then it was ridiculed for its optimism and idealism. Two generations of seminarians learned about the Social Gospel by reading Niebuhr. After Niebuhr's generation passed, liberationists judged that the Social Gospel *and* Christian realism were too middle class, white, male dominated, nationalistic, and socially privileged to be agents of liberation.

Yet the Black Social Gospel has an unsurpassed legacy, and the White Social Gospel is not far behind it. Rauschenbusch did not rest on ethical idealism alone. He had a deep Christian basis and a realistic sense of the class struggle, and he preached the coming commonwealth of God with unsurpassed brilliance. I am going to end with a proof-text on each of these points. Near the end of his life, dying from cancer and battered from the hate mail he received for criticizing the war, Rauschenbusch told Lemuel Barnes that he was deeply lonely because of his deafness and tormented by attacks from conservatives and war boosters: "But I have been upheld by the comforts of God. Jesus has been to me the inexhaustible source of fresh impulse, life, and courage.... My life would seem an empty shell if my personal religion were left out of it."[15]

He realized that moral idealism alone is powerless to change society: "We must not blink the fact that idealists alone have never carried through any great social change.... The possessing classes rule by force and longstanding power. They control nearly all property. The law is on their side, for they have made it.... For a definite historical victory a given truth must depend on the class which makes that truth its own and fights for it."[16]

But that was never his first or last word. First and last, he said that the commonwealth of God is the very life and word of Jesus, which must be struggled for even though it cannot be fully attained. "We shall never have a perfect social life, yet we must seek it with faith. The kingdom of God is

[15] Walter Rauschenbusch to Lemuel Call Barnes, 10 May 1918 (Box 32, Rauschenbusch Family Collections, ABHS).

[16] Rauschenbusch, *Christianity and the Social Crisis*, 400, 401.

always but coming. But every approximation to it is worthwhile." That was the radical core of the Social Gospel.[17]

[17] Ibid., 421.

Chapter 2

Walter Rauschenbusch: The Soul of the Social Gospel

Christopher H. Evans

In the years since I published my biography of Walter Rauschenbusch in 2004,[1] I still find myself coming back to the question: who was Walter Rauschenbusch, and how does his personality manifest itself in his theology? Details of Rauschenbusch's life are well known. A German-American born in Rochester, New York, in 1861, Rauschenbusch grew up in a conservative Baptist family, where his father served as the longtime head of the German Department at Rochester Theological Seminary (RTS). After spending a formative eleven years as pastor of a German immigrant church in the Hell's Kitchen section of New York, he returned to his native Rochester to serve on the faculty of RTS until his death in 1918. Rauschenbusch was a prolific writer; however, much of his notoriety as the chief proprietor of the Social Gospel rests on what I like to call his "Social Gospel trilogy," *Christianity and the Social Crisis* (1907), *Christianizing the Social Order* (1912), and *A Theology for the Social Gospel* (1917).[2]

The concept that mostly defines Rauschenbusch's theology is the kingdom of God. Using the model of the Hebrew prophets from the Old Testament and Jesus's words from the Synoptic Gospels, Rauschenbusch saw scriptural teaching pointing toward the creation of a just society. Emphasizing what he and other contemporaries referred to as "social salvation," Rauschenbusch pushed for a democratic Socialist alternative to the predatory economic practices associated with capitalism. While expressing his optimism in the possibility of reform, he also cautioned, "At best there is al-

---

[1] Christopher H. Evans, *The Kingdom Is Always but Coming: A Life of Walter Rauschenbusch* (Grand Rapids, MI: William B. Eerdmans Co., 2004).

[2] Numerous anthologies of Rauschenbusch's writings have been published since his death. See, for example, Benjamin E. Mays, ed. *A Gospel for the Social Awakening* (New York: Association Press, 1950), Benson Y. Landis, ed. *A Rauschenbusch Reader* (New York: Harper & Row, 1958), and Winthrop S. Hudson, ed. *Walter Rauschenbusch: Selected Writings* (New York: Paulist Press, 1984).

ways but an approximation to a perfect social order. The kingdom of God is always but coming."[3]

Rauschenbusch was part of a broader historical landscape of late nineteenth- and early twentieth-century reformers that shaped the Social Gospel as one of the most important movements in American religious history. These individuals included John Ryan, whose ethical formulations of Catholic social teaching found expression in New Deal economic policies; Jane Addams, pioneer of the settlement-house movement; Reverdy Ransom, African American civil rights leader; and Harry F. Ward, one of the most radical American activists between the world wars. These persons contributed to what their peers often called "the social awakening," where church leaders struggled over issues of "applied Christianity," believing religion's chief ends pointed toward the alleviation of social injustices.[4] Yet Rauschenbusch's name still stands out as the exemplar of this arising social conscience in American Christianity, and he remains today the embodiment of the Social Gospel movement.

I think a critical point about Rauschenbusch is he was, in many respects, always a pastor. Several of the most important figures who shaped the development of nineteenth-century American liberal theology, such as William Ellery Channing, Theodore Parker, Horace Bushnell, and William Newton Clarke, were ministers of congregations.[5] Even though Rauschenbusch spent the bulk of his professional career as a professor in a theological seminary, he always wore his pastoral identity on his sleeve. One of his friends, Rabbi Stephen Wise, commented to Rauschenbusch's widow, Pauline, in 1928 that her late husband's book of prayers, *Prayers of the Social Awakening*, captured Rauschenbusch's personality. "The spirit of the man is in these prayers. It is that which makes them so precious."[6]

---

[3] Walter Rauschenbusch, *Christianity and the Social Crisis* (New York: Macmillan Co., 1907), 421.

[4] For a broader history of the Social Gospel movement in American religion, see Christopher H. Evans, *The Social Gospel in American Religion, A History* (New York: New York University Press, 2017).

[5] On the historical connection between the growth of liberal theology and pastoral ministry, see Gary Dorrien, *The Making of American Liberal Theology: Imagining Progressive Religion, 1805–1900* (Louisville, KY: Westminster John Knox Press, 2001), and Evans, *Liberalism without Illusions: Renewing an American Christian Tradition* (Waco, TX: Baylor University Press, 2010).

[6] Evans, *The Social Gospel*, 131.

Such statements about Rauschenbusch's godly and pastoral nature were repeated by scores of contemporaries who knew him well, including his first biographer—Rauschenbusch's former student assistant at Rochester Theological Seminary, Dores Robinson Sharpe.[7] Chock-full of anecdotes, Sharpe's 1942 biography captures the magnetic pull that Rauschenbusch had upon people who knew him. Yet Sharpe's biography does veer into hagiography, creating a sentimental view of Rauschenbusch that has made interpreting his life, and his subsequent legacy, somewhat difficult.

In a review of Paul Minus's 1988 Rauschenbusch biography in *Christian Century*,[8] Max Stackhouse titled his article "The Legacy of a Loving Prophet."[9] Stackhouse largely supported the commonly held view that Rauschenbusch's central significance was in setting the stage for the more rigorous theological coming of Reinhold Niebuhr. Stackhouse carried a deep love for Rauschenbusch. However, one gets the sense from reading his review that Rauschenbusch was kind of a theological lightweight compared to figures residing on the Mount Olympus of later twentieth-century theology, such as Karl Barth, Paul Tillich, Rudolf Bultmann, and Reinhold Niebuhr.

The view of Rauschenbusch as an important, but secondary, theologian has carried over into most interpretations of American religious history. Narratives on twentieth-century Protestantism inevitably turn to the impact of Reinhold Niebuhr and the broader tradition of crisis theology, or neoorthodoxy. The standard interpretive arc emphasizes how Niebuhr challenged the naïve liberalism of the Social Gospel by calling the church back to a more biblical-reformation-based grounding in human sinfulness and God's sovereignty. This tradition of historical writing frequently emphasizes the intellectual vitality of the Reformed Protestant tradition as the intellectual heart of American Christianity. [10] My intention is not to refute Niebuhr's

---

[7] Dores Robinson Sharpe, *Walter Rauschenbusch* (New York: Macmillan Co., 1942).

[8] Paul Minus, *Walter Rauschenbusch: American Reformer* (New York: Macmillan Co., 1988).

[9] Max L. Stackhouse, "Rauschenbusch Today: The Legacy of a Loving Prophet," *The Christian Century* 106 (25 January 1989): 75–78.

[10] For much of the twentieth century, the historiography of American Christianity was largely shaped by Perry Miller. Miller not only saw the legacy of Puritanism as the dominant American theological tradition, but he tied the development of American Reformed theology to broader trends in American intellectual history.

importance. Rather, we need to see Rauschenbusch's thought as making an equally vital contribution to the history of American theology, in ways often overshadowed by Niebuhr's polemics. If one peels back the layers of hagiography written by apologists like Sharpe, one not only can cast aside some of the most common caricatures about Rauschenbusch's naiveté, one also gets a better portrait of how Rauschenbusch's pastoral personality left an indelible imprint on his theology.

A key to understanding who Rauschenbusch was as a person and theologian comes from the introduction to Sharpe's biography penned by the great Baptist preacher Harry Emerson Fosdick. Fosdick wrote that Rauschenbusch "approached the social applications of Christ's gospel by way of a deep, well-informed care for people, one by one."[11] While Walter Rauschenbusch's identity will always be linked with the social aspects of religious belief, his understanding of "social salvation" was inseparable from the importance of the individual. This provides us insight into why 100 years after his death, Rauschenbusch remains the heart and soul of the Social Gospel movement.

FINDING WALTER RAUSCHENBUSCH

Historian William McGuire King has observed that the Social Gospel emphasized the fulfillment of personal religion, not its negation.[12] The more I read Rauschenbusch, the more I agree with this assertion. If one examines details of his life—his German-American heritage, his Hell's Kitchen ministry, his lifelong struggles with deafness, his identity as a Baptist, and his teaching career—one sees how his personality impacted his theology. In this paper, I'd like to examine three components of Rauschenbusch's life that I

See, for example, Miller, *Errand into the Wilderness* (Cambridge, MA: The Belknap Press, 1956). The textbook that symbolizes this Puritan arc for interpreting American Christianity was Sydney Ahlstrom, *A Religious History of the American People* (New Haven, CT: Yale University Press, 1972).

[11] Sharpe, *Rauschenbusch*, xii.

[12] William McGuire King, "'History as Revelation' in the Theology of the Social Gospel," *Harvard Theological Review* 76/1 (1983): 109–29, and "An Enthusiasm for Humanity: The Social Emphasis in Religion and Its Accommodation in Protestant Theology," in *Religion and Twentieth Century American Intellectual Life*, ed. Michael J. Lacey (Cambridge: Cambridge University Press, 1989), 49–77.

wish I had explored in greater depth in my biography. These factors help us understand his ongoing theological appeal today.

First, *Walter Rauschenbusch was an evangelist.* One of Dores Sharpe's most moving recollections concerns the time when he accompanied Rauschenbusch on a series of lectures in Chicago. As the two men were enjoying a meal on the banks of Lake Michigan, Rauschenbusch asked Sharpe, "How do you think of me and my work?" Sharpe responded, "I think of you as an evangelist and of your work as evangelism of the truest sort." This response pleased Rauschenbusch, who noted, "I have always wanted to be thought of in that way. Your testimony gives me new fighting power."[13] Sharpe made a vital point about Rauschenbusch's core identity—he was an evangelist who wanted to share his faith in the power of Jesus's message for his generation.

If this makes Rauschenbusch an "evangelical," he was a very different evangelical from how that term is generally understood. He exemplified a paradigm of what theologian Kenneth Cauthen called an "evangelical liberal,"[14] in that his theology balanced a deep pietism with a positive view of the individual. Rauschenbusch hung on to his father's Pietism that highlights a broader tradition of antebellum Protestant perfectionism associated with early nineteenth-century revivalists such as Charles Grandison Finney and Phoebe Palmer. The evangelical emphasis on religious perfectionism believed that individuals could be cleansed of the power of sin in order to live lives of holiness in thought, word, and deed. This perfectionism was essential to the early nineteenth-century abolitionist and women's rights movements, and it created a template for the rise of the Social Gospel movement after the Civil War.

Rauschenbusch was especially influenced by William Arthur's 1856 book, *The Tongue of Fire.* An Irish Methodist, Arthur's emphasis on the Holy Spirit's power to transform sinners to conform to the image of Christ affected a very wide range of late nineteenth-century evangelicals—including leaders of the burgeoning holiness and Pentecostal movements as well as the "liberal" Social Gospel.

Personal holiness was at the root of Walter Rauschenbusch's Christianity. As he noted in an 1897 address, "The main thing is to have God; to live

---

[13] Sharpe, *Rauschenbusch*, 393.

[14] W. Kenneth Cauthen, *The Impact of American Religious Liberalism* (New York: Harper & Row, 1962).

in him; to have him live in us; to think his thoughts; to love what he loves and hate what he hates; to realize his presence; to feel his holiness and to be holy because he is holy...to join in the great purposes of God and to be lifted to greatness of vision and faith and hope with him—that is the blessed life."[15] However, "the blessed life" of a robust personal faith was always interconnected to the attainment of a just society.

Of all of Rauschenbusch's works, two books that clearly summarize the interrelationship between personal and collective salvation are *Prayers of the Social Awakening* (1910) and a short devotional book, *Dare We Be Christians?* (1914). Like other Social Gospel figures, for Rauschenbusch the cross of Christ was always a reminder to him that Christian discipleship requires sacrifice, suffering, and perhaps the cost of one's life. At the same time, Rauschenbusch's understanding of love radiates with life-giving energy. Many aspects of *Dare We Be Christians?* speak to various pastoral occasions, such as weddings. He held to a belief in the mutuality and diverse expressions of love, encompassing physical intimacy on one end with a sense of interconnection that bonded individuals to communities. "Love demands sacrifice, and sacrifice seems the denial and surrender of life. Actually, love is the great intensifier of life and giving our life preserves it. By seeking life selfishly, we lose it; when we lose it for love we gain it." [16]

Rauschenbusch and other Social Gospel liberals often used terms like "the sacredness of personality" to describe an individual's quest to become more Christlike. As historian Eugene McCarraher notes, this Social Gospel emphasis on "personality" reflects "the highest achievement of humanity: sensitivity in feeling, rationality of judgement, and capacity for spiritual insight, all nurtured in a supportive community setting."[17] These themes come through in Rauschenbusch's interpretation of the Lord's Prayer, whereby in prayer "we are one with our fellow-men in all our needs. We are one in our sin and our salvation. To recognize that oneness is the first step toward praying the Lord's Prayer aright. That recognition is also the foun-

---

[15] Walter Rauschenbusch, "The Laity and the Spiritual Life," in Hudson, *Rauschenbusch*, 98.

[16] Walter Rauschenbusch, *Dare We Be Christians?* (Boston. MA: Pilgrim Press, 1914), 39–40.

[17] Eugene McCarraher, *Christian Critics: Religion and the Impasse in Modern American Social Thought* (Ithaca, NY: Cornell University Press, 2000), 12.

dation of Social Christianity."[18] There were many late nineteenth- and early twentieth-century derivations of what is often called "personalism," a movement that would ultimately have a major impact on the theology of Martin Luther King Jr.[19] The belief that we understand God ontologically through categories of human personhood is important for interpreting Walter Rauschenbusch's Social Gospel—especially his critique of capitalism.

A movie that I love to show my students is Charlie Chaplin's 1936 film *Modern Times*. Through Chaplin's slapstick humor, the film represents a sophisticated criticism of early twentieth-century capitalism (a point underscored in the movie's opening depiction of a flock of sheep that fades into a horde of persons pushing through a subway station on the way to work). Throughout the film, Chaplin illustrates why Rauschenbusch considered capitalism antithetical to the spirit of modern Christianity—its disregard for the individual, its routinization, and, most especially, its parasitic qualities, whereby a select group of individuals accumulate wealth which they do not create. One of the main reasons Rauschenbusch attacked industrial capitalism was that it debased the individual, making persons of little or no value to the larger ends of society. In one of my favorite passages from *Christianizing the Social Order*, he summarized his belief that individuals had a God-given right to a living wage, not just because it was good economics:

> The workingman must be protected in sickness and age by the collective wealth of the community. He must have a recognized property right in the industrial organization. The minimum form of that right is the right to get employment and to stay in his job as long as he does honest and efficient work. How long it will take us to reach this condition I do not know. That we must move in this direction seems to me clear. A condition in which one fourth of the race holds all the opportunities of livelihood in its arbitrary control, and the other three fourths are without property, without access to the earth, and without an assured means of even working for a living is neither

---

[18] Rauschenbusch, *Prayers of the Social Awakening* (Boston, MA: Pilgrim Press, 1914), 17–18.

[19] See Gary Dorrien, *The Making of American Liberal Theology: Imagining Progressive Religion*, and *The Making of American Liberal Theology: Idealism, Realism, and Modernity, 1900–1950* (Louisville, KY: Westminster John Knox Press, 2003).

> American nor Christian. *Property is a means of grace, and a good job is another.*[20] [emphasis mine]

Rauschenbusch contributed to a broader tradition of natural-law theology that emphasizes that any vision of a just society needs to honor the dignity and worth of the individual in order to have any lasting value. He repeatedly came back to the theme that an individual's personal devotion to God was only fully realized when it was connected to a broader tapestry of community. "Because we are bound together in unity of life, the good or the evil in one man's soul affects the rest.... No torch is kindled of itself, but when one man has lighted his at the altar fire of God, hundreds will take their light from him."[21]

Second, *Walter Rauschenbusch was a Baptist theologian.* He loved his Baptist identity and saw it as the core of who he was as a Christian. "I am a Baptist, then, because in our church life we have a minimum emphasis on ritual and creed, and a maximum of emphasis on spiritual experience, and the more I study the history of religion, the more I see how great and fruitful such a position is."[22] Like his father, he treasured the legacy of the sixteenth-century Anabaptists, yet he valued these traditions for their emphasis on individual freedom, not their sectarianism. Rauschenbusch often spoke the common language of liberal Protestantism of his era, emphasizing applied ethics over doctrine. However, he worried that too many Baptists were taking obscure doctrines and scriptural texts and creating a religious individualism that would lead them into an unhealthy sectarianism. He used the following anecdote:

> A near-sighted child was taken to the zoo and stood in front of the lion's cage. The lion's tail was hanging down through the bars. "But I thought the lion was different," said the child, "it looks like a yellow rope." So there are Baptists who have hitherto discovered only

---

[20] Walter Rauschenbusch, *Christianizing the Social Order* (New York: Macmillan, 1912), 350.

[21] Ibid., 461.

[22] "Why I am a Baptist," Rochester/Genesee Region, American Baptist Churches, http://www.abcrgr.org/component/content/article?id=14:why-i-am-a-baptist. Accessed 20 April 2018).

> the tail-end of our Baptist ideals and convictions, and it is no wonder that they turn out as narrow as the tail they devoutly believe in.[23]

Specifically, Rauschenbusch worried that this narrow tail was leading Baptists to embrace a theological pessimism that increasingly defined his generation.

Perhaps the theological development that most disturbed Rauschenbusch was the rise of apocalyptic premillennialism. He pushed back against the strict biblicism among Baptists who interpreted the Bible as a codebook for predicting the end-times. Rauschenbusch lived when various forms of dispensationalism (beliefs that many people associate with today's *Left Behind* books and films) were finding a hearing among Baptists and other Protestants.

Rauschenbusch frequently voiced his fears about the negative impact of end-time speculation upon the church's ministry and mission. "The apocalyptic hope has always contained ingredients of religious force and value," he conceded in *Christianizing the Social Order*. However, "its trail through history is strange and troubled reading. It has been of absorbing fascination to some Christian minds, but it has led them into labyrinths from which some never emerged."[24] Rauschenbusch repeatedly expressed his worry about the popular appeal of dispensationalism and frequently locked horns with some of the most prominent Baptist premillennialists of his generation, such as the Baptist Isaac Haldeman in New York and William Bell Riley in Minneapolis. In a 1914 response to Riley's accusations of heresy, Rauschenbusch expressed his hurt at the accusation and his worry that Riley's tactics went against a spirit he treasured in his ministry: Christian unity. "When you charge me with 'denying the Lord that brought me' you hurt me just as if you charged me with being false to my wife or cruel to my children.... I have written you as a Christian man to a Christian man, and I should be glad if this letter served as a warning, not only in my case, but in general against the methods often used by your school of thought."[25]

---

[23] Rauschenbusch, "Why I am a Baptist."

[24] Rauschenbusch, *Christianizing the Social Order*, 55. For an account of Rauschenbusch's critique of dispensationalism, see Evans, "Walter Rauschenbusch and the Second Coming: The Social Gospel as Baptist History," in *Through a Glass Darkly: Contested Notions of Baptist Identity*, ed. Keith Harper (Tuscaloosa: University of Alabama Press, 2010), 145–71.

[25] Evans, *The Kingdom Is Always but Coming*, 258.

Rauschenbusch died before the Fundamentalist-Modernist controversy of the 1920s, but he became for later generations of religious conservatives a symbol of all that was wrong with the so-called "Modernist" position. However, he worried that too many Baptists were being swayed by ahistorical readings of Scripture that characterized many forms of premillennialism. Rauschenbusch saw chief characteristics of Baptist identity—believer's baptism, congregational autonomy, and soul liberty—as gifts to the wider Christian movement. For Rauschenbusch, being a Baptist was a means to a greater end, not an end in itself. I think if he were here today, he'd be heartbroken that many Baptists continue to worship the "yellow rope" without necessarily seeing the "lion."

Finally, his Baptist identity leads to a third aspect of his vocational identity: *Walter Rauschenbusch was a teacher*. The primary field of Rauschenbusch's teaching was church history, and those who experienced him in the classroom recall him with a mixture of awe, intimidation, and humor. My favorite account, conveyed by one of his former students, Edwin Dahlberg, future president of the National Council of Churches, is that after he submitted a paper that he knew was subpar, Dahlberg received back from Rauschenbusch one comment written at the top, "cockle-doodle-doo."[26] As Dahlberg made clear, however, the true nature of Rauschenbusch's theology of love, focused upon the God-given uniqueness of the individual, was manifested in the relationships that he maintained with his former students. The Rauschenbusch Family Papers are filled with correspondence with his students who frequently sought his vocational counsel, asked him for advice on personal problems, and, on occasion, debated him.

It is also important to note how his passion for his primary classroom discipline found its way into his writings. Rauschenbusch was a church historian at a time when this was a relatively new field of theological inquiry. Derived from German liberals Albrecht Ritschl and Adolf von Harnack, as well as his Baptist contemporary, Shailer Mathews, Rauschenbusch helped popularize in the United States the belief that Christianity was an historically conditioned faith. While earlier theologians often chalked up historical events to God's providence, Rauschenbusch emphasized that church history was as much a story of failure as it was success. Additionally, Rauschenbusch helped popularize the study of American church history, recognizing unique patterns of religious formation in the United States at a time when

[26] Ibid., 157.

European Christianity tended to see American religious developments as inconsequential to Christendom.[27]

Rauschenbusch's understanding of history was at times problematic. Like many Protestant contemporaries he could equate the kingdom of God with western democratic institutions and often reflected the distrust, typical of his era, of Roman Catholicism. Yet in discussing the historical development of Christianity, he was part of a generation that took seriously the ways that different beliefs and doctrines emerged out of specific historical contexts. While later criticized for being too optimistic about historical processes, Rauschenbusch's view of history did not fall into any sort of preordained outcome, as predicated by Marxism on one extreme and dispensationalism on the other. As he noted in *Christianity and the Social Crisis*, "History laughs at the optimistic illusion that 'nothing can stand in the way of human progress.'"[28] While Reinhold Niebuhr later drew attention to the often tragic consequences of historical paradox and irony, Rauschenbusch was under no illusion that historical processes on their own would lead one to a primrose path. "If any one can read history without a sickening sense of the enormous extent of injustice and oppression in all nations, he has a mental make-up which I both envy and abhor."[29]

Rauschenbusch's optimism never ventured far from his belief that solving the nation's social problems would require people of faith to make tremendous personal sacrifice—perhaps even losing their lives. Yet he also cautioned that Christians should never see social action alone as a substitute for a vibrant faith. As he summarized,

> If the Church comes to lean on social preachings and doings as a crutch because its religion has become paralytic, may the Lord have mercy on us all!... To concentrate our efforts on personal salvation, as orthodoxy has done, or on soul culture, as liberalism has done, comes close to refined selfishness. All of us who have been trained in

---

[27] See Henry Warner Bowden, "Walter Rauschenbusch and American Church History," *Foundations* 9/3 (July–September 1966): 234–50, and *Church History in the Age of Science: Historiographical Patterns in the United States, 1876–1918* (Chapel Hill: University of North Carolina Press, 1971), 170–95.

[28] Rauschenbusch, *Christianity and the Social Crisis*, 279.

[29] Rauschenbusch, *Christianizing the Social Order*, 333.

> egotistic religion need a conversion to Christian Christianity, even if we are bishops or theological professors.[30]

Rauschenbusch was optimistic about the possibility of social change in his lifetime. But he was enough of a realist to know that change was never going to be easy. As he stressed in his many letters to tired and burned-out ministers, he encouraged them to recognize the ways their work made a difference—even amid times when they didn't necessarily see the fruits of their labors. As he wrote in the conclusion of *Christianizing the Social Order*:

> The sacrifices demanded by a religious conversion always seem sore and insuperable, but every religious [person] will agree that after the great surrender is made, there is a radiant joy that marks a great culmination of life.... God is the great joy. Whenever we have touched the hem of his garment by some righteous action, we get so much satisfaction that we can be well content...even if we suffer hurt and persecution for it. Not the memory of power wielded, not even the memory of love, is so sweet as the consciousness that we once suffered for a great cause.[31]

A VINDICATION OF WALTER RAUSCHENBUSCH

Many of us who have written on aspects of Walter Rauschenbusch's life and thought share Dores Sharpe's affection for the person who was called by his closest friends "Rauschy." In my own research, I found myself caught up in his personal struggles, seeing how he was an individual who at times wore his heart on his sleeve. I recognize that as much as I tried to avoid it, I probably veered into some of the sentimentalism that Sharpe expressed. I was especially struck by Rauschenbusch's love for his family—his beloved spouse, Pauline, and their five children.

There is no doubt that Rauschenbusch had a melancholy side. His struggles with deafness, the attacks of critics, and conflicts in his family could drive him into a depression that is unmistakable in many of his letters. Yet I reject the frequent argument that Rauschenbusch died of a broken heart—a man whose love of humanity left him shattered in the midst of the carnage of World War I. It is unfortunate that American Protestantism lost Rauschenbusch before he had an opportunity to address the confusing

---

[30] Ibid., 464–65.

[31] Ibid., 473.

theological climate of the 1920s and 1930s. However, it is a testament to the power of his idealism that Rauschenbusch remained the standard bearer of the Social Gospel in the decades to come.

One of the problems with a broken-hearted interpretation of Rauschenbusch's final years is that it feeds into a belief that the Social Gospel collapsed after World War I. Despite his criticisms, Reinhold Niebuhr never doubted the indelible core of the Social Gospel—mainly, that the primary thrust of Christianity was to seek a just society through the transformation of social structures. Yet for all the ways that Christian theology has benefited from his critiques, I'm not sure that Niebuhr offered a better way forward for the church. Rauschenbusch's influence, while perhaps muted, never disappeared, as many of his critiques of economic injustice and the Christian's ethical relationship to society became foundational to a wide range of social movements, both inside and outside of institutional Christianity.

An example of Rauschenbusch's influence can be seen in the career of one of the most important twentieth-century American social activists, A. J. Muste. Introduced to Rauschenbusch's writings as a student at Union Theological Seminary in the 1910s, Muste became one of the most significant religious-based activists in the United States, whose leadership of the Fellowship of Reconciliation played a pivotal role in crafting Gandhian nonviolence into a workable political strategy. Writing in the early days of the Cold War, he offered a salient critique of Reinhold Niebuhr that embodies key aspects of Rauschenbusch's thought. While conceding that liberals needed to take doctrines of sin seriously, Muste worried that too much emphasis on depravity would not necessarily make people more aware of the need for God's grace, but instead provide a rationale to do nothing. He wrote:

> When we become obsessed with human helplessness and corruption instead of being caught up in transcending them by the grace of God, we are still preoccupied with self, still self-centered and, therefore, still self-righteous....If we do not end with the experience of the grace and power of God as that which overcomes and blots out our

preoccupation with our sinful selves, we are but giving another demonstration of the pretension and corruption of humanity.[32]

Today, I hear Walter Rauschenbusch's voice making the point that Christian love is not naïve. Rather, it is what enables us to carry on, in the face of our own pessimism, the work for justice. Rauschenbusch's words from 1896 might serve us well as an appropriate response to various theologies of pessimism:

> Faith in salvation by catastrophe cuts the nerve of action, but only in the unselfish pursuits of life.... I have yet to see proof that those who believe in the imminence of Christ's coming are indifferent to the security of real estate titles, the length of leases, the education of their children, and other things that involve a long look ahead.... The question is, which will do more to make our lives spiritual and to release us from the tyranny of the world, the thought that we may at any moment enter into the presence of the Lord, or the thought that every moment we are in the presence of the Lord?[33]

CONCLUSION: DARE WE BE CHRISTIANS?

When we talk about Walter Rauschenbusch being the "soul of the Social Gospel," it is not simply about how he articulated unique theological insights. It reflects how his theology embodied his own God-given personality that believed in the potential of persons and faith communities to change the world. As he affirmed in *Dare We Be Christians?*,

> Love is preparing to connect the present and the future generations. To lovers their love seems their own peculiar joy and apart from all the world. But Humanity stands in the shadow behind them and lifts the majestic hands of blessing above them. The indomitable spirit of the race is reaching out in them toward the better days that are to be and is flinging a new defiance to death as they affirm life together.[34]

---

[32] Muste, "Pacifism and Perfectionism" (*Fellowship*, March and April 1948): 219–20.

[33] Rauschenbusch, "Our Attitude toward Millenarianism," in Hudson, *Rauschenbusch*, 94.

[34] Rauschenbusch, *Dare We Be Christians*, 21.

No one will doubt Reinhold Niebuhr's theological legacy. Yet I don't think the evidence is there to support an argument that Niebuhr's theology on its own created permanent social movements. Niebuhr's theology helps give guidance to movements; the religious idealism of Walter Rauschenbusch creates them.[35]

Rauschenbusch's theology is not perfect. He had blind spots, some because of his historical era and others by his own omissions. Yet his personality shaped a vision of prophetic Christian thought that projected a long arc throughout the twentieth century. That legacy emphasizes that Christian love does not exempt us from being under judgement for our failure to act in the face of injustice. Rauschenbusch wrote that "nations die of legalized injustice,"[36] and unfortunately the wisdom of that comment is all too pertinent in our era.

In remembering the fiftieth anniversary of the death of Martin Luther King Jr., I hear echoes of Walter Rauschenbusch in King's final Sunday sermon preached at the National Cathedral in Washington DC. In preparing for a Poor People's March on the nation's capital, King noted that America stood at a historical moment when the nation had to decide whether "to help bridge the gulf between the haves and the have-nots." For King, the question was not whether America had the ability "to get rid of poverty. The real question is whether we have the will." [37]

As King and Rauschenbusch remind us, we all are accountable to the God of history for the ways that we've turned our backs on our Creator. Yet as Rauschenbusch affirmed in one of his prayers, entitled "On the Harm We Have Done," each day offers us the possibility to be renewed by God's grace and love:

> Change us by the power of thy saving grace from sources of evil into forces for good, that with all our strength we may fight the wrongs we have aided, and aid the right we have clogged. Grant us this

---

[35] Rauschenbusch and the broader Social Gospel movement that he helped shape contributed to the development of what is today called "the religious left." See *The Religious Left in America: Doorkeepers of a Radical Faith*, eds. Leilah Danielson, Marian Mollin, Doug Rossinow (New York: Palgrave Macmillan, 2018).

[36] Rauschenbusch, *Christianizing the Social Order*, 333.

[37] Martin Luther King Jr., "Remaining Awake through a Great Revolution," in *A Testament of Hope: The Essential Writings of Martin Luther King, Jr.*, ed. James Melvin Washington (San Francisco, CA: Harper & Row, 1986), 274.

boon, that for every harm we have done, we may do some brave act of salvation, and that for every soul that has stumbled or fallen through us, we may bring to thee some other weak or despairing one, whose strength has been renewed by our love, that so the face of thy Christ may smile upon us and the light within us may shine undimmed.[38]

[38] Rauschenbusch, *Prayers of the Social Awakening*, 127.

Part II

The Extent of the Rauschenbusch Legacy

Chapter 3

The Reality of Hope: Walter Rauschenbusch's Theology in German Context

Andrea Strübind

INTRODUCTION

In his first book, *Stride Towards Freedom*, published in 1958, Martin Luther King Jr. described how Walter Rauschenbusch's principal work, *Christianity and the Social Crisis*, had made a deep and unforgettable impression on him. In this work, King discovered the theological basis for his social orientation, which he had already developed through his own experiences with racism.[1] Aside from some critical moments with regard to the Social Gospel, which was very much in vogue at that time, King praised Rauschenbusch for his view of the entire person—body and soul—of both intellectual and material well-being. It was my own specialized study of Martin Luther King Jr. that formed my path to Walter Rauschenbusch.

The most important reference to Rauschenbusch for King proved to be the uptake of Rauschenbusch's theology of the kingdom of God as an eschatology of the present.[2] Therefore, this forms a focal point of my presentation to follow. In his teachings on the kingdom of God, Rauschenbusch brought together concern for the individual with his social vision for a redeemed society. It is entirely valid to see the Social Gospel movement, of which Rauschenbusch is regarded as the father, as a response to the hardships of industrialization and the associated mass suffering and poverty. The movement combined a social dimension with traditional soteriology, contrary to the predominant concentration on the individual so typical of mainstream Protestantism in the United States.

---

[1] Cf. Martin Luther King, "Pilgrimage to Non-violence," in *Stride Toward Freedom: The Montgomery Story* (New York: 1958), 90–107.

[2] Cf. Kenneth L. Smith and Ira G. Zepp, *Search for the Beloved Community. The Thinking of Martin Luther King Jr.* (Valley Forge, PA: Judson Press, 1998), 31.

For Rauschenbusch, God's kingdom was *the* central focus of theology, of belief, and of Christian practice. He explained this in detail in his work *A Theology for the Social Gospel.* All theological topics ought to be determined by this fundamental theme.[3] The concept of the kingdom of God was a guiding principle for Rauschenbusch, meaning that references to the analogy between God's kingdom and a transformed and renewed society can be found in all his works from 1891. He outlines this interpretation clearly and deliberately in his book *Christianizing the Social Order* (1912): "The Kingdom of God is the first and the most essential dogma of the Christian faith. It is also the lost ideal of Christendom. No man is a Christian in the full sense of the original discipleship until he has made the Kingdom of God the controlling purpose of his life, and no man is intellectually prepared to understand Jesus Christ until he has understood the meaning of the Kingdom of God."[4]

As far as Rauschenbusch was concerned, hope for the kingdom of God did not exist simply in relation to the hereafter, but was deemed to be a social and collective hope in history, in the here and now. Implicit in the implementation of God's kingdom was an increasing humanization of society, consisting of a reality where all the differences of nationality, race, and religion would be transcended. Ultimately, in Rauschenbusch's eyes, God's kingdom was identical with a transformed and regenerated society.

The kingdom of God remained for him a concept that was always in progress, or constantly in the process of creation. Likewise, he also viewed the improvement of human society more as an ongoing process than as an attainable fact or reality. However, the attitude should be one of striving and seeking for the fulfillment of the standards inherent in the kingdom of God. The strength of this conception of God's kingdom lies in the linking of Christian perspectives of hope and the living environment. The applied eschatology serves here as an engine for social change.

An explicitly present eschatology such as this is easy to criticize and dismiss in an era of critique of all utopias. Libraries are filled to overflowing with critiques of the nineteenth-century belief in progress, which was granted the utmost legitimacy until the various catastrophes of the twentieth century, and the concepts of this criticism have basically become common-

---

[3] Ibid., 39.

[4] Walter Rauschenbusch, *Christianizing the Social Order* (New York: MacMillan Co., 1912), 49.

place.[5] Nevertheless, Rauschenbusch's vision of the kingdom of God is forcing even current-day theology to review its perspectives of hope with an eye to the inner-worldly implications and consequences for a righteous, humane, and *coram deo* living human race.

Walter Rauschenbusch's kingdom of God theology has been repeatedly attributed to his research visit to Germany in 1891, with justifying grounds being given as his response to Albrecht Ritschl's approach.[6] Likewise, his rereading of the Holy Scriptures, which revealed to Rauschenbusch the significance of the prophets' social criticism and the political dimension of the Sermon on the Mount, is seemingly attributable to the enhanced "aid to vision" gained from the more critical and liberal German theology.[7] His identification with the great German theologians Albrecht Ritschl and Adolf von Harnack is also highlighted and described in various encyclopedia articles.[8] In the following, the influences stemming from his German heritage and his response to liberal positions by virtue of his research visit to Berlin in 1891 will be examined.

Due to the limitations of this article, I will not be able to explore Rauschenbusch's relationship with Martin Rade (1857–1940),[9] with whom he was in close cooperation, and Rauschenbusch's second German research trip to Marburg.[10] Rauschenbusch published a number of articles in Rade's periodical magazine *Christliche Welt*, which primarily dealt with the eco-

---

[5] Cf. Gangolf Hübinger, *Kulturprotestantismus und Politik. Zum Verhältnis von Liberalismus und Protestantismus im wilhelminischen Deutschland* (Tübingen: 1994); Johannes Paulmann, *Globale Vorherrschaft und Fortschrittsglaube* (München: 2018); Friedrich Wilhelm Graf, *Die Wiederkehr der Götter. Religion in der modernen Kultur* (München: 2004).

[6] Cf. Reinhart Müller, *Walter Rauschenbusch* (Leiden: Köln 1957), 19–20; cf. Christian Oelschlägel, "'Reich Gottes' im Sozialprotestantismus der USA. Walter Raischenbuschs Theology for the Social Gospel," in Johannes Eurich (ed.), *Diakonische Orientierungen in Praxis und Bildungsprozessen* (Heidelberg: 2005), 69–82; Ralf Dziewas, "Social Gospel und moderne Sozialtheologie," in *ZThG* 18 (2013): 199–214, esp. 202.

[7] Müller, *Rauschenbusch*, 21.

[8] Mark G. Toulouse, "Walter Rauschenbusch" in *TRE* 7, 67–68.

[9] Anne Christine Nagel, *Martin Rade, Theologe und Politiker des Sozialen Liberalismus. Eine politische Biographie* (Gütersloh: 1996).

[10] Müller, *Rauschenbusch*, 20–21; Erich Geldbach, "Die Social Gospel Bewegung. Entstehung und Inhalte," *ZThG* 18 (2013): 124–42, esp. 126.

nomic situation in the United States and unresolved social issues, including the question of women's rights, alcoholism, racism, and the underprivileged status of Native Americans.[11] A comparison between the Evangelical Social Congress in Germany and the Social Gospel remains a desideratum for research.[12]

HERITAGE AND FAMILY—THE GERMAN REVIVALIST MOVEMENT

Walter Rauschenbusch originated from a family that can be traced back through six generations of Lutheran pastors to the seventeenth century in Westphalia, Germany.[13] His grandfather and his father,[14] who ultimately converted to the Baptists and emigrated to the United States, were closely affiliated to the revivalist movement in the Minden-Ravensberg region.[15] Rauschenbusch grew up in a German family, speaking German as his first language, and the family was very mindful of their heritage that was steeped in tradition. As Walter and his siblings grew up, their father was most insistent that the children should be very aware of and should resolutely maintain their German language, culture, and history. Even after emigrating to the United States, his father, August Rauschenbusch, worked exclusively among German migrants. Within this context, he strongly advocated the view that these migrants should not give up their status as an independent population group with German origins.[16] In his old age, August Rauschenbusch returned to Germany, which had always remained his spiritual homeland, where he died in 1899.[17]

On the basis of his father's attitudes, Walter Rauschenbusch was naturally raised within the church in a German-speaking Baptist congregation. His childhood and youth were, on the one hand, shaped by the context of

---

[11] Geldbach, "Bewegung," 137.

[12] Ibid., 136.

[13] Christoph Bresina, "Von der Erweckungsbewegung zum 'Social Gospel': Walter Rauschenbuschs Herkunft, Umfeld und Entwicklung bis 1891" (Unpublished PhD dissertation, Marburg University, 1993), 1.

[14] Cf. Andreas Schumacher, *August Rauschenbusch (1816–1899). Ein Pionier der deutschen Baptisten in Nordamerika* (Bern: 2010), 33–35.

[15] Josef Mooser, *Frommes Volk und Patrioten: Erweckungsbewegung und soziale Frage im östlichen Westfalen 1800–1900* (Bielefeld: 1989).

[16] Bresina, "Erweckungsbewegung," 81.

[17] Schumacher, *Rauschenbusch*, 141–44.

growing up in a German migrant community in the United States; however, on the other hand, he also spent four years of his childhood in Germany with his mother and siblings. His close connection to and identification with his German homeland are also shown in the fact that—at the behest of his father—a major part of Walter Rauschenbusch's education took place in Germany. He attended the *Evangelisch Stiftische Gymnasium* (Protestant Secondary School) in Gütersloh, which was specifically sought out for his education on the basis of its revivalist influence and theologically conservative orientation.[18] Walter Rauschenbusch was very aware of his family tradition, which included an academic education described as an important constant in his life.[19] In his (as-yet-unpublished) study, Christoph Bresina has presented an excellent account of Walter Rauschenbusch's development, analyzing those elements of the German revivalist movement which played a significant role in shaping his theology. This includes, first and foremost, his spirituality, which derives its inspiration from a personal relationship to Jesus Christ, a clear awareness of his own sinfulness, and constant reading of the Bible. He was equally familiar with concepts ranging from revelatory and salvation interpretations of God's kingdom through to pre- and post-millenarianism, such as the new approaches in the *diaconia* that were closely associated with the revivalist movement.

Nevertheless, Walter Rauschenbusch decided on quite a different pathway, possibly in an initially unconscious act of distancing himself from his father. This path led Rauschenbusch to open himself up to the English-speaking world around him. As a consequence, he undertook a course of study at the Rochester Theological Seminary, working solely in the English-speaking department at a time when his father was certainly a lecturer at the same institution, but in the German Department.[20] His teachers, including William Arnold Stevens, came from the background of American Evangelicalism. Having said this, Rauschenbusch always retained a close association with the German Baptists on both sides of the Atlantic, through his family links and also due to his reputation.

---

[18] Wolfgang E. Heinrichs, *Freikirchen eine moderne Kirchenform. Entstehung du Entwicklung von fünf Freikirchen im Wuppertal* (Gießen: 1989), 244–50.

[19] Bresina, "Erweckungsbewegung," 48.

[20] Cf. Ibid., 166; Christopher H. Evans, *The Kingdom Is Always but Coming. A Life of Walter Rauschenbusch* (Grand Rapids, MI: Eerdmans, 2004) 32–44.

Walter Rauschenbusch did not develop the complex understanding of his theology of God's kingdom as a social structure in the sense of a transformed righteous society through discussions with liberal German theologians. On the contrary, he absorbed various approaches and inspirational concepts from English and American authors—from the realms of theology, sociology, and economics—which he then coalesced in the follow-up to his own rereading of the Holy Scriptures. Even prior to his research visit to Berlin in 1891, he had already acquired fundamental elements of his later theology of God's kingdom and of the Social Gospel. Given his upbringing within the German revivalist movement, it comes as no surprise that the emphasis on practical Christianity, on an active life in discipleship, was a concept that he cared deeply about. For Rauschenbusch, this outlook was associated from the very early stages with a component that was hostile to dogma and tradition. He rejected speculative theology as unproductive and countered it with an understanding of the Gospel within the living world. Both during his school years in Gütersloh, as well as in his tertiary study in Rochester, he became closely acquainted—in accordance with the theological "fashion" of the time—with the exegetical concentration on the life of Jesus. Admittedly, this was not in the spirit of David Friedrich Strauss (1808–1874), who subjected the Gospels to a radical demythologization, leading to a critical destruction of the story of Jesus.[21] Instead, Rauschenbusch studied August Neander's life of Jesus[22]—a standard reference and alternative concept to Strauss—which had also made a strong impact on his father. Neander was the first church historian to be employed at the newly established Faculty of Theology in Berlin.

DISCOVERY OF SOCIAL ISSUES

In the period of his pastorate at the German-speaking Baptist congregation in New York, Rauschenbusch was confronted with the genuine existential

---

[21] Peter Stuhlmacher, *Vom Verstehen des Neuen Testaments* (Göttingen: 1979), 139–42.

[22] Johann August Wilhelm Neander, *Das Leben Jesu Christi in seinem geschichtlichen Zusammenhange und seiner geschichtlichen Entwicklung* (Hamburg: 1837); Kurt Viktor Selge, "Die Berliner Kirchenhistoriker," in *Geschichtswissenschaft in Berlin im 19. und 20. Jahrhundert. Persönlichkeiten und Institutionen*, eds. Reimer Hansen und Wolfgang Ribbe (Berlin, New York: 1992), 409–47.

hardships that were a daily reality for his parishioners.[23] As a result of these experiences and, more particularly, as a direct consequence of his very close friendships with Leighton Williams (Amity Baptist Church) and Nathaniel Schmidt (First Swedish Baptist Church in New York City), Rauschenbusch acquired a new appreciation for the very tangible importance of social issues and the theological legitimization of demands for social reform.[24]

According to Rauschenbusch, in retrospect, neither his family home nor his time studying at the seminary had caused him to face the question of social issues: "There was absolutely nothing in our Seminary at that time to turn my attention to social questions or to impart social passion. Nothing in my home life either."[25] Through his involvement with the publications and works of Henry George, a candidate for the post of mayor of New York, the contemporary social context and, in particular, the economic situation were revealed to Rauschenbusch, which he came to understand as being a part of an evolutionary process. Rauschenbusch grappled with the labor movement as well as with Socialist and Communist strategies. At this stage, he recognized, in addition, traditional Protestantism's focus on the individual, and his or her path to salvation, as an aberration and a reduction of Jesus's message, whereby it had developed an ethical shortfall. The kingdom of God as an inner-worldly value, and an expression of eschatology of the present was a concept that developed for Rauschenbusch in consultation with many providers of ideas, where Leo Tolstoy and his interpretation of the Sermon on the Mount effectively became a *leitmotif* for him.[26] Prior to his journey to Europe he also undertook an intensive analysis of religious Socialism, which he believed merited legitimate consideration in the light of the contemporary critical social situation.

Rauschenbusch felt it was important to attract attention to religious Socialism's potential solutions, and he sought to achieve this through a publication established together with a number of friends.[27] In the January 1889 edition of *For the Right*, the following statement was printed regarding the publication's intentions: "Most Christian people look only to the renewal of

---

[23] Evans, *The Kingdom Is Always but Coming*, 57–67

[24] Bresina, "Erweckungsbewegung," 281–85.

[25] Letter from Rauschenbusch to John S. Philipps, 24 May 1909, in Bresina, "Erweckungsbewegung," 242, (n)324.

[26] Evans, *The Kingdom Is Always but Coming*, 78–80.

[27] Bresina, "Erweckungsbewegung," 362ff.

the individual. Most social reformers look only to the renewal of society. We believe that two factors make up the man, the inward and the outward, and so we work for the renewal and the Christianization of the individual and of society."[28]

On the basis of his development through to 1891, it can be demonstrated that the development of Rauschenbusch's specific understanding that the kingdom of God should be the central focus of Christian belief and its teachings, together with its social and collective perspectives for hope—all of which was in direct contrast to the common belief at the time—was not initially associated with his response to Albrecht Ritschl.

Thus, in an 1889 sermon, Rauschenbusch directly connected the kingdom of God with social salvation and societal transformation: "I do most profoundly believe that Jesus Christ has salvation for society as well as for the individual. The two things formed the burden of his preaching: eternal life for the individual, the kingdom of God for the world."[29]

Among the many varied sources of inspiration for Rauschenbusch, his own study of the Bible similarly shines out as a significant component that triggered in him a new method of interpreting Scripture, leaving conservative Biblicism far behind. Contrary to claims made particularly in German publications about Walter Rauschenbusch, it needs to be emphasized that the development of his specific understanding of the kingdom of God as an inner-worldly value should not be attributed first and foremost to his German upbringing and education. Possibly Charles Howard Hopkins's dictum with respect to Rauschenbusch should be endorsed, that the Social Gospel movement was, in fact, a "typical American movement."[30] In any case, it should be noted that there quite simply was no comparable movement in Germany, in spite of clear theological analogies.

---

[28] "Editorial," *For the Right* (2 January 1891): 2; Bresina, "Erweckungsbewegung," 87.

[29] Bresina, "Erweckungsbewegung," 424.

[30] Charles Howard Hopkins, *The Rise of the Social Gospel in American Protestantism 1865–1915* (New Haven, CT: Yale University Press, 1940), 3; Geldbach, "Die Social Gospel Bewegung. Entstehung und Inhalte," in *ZThG* 18 (2013): 124–42.

RESEARCH STAY IN BERLIN 1891— THE FACULTY OF THEOLOGY

In 1891, Walter Rauschenbusch, accompanied by his sister Emma, spent nine months in Germany.[31] He used the visit as an opportunity to draft the manuscript of his book under the working title of "Christianity Revolutionary."[32] He spent the first months in Berlin, where a relative assisted him in gaining access to the libraries. At the invitation of Hermann Cremer, whom he knew from his years in Gütersloh, he then shifted to Greifswald to continue working on his book.[33] Rauschenbusch regarded Cremer in quite a critical light during this stay due to his conservative religious stance. The same applies with regard to Adolf Stoecker[34] and his attempt to establish a political force against social democracy by founding the Christian Social Worker's Party (CSP) in 1878. Stoecker's aim with this action had been to win the hearts of the working classes back to the church.

Rauschenbusch's reception of German liberal theology occurred first and foremost in a literary context. I believe it is not reasonable to claim that he was significantly influenced by discussions with leading theologians in either Berlin or Greifswald. Account also needs to be taken of the fact that, from the mid-nineteenth century, the Senior Church Council exerted clear influence to ensure the formative influence of conservative Confessionalism was well established at the Faculty of Theology in Berlin.[35] From the 1860s, a turnaround began to take place, primarily as a result of influence from the school of thought originating with Albrecht Ritschl, the systematic theologian in Göttingen. Ritschl was able to exert influence by means of appointments and vocations to Berlin. From 1888, Adolf von Harnack (1851–

[31] Evans, *The Kingdom Is Always but Coming*, 89;

[32] Paul M. Minus, *Walter Rauschenbusch. American Reformer* (New York: MacMillan Co., 1988), 78.

[33] Ibid., 78.

[34] Günter Brakelmann, *Adolf Stöcker als Antisemit, Teil 1, Leben und Wirken Adolf Stoeckers im Kontext seiner Zeit* (Waltrop: 2004); Günter Brakelmann, Martin Greschat, Werner Jochmann: "Protestantismus und Politik. Werk und Wirkung Adolf Stoeckers," *Beiträge zur Sozial- und Zeitgeschichte*, 17 (Hamburg: 1982); Grit Koch, *Adolf Stoecker 1835–1909. Ein Leben zwischen Politik und Kirche* (Erlangen/Jena: 1993).

[35] Cf. Notger Slenczka, *Die Theologische Fakultät 1880-1945,* in Heinz-Elmar Tenorth (ed.), *Geschichte der Universität Unter den Linden 1810-2010, Vol. 5, Transformation der Wissensordnung* (Berlin: 2010), 53-108, 54.

1930) was a leading representative of contemporary scientific-historical research, and Rauschenbusch repeatedly gave positive acknowledgement to von Harnack in a number of his works. Having said this, it is also important to state that this was only a literary connection. Rauschenbusch did undoubtedly use German literature in developing his book and integrated the findings of a range of exegetes, historians, and sociologists.

Church history was the primary discipline studied in the Faculty of Theology in Berlin. This priority position for historical research certainly had a lasting impact on Walter Rauschenbusch. "What really matters here is that the scientific source-critical retreat into history is always connected with curiosity for an explanation for the respective present and the justification for present day claims to validity."[36] The historical contextualization and relativization of biblical texts had the potential to subject the traditional dogmatic content of Christianity to a radical and contemporary critique. After Rauschenbusch's close friends Leighton Williams and Nathaniel Schmidt expressed their fundamental difficulties with the manuscript he had drafted in Germany, criticizing its lack of inclusion of more recent exegetical literature, it would be sixteen more years before Rauschenbusch would publish the completely revised work under the new title of *Christianity and the Social Crisis* in April 1907—shortly before his second research trip to Germany.[37]

DISCOVERIES IN HIS WORK, CHRISTIANITY AND THE SOCIAL CRISIS

The following section presents some observations based on Rauschenbusch's book *Christianity and the Social Crisis.*[38] In this review, I will concentrate on the German authors that he names and references. Rauschenbusch begins his work with a detailed "historical" section, which lays the biblical foundation for his statements. In this respect, the consistent application of the historical perspective is particularly striking. He began with the Old Testament, making clear and specific reference to the prophetic tradition. In his introductory chapter on the significance of the prophets, Rauschenbusch

---

[36] Slenczka, *Fakultät*, 56–57.

[37] Minus, *American Reformer*, 79.

[38] Walter Rauschenbusch, *Christianity and the Social Crisis* (New York, London: MacMillan 1907); Walter Rauschenbusch, "Christianity and the Social Crisis," in *Walter Rauschenbusch. Published Works and Selected Writings, Vol. I*, ed. William H. Brackney (Macon, GA: Mercer University Press, 2018), 1–293.

refers to Emil Kautzsch (1841–1910), professor of Old Testament and Hebrew in Basel, Tübingen, and Halle, who assumed an approach critical of the Bible, very similar to Julius Wellhausen.[39] Rauschenbusch quotes Kautzsch regarding the socially critical orientation of the prophecy of Amos. In doing so, Rauschenbusch was making reference to the newest findings from historical and critical research into the Old Testament. Additional reference is made to Frants Peter William Meyer Buhl (1850–1932), a Danish Old Testament and Oriental studies specialist at the University of Leipzig, who was the first Protestant theologian to present a biography of Mohammed.[40]

In the second chapter, which examined Jesus's social goals,[41] Rauschenbusch called for the Bible and the New Testament to be read from a social and historical contextual perspective. This would enable the choice of a new, innovative, and up-to-date approach after the many approaches that concentrated primarily on the individual. Karl Hase (1800–1890)—associate professor of theology in Jena—described Rauschenbusch as the source of the first scientific approach to the life of Jesus. In his textbook, *Geschichte Jesu* (*History of Jesus*), first published in1876, Hase was already able to look back on fifty years of research into the life of Jesus (*Leben Jesu Forschung*).[42] In his series of lectures in 1819, Schleiermacher had initially mapped out the topic as being particularly relevant. The textbook also forms a replica of the controversy surrounding Johann David Strauss's book on the life of Jesus. In his account, Hase understood the Gospels to be credible sources, but that they also need to be subject to historical review. Hase portrayed Jesus primarily for his religious creed and morality. This corresponded to an ethical understanding of the kingdom of God that was typi-

---

[39] Cf. Andreas Freye, *Emil Kautzsch (1910). Alttestamentler und Orientalist* (Berlin: 2018); Rudolf Smend, *Traditionsbewußte Erneuerung der alttestamentlichen Wissenschaft: Emil Kautzsch (1841–1910,* in Andreas Urs Sommer (Hrsg.), *Im Spannungsfeld von Gott und Welt. Beiträge zu Geschichte und Gegenwart des Frey-Grynaeischen Instituts in Basel 1747–1997* (Basel: Schwabe, 1997), 111–22.

[40] Knud Jeppesen, "Frants Buhl as an Old Testament Scholar" *The Isaiah Commentary in Danish,* in Katherine Dell, Graham Davies, and Yee von Koh, eds., "Genesis, Isaiah and Psalms. A Festschrift to honour Professor John Emerton for his eightieth birthday," *Vetus Testamentum, Supplements* 135 (Amsterdam: 2010): 153–62.

[41] Rauschenbusch, *Christianity and the Social Crisis,* 49.

[42] Werner Zager, *Jesusforschung in vier Jahrhunderten* (Berlin, Boston: 2014), 64.

cal of liberal theology. "Jesus' purpose was not, in the first instance, the proclamation of doctrine, but the awakening of a spirit, which, as a holy common spirit, would establish a kingdom of religious community."[43] Rauschenbusch was clearly and evidently able to relate to these statements, as he himself sought to understand Jesus in the historical context. It is interesting, however, that Rauschenbusch does not simply reproduce Strauss's controversial theses, choosing instead to affiliate himself with Hase's measured historical-critical point of view.

Rauschenbusch began his historical introduction to the works of Jesus with John the Baptist, whom he portrayed primarily for his call to repentance and ethical obedience.[44] His proclamation of the kingdom of God following on from the prophets was a vision for a national revival. Jesus raised the anticipated kingdom onto an ethical foundation and, thus, it came to represent social hope. Rauschenbusch presented the close interconnection between Jesus and John the Baptist in careful detail, as well as the popular movement that shaped Jesus's messianic expectation and his mission. In this way, Jesus is placed in the tradition of the prophets. Thus, an almost prophetic type of religion took shape. In order to depict the continuity of the prophetic legacy and, at the same time, to present Jesus's very clear exceeding of this legacy, Rauschenbusch referred to the renowned Old Testament specialist Julius Wellhausen (1844–1918) and his work *Israelitische und Jüdische Geschichte* (*Israelite and Jewish History*).[45] Wellhausen had clearly differentiated between Jesus as the bearer and Jesus as the subject of the Gospel. In Wellhausen's view, the Gospels did not offer direct access to the historical Jesus.

It is very interesting to note how strongly Rauschenbusch repeatedly highlighted the historical contextualization of Jesus. In this respect, he followed both the historical-critical research approach in the Old and New Testament, as well as Adolf von Harnack's new dogma-critical approach of church historical research.[46] In his standard reference on the history of dogma, Harnack traced the path of the original Gospel in its analysis of the

---

[43] Karl Hase, *Geschichte Jesu. Nach akademischen Vorlesungen* (Leipzig: 1876), 403.

[44] Rauschenbusch, *Christianity and the Social Crisis*, 51.

[45] Ibid., 53; Rudolf Smend, *Julius Wellhausen. Ein Bahnbrecher in drei Disziplinen* (München: 2006).

[46] Slenczka, *Fakultät*, 59.

Hellenistic world, which ultimately led to its reshaping by the objectivizing dogma. This essentially negative display of history and this dogma-critical approach are also to be found time and again in Rauschenbusch's statements.[47] He repeatedly presented the history of Christendom as an aberration, which would appear ultimately to have made the creator of an ecclesiological machinery out of Jesus.[48]

Rauschenbusch developed the theology of Jesus's kingdom of God in connection with, and yet detached from, the messianic hopes of his time. In doing so, he emphasized incessantly the social and collective dimension of his statements, which were already being positioned as the universal transformation of national hopes.[49] "But Jesus never fell into the fundamental heresy of later theology; he never viewed the human individual apart from human society; he never forgot the gregarious nature of man."[50] With its development into a social understanding of God's kingdom, Rauschenbusch's revivalist legacy was clearly and significantly broken apart. His interpretation of Scripture followed historical-critical methodology, which he consistently used on everything from biblical texts through to text-critical and literary critical comments or notes on the resources.[51] Likewise, synoptic comparisons and elaborations of different perspectives on the Gospels all followed the same core structure. What is striking in this context is that the largest proportions of his text are based on his rereading of Bible passages from the Gospels, and there are basically very few references to the related secondary literature.

The third chapter of his book dealt with social initiatives from early Christendom.[52] Once again, the negative view of history is explicitly set against Jesus's preaching and his works. Rauschenbusch presents a particularly critical assessment of the development of sacramental theology, correlating this to the implanting of superstitious rituals.[53] However, even the formulation of doctrines relating to the teaching of the Trinity and to

---

[47] Rauschenbusch, *Christianity and the Social Crisis*, 55. In this work, he traced the path of the original Gospel into the Hellenistic world.

[48] Rauschenbusch, *Christianity and the Social Crisis*, 92.

[49] Ibid., 61.

[50] Ibid., 65–66.

[51] Ibid., 76 –79.

[52] Ibid., 93.

[53] Ibid., 94.

Christology in the early church are represented mercilessly as aberrations by Rauschenbusch and without any apparent differentiation. In this inventory of church history, Rauschenbusch refers repeatedly and explicitly to Harnack's *Die Mission und Ausbreitung des Christentums in den ersten drei Jahrhunderten* (*The Mission and Spread of Christianity in the First Three Centuries*).[54] The plurality of Christian movements, which have undoubtedly taken place, were suppressed, or even eliminated, by the standardizing mainstream church. This had a direct impact on the primary sources, which were deemed to be heretical trends and were not handed down through the process of canonization.

Rauschenbusch refers to Heinrich von Weizsäcker (1822–1899) and his work *Das apostolische Zeitalter der christlichen Kirche* (*The Christian Church in the Time of the Apostles*), which has been described as a classical work from the epoch of the reconstruction of the origins of early Christianity, and which should be seen as a rigorous, historical-critical, analytical writing of history.[55] In order to trace the suppressed social ideals associated with the Jewish-Christian movement, Rauschenbusch also raised apocryphal writings that were published, among others, by Adolf Hilgenfeld, professor of the New Testament and Early Church History in Jena. By highlighting these, he also implied an approach that is critical of the canon and the process of canonization. Rauschenbusch contrasted Paul with the preaching and traditions of Jesus.[56] However, with a reference to Bernhard Weiss and his textbook on the biblical theology of the New Testament from 1868,[57] Rauschenbusch also acknowledged the moderate critical school, which sought to follow the middle ground and, thus, distinguish itself from the direction assumed in Tübingen.[58]

Rauschenbusch steadily covered the history of the early Christian communities and examined them for their social components, such as the new community comprising Jews and heathens, or the joint property of the

---

[54] Ibid., 95; 112; 129; 130; 132; 156.

[55] Ibid., 100; Weizsäcker, *Konrad Hammann, Rudolf Bultmann. Eine Biographie* (Tübingen: 2012), 375.

[56] Rauschenbusch, *Christianity and the Social Crisis*, 102.

[57] Ibid., 104.

[58] Leonhard Goppelt, *Theologie des Neuen Testaments* (Göttingen: 1980), 42. An additional author that he quoted: Ernst Dobschütz, *Urchristliche Gemeinden* (118).

early Christian community in Jerusalem.[59] In his account, Rauschenbusch drew on statements made by Rudolph Sohm, albeit without broaching the issue of Sohm's controversy with Harnack.[60] This allowed his references to appear eclectic.[61]

In order to clarify the continuity of Christian love and deaconry, Rauschenbusch did not just refer once again to Harnack, but he also even cited Karl Kautsky (1854–1938). Kautsky was a prominent journalist and member of the Social Democratic Party of Austria (SPÖ).[62] His argument was supported with references to authors from the field of history, such as Hermann Schiller.[63]

In the fourth chapter,[64] Rauschenbusch addressed the question of why the church had not played a role in renewing society or, alternatively, why it had not made a significant contribution to social development—in spite of its clearly existent potential. The historical analysis tends to become more superficial at this point and less differentiated. He described the history of Christianity by means of rough lines from its growth into a state religion through to the end of the Middle Ages. He saw the primary problem in the fact that while Christianity has campaigned time and again against social hardships and injustices, it has never genuinely challenged the social order of any respective epoch.[65] The church did not stand up for social reform according to the principles advocated by Jesus. It was not the pioneer of women's emancipation, and it did not fight for the implementation of democracy, quite the contrary. From the time of the apostles, the church was not, and has not been, socially politically active.

---

[59] Rauschenbusch, *Christianity and the Social Crisis*, 123.

[60] Stefan Seit, "Charisma oder Recht? Webers Charisma-Konzept und das Bild der Kirche in Rudolph Sohms Interpretation des Ersten Clemensbriefs. Vorüberlegungen zu einem schwierigen Begriff," in *Das Charisma. Funktionen und symbolische Repräsentationen*, eds. Pavlína Rychterová, Stefan Seit, and Raphaela Veit (Berlin: 2008), 13–58, esp. 13–31.

[61] Cf. Rauschenbusch, *Christianity and the Social Crisis*, 125. Further reference: Gerhard Uhlhorn, *Die christliche Liebesthätigkeit in der alten Kirche*, 1882–84, 2 vols.

[62] Harald Koth, "Meine Zeit wird wieder kommen ..." *Das Leben des Karl Kautsky* (Berlin: 1993).

[63] Rauschenbusch, *Christianity and the Social Crisis*, 133;

[64] Ibid., from 143.

[65] Ibid., 149.

Rauschenbusch used the example of slavery to make it crystal clear how long the church was willing to accept the existing order and the oppression of slaves, having even held slaves itself. Sadly, the attitude continues in the modern-day church; Paul was by no means a social revolutionary, but the fact that he lived under a repressive political system should not perpetuate the concept that Christians today should do the same. Because of the constant concentration on eternal life—a development from the early church—the proclamation of the kingdom of God was pushed into the background. In this passage, Rauschenbusch repeated his degenerating view of church history (see above), similar to that of Harnack.

The concentrated fascination with the hereafter has made the church blind to social hardships in the present time, Rauschenbusch believed. The same applied to the antagonism of spirit and flesh—the ascetic orientation of Christendom since the early church—which was later transformed into monastic life. Rauschenbusch reiterated his proposition that Christianity had lost its potential for social direction-setting very early on, as it became preoccupied with the introduction of a new ceremonialism and attachment to rituals.[66] Once again, he returned to his criticism of the development of sacramental theology and practice. "But when Christianity turned its deepest interest from ethical conduct to sacramental ritual, it thereby paralyzed its power of moral transformation."[67] Through this fundamental assessment, renewed criticism is attached to doctrinal education. "A type of Christianity in which pagan superstition and Greek intellectualism had paralyzed the original social and ethical impetus, was in no condition to undertake the immense task of reorganizing social relations on a Christian basis."[68] Likewise, in his analysis of the development of church history, Rauschenbusch did not hold back his sharp criticism of the Roman Catholic Church.[69]

The Reformation was also not particularly effective in achieving any major change in the relationship between church and state. If anything, the church actually fell even deeper into dependence on leaders and authorities. Rauschenbusch identified potential solutions for this historical church legacy, which he clearly saw as a burden, in the writings of the sociologist Eberhard Friedrich Schäffle (1831–1903). As an economist, Schäffle was a pro-

[66] Ibid., 177.
[67] Ibid., 177.
[68] Ibid., 179.
[69] Ibid., 192.

ponent of the "Organismal Theory" in the social sciences.[70] Moreover, the transformation of society, in his opinion, cannot make any genuine progress without the contribution of the science of sociology, which at the time was still in its infancy as an academic field.

In the end of this chapter, he returned once again to the traditional interpretation of Scripture, which is equally lacking the social and political dimension of biblical sources.[71] In Rauschenbusch's opinion, the church had allowed foreign influences to determine its path and has therefore missed its great mission. In this way, he summarized his critical viewpoint on church history once more. He believed the time had come with the development of the modern age when it would finally be possible to overcome all the old aberrations and undesirable developments, including otherworldliness and asceticism among a long list. "We are standing at the turning of the ways. We are actors in a great historical drama. It rests upon us to decide if a new era is to dawn in the transformation of the world into the kingdom of God, or if Western civilization is to descend to the graveyard of dead civilizations and God will have to try once more."[72]

In the fifth chapter,[73] Rauschenbusch turned towards the crises of the present day, although I will not be able to give a close analysis of these. In this section, he summarized sociological observations, which he had made during his pastorate in New York, and the proceeds from the pursuit of economic approaches.

In the subsequent sixth chapter, Rauschenbusch dealt with the position of the church in the contemporary crisis of his time, its earning capacity and its conflicts of interest in the light of the social developments.[74] Just as in the previous chapter, the focus is not primarily on the *theological* integration or evaluation, but it presents a harsh critique of the capitalist economic system and the entanglement of the Christian churches with the system. In this context, Rauschenbusch took a stand regarding the situation in Germany.[75] The German state church had not expressed any sympathy at all

---

[70] *Albert Schäffle (1831-1903): The Legacy of an Underestimated Economist*, ed. Jürgen G. Backhaus (Frankfurt: 2010).

[71] Rauschenbusch, *Christianity and the Social Crisis*, 197

[72] Ibid., 210.

[73] Ibid., from 211.

[74] Ibid., from 287.

[75] Ibid., 320–21.

for the Socialist movement. On the contrary, it preached the need for absolute loyalty towards the authorities, expounded the divine order of social classes, promoted subordination, and advocated for patience. Apparently, Socialism and Christianity were incompatible. As a consequence, the Socialist camp viewed the church as a powerful instrument supporting those in power and as a bulwark of conservatism. It comes, then, as no surprise that the Socialist movement in Germany assumed a clearly anti-church stance. In spite of all the church's social advocacy and commitment, which it ultimately did put into practice, it lost the support of the workers and working classes. Now, at last, the clergy in Germany might have awakened to its reality and acknowledged the central importance of social issues. However, the reality remained that Rauschenbusch had cited Germany as a warning example, not as a role model.

The final chapter[76] addressed the question of what is to be done now, and contains concrete examples for social change, which the church should actively introduce and support. It should not be acceptable that social regeneration is postponed to an indeterminate future simply because of historical church developments. On the contrary, the church should become actively involved in Christianization of social and societal life. In this chapter, Rauschenbusch makes virtually no reference to German authors or sources. However, it is interesting that he did describe at the very end some Christian "martyrs" who have given their all for social issues. He refers specifically to Rudolf Todt, who campaigned both as a pastor and as a writer for dialogue to be opened up between the church, workers, and Socialism.[77]

CONCLUSION

The first half of the book, which I have examined for its background, as well as its interconnection with German theology, addresses biblical sources and presents a critical analysis of church history. This concludes with the quoted climax, according to which the present day represents an irretrievable situation for Christianity requiring definitive decision making.

[76] Ibid., from 343.

[77] Ibid., 417; Günter Brakelmann, *Kirche und Sozialismus im 19. Jahrhundert. Die Analyse des Sozialismus und Kommunismus bei Johann Hinrich Wichern und bei Rudolf Todt* (Wittenberg: 1966); Christian Buchholz, "Der vergessene und unterschlagene Rudolf Todt. Historischer Versuch eines Dialogs zwischen Kirche und Sozialismus," in *Deutsches Pfarrerblatt* 78 (1987): 360–62.

The reading matter makes it clear that Rauschenbusch had comprehensively considered and acknowledged the products of historical-critical research in Germany. In doing so, there is no doubt that he dealt quite eclectically with the fruits of his reading. In the development of Rauschenbusch's interpretation with respect to critique of doctrine and the transformation of Christian origins, he quite clearly followed Adolf von Harnack's perspectives, with Harnack leading the list of references. Rauschenbusch's statements presented the historical approach that became increasingly well established in theological study in Germany towards the end of the nineteenth century. This approach was also evident in the general culture, whereby almost nothing remained of the revivalist piety or any trace of his father's biblical literalism. However, in Rauschenbusch's vision of a church that actively initiates fundamental and radical social reform, he did not fall back on the tenets of German theology. That was quite simply too politically conservative.

Chapter 4

Everybody Is God's Somebody: Samuel DeWitt Proctor and the Black Social Gospel

Adam L. Bond

The emerging scholarship on the Black Social Gospel has brought new names and ideas to the attention of the American religious historian.[1] Some notable leaders within the African American experience have received recognition for their social engagement, but their writings are not appraised as worthy theological treatises. The black church, however, has always been a Social Gospel institution. Its leaders, when less concerned about doctrinal orthodoxy than human flourishing, have debated the path to uplift for the race *and* sought to land the "souls" of its people upon the shores of paradise—earthly or ethereal. Over a century before the Social Gospel musings of Walter Rauschenbusch (1861–1918), Washington Gladden (1836–1918), and Shailer Mathews (1863–1941) were etched out in the lecture halls and sanctuaries of their respective institutions and churches, black churches heard and shaped a Gospel that responded to the ills of society. Their plight was grounded in a global white supremacy that lasted in the forms of slavery, Jim Crow, and varied iterations of racism in the United States. And with time, the dialogue between the African American quest for liberation and the "formal" theological strands of a Social Gospel theology intersected in the minds and literature of numerous black religious intellectuals. Among them is the Reverend Dr. Samuel DeWitt Proctor.

A celebrated educator and churchman, Proctor (1921–1997) considered himself to be an heir of the black prophetic tradition of the Social Gospel and intellectual son of Walter Rauschenbusch. Proctor was born on July 13, 1921, in Norfolk, Virginia, growing up in the segregated community of Huntersville. He understood the weight of being a "race man" and laid claim to the liberal trajectory of African American Christianity in the

---

[1] Portions of this essay are adapted from my book on Proctor. See *The Imposing Preacher: Samuel DeWitt Proctor and Black Public Faith* (Minneapolis, MN: Fortress Press, 2013).

twentieth century. Although his name is not yet a part of the canon of modern American church history, he is a saint in black church circles. Numerous African American clergy members with activist concerns, moreover, have placed their work for social justice under the banner of his name. The Samuel DeWitt Proctor Conference, Inc., grew out of the spirit of his ministry and the social justice advocacy of his protégés.

Proctor rose to positions of influence in a period of heightened racial conflict. He was a prominent Baptist minister, college president (of two historically black universities) from 1955 to 1962, a former associate director of the Peace Corps during the Kennedy-Johnson administration(s), and the pastor of the historic Abyssinian Baptist Church in Harlem from 1972 to 1989, succeeding Adam Clayton Powell Jr (1908–1972).[2] Proctor witnessed, participated in, and lived beyond the modern civil rights struggle. His actions and ideas were informed by a sense of duty to the cause of black freedom. He accepted, therefore, the mantle of prophet of a black public faith flavored with a Social Gospel theology. Proctor relied upon his instruction within the black church and theological education in American theological liberalism when framing the Gospel of uplift that informed his five decades of public leadership. To be sure, he leveraged a Black Social Gospel theology within the pulpit and classroom, church and academy, as a platform to advocate for the personhood of African Americans—the equality of black being—in ways that would create awareness of the social crisis caused

---

[2] For biographical information on Proctor, see Samuel DeWitt Proctor, *The Substance of Things Hoped For: A Memoir of African-American Faith*, with a foreword by Marian Wright Edelman (New York: G. P. Putnam's Sons, 1995); Samuel D. Proctor, *Samuel Proctor: My Moral Odyssey*, with a foreword by Bill Moyers (Valley Forge, PA: Judson, 1989); and Marvin A. McMickle, "Proctor, Samuel D.," in *An Encyclopedia of African American Christian Heritage* (Valley Forge, PA: Judson, 2002). Proctor published many books, mostly pastoral in nature. He published numerous books on preaching, and though his earliest text, *The Young Negro in America: 1960–1980* (New York: Association Press, 1966), would probably be considered by most as outside of the theological genre, it reflects his practical theology. His contribution extends to the field of education as well. He published several articles in education journals. Yet his popularity is somewhat limited to the African American tradition. This may be the product of his time in historic black colleges and universities, his time on the black "preaching circuit," and his work in seminaries with African American church leaders.

by racism in American society and as the foundation for promoting "genuine community."

THE MISSION AND PURPOSE OF THE BLACK SOCIAL GOSPEL

Gary Dorrien's definition of the Black Social Gospel is useful for the conversation in this essay. Dorrien writes:

> The black Social Gospel was a complex phenomenon from its beginning. It was a form of social Christianity that imagined what a new abolitionism needed to be under the conditions of modern social consciousness and racial segregation. Most of it powerfully identified with U.S. Americanism despite its variable strains of black nationalism, especially cultural nationalism. Black Social Gospel theology featured evangelical and modernist tropes, a politics of racial justice opening out to a comprehensive politics of social justice, and, usually, an aspiration to forge alliances with white progressives on both counts.[3]

The Black Social Gospel is a Social Christianity and/or philosophical and political tradition that emerged as an intellectual—not merely practical—force in the late nineteenth century. It found its "formal" voice in the early years of the twentieth century and began to wane in the latter years of the civil rights movement. The Black Christian Social Gospel identifies race as the point of departure for discerning a religious solution for the racialized political and economic ills of society. Persons such as Ralph Luker, among other thinkers, have documented the ways in which the Black Social Gospel has operated as an ideological force and social-political philosophy behind the creation of organizations and clubs such as the NAACP and the Urban League. And studies by persons such as Peter Paris, Gary Dorrien, Susan Lindley, Judith Weisenfeld, and Christopher Evans have helped us distinguish the theological merits of Black Social Gospel traditions within the larger canon of black religious thought.[4] Samuel DeWitt Proctor, Howard

---

[3] Gary Dorrien, *Breaking White Supremacy* (New Haven, CT: Yale University Press, 2018), 96.

[4] See Peter J. Paris, *The Social Teaching of the Black Churches* (Philadelphia, PA: Fortress Press, 1985); Susan Hill Lindley, "'Neglected Voices and Practice in the Social Gospel,'" *Journal of Religious Ethics* 18/1 (1990): 75–102; Judith Weisenfeld, *African American Women and Christian Activism: New York's Black YWCA,*

Thurman (1899–1981), Nannie Helen Burroughs (1879–1961) and others were committed to a reading of the Christian faith that made a theological case for the Gospel as something that was/is socially oriented. They were guided by what Peter Paris calls the non-racist black prophetic principle (i.e., a belief in the parenthood of God and kinship of humanity), and they envisioned a "beloved" or "genuine" community that celebrated the inherent personhood of all humanity. In most instances, Black Social Gospelers privileged a historical Jesus who was or became Christ through his paradigm-shattering life as a human being. (In other words, Jesus raised the bar for human existence.) And they saw the church as one vehicle for transforming society. The Social Gospel of Walter Rauschenbusch and others gave some of these black religious leaders new language for what they already believed; notions that were already embedded in their congregational and cultural DNA.

Proctor's public faith had at its foundation a concern for black humanity. His numerous sermons and publications reflected a belief in the worth of persons, especially, but not limited to, African Americans. Race remained a constant in his religious reflections. As Dwight Hopkins has noted, one cannot speak of theological anthropology in America without race entering into the conversation.[5] Proctor's experience as a black man in this nation included the life and death of Jim Crow, the civil rights movement, and the

---

1905–1945 (Cambridge, MA: Harvard University Press, 1997); and Christopher H. Evans, *The Social Gospel in American Religion: A History* (New York: New York University Press, 2017). See also Barbara Dianne Savage, *Your Spirits Walk Beside Us: The Politics of Black Religion* (Cambridge, MA: Belknap Press; Harvard University Press, 2008).

[5] Dwight N. Hopkins, *Being Human: Race, Selves, Culture* (Minneapolis, MN: Fortress Press, 2005), 118. Hopkins writes, "In the United States an obsession with race is deeply embedded in the concept of a human being. The 1607 Jamestown, Virginia, and 1620 Plymouth, Massachusetts, arrivals of White Christians from Europe created a ranking in which human beings were placed on a racial scale in the so-called New World. This racial hierarchy inspired the Christian genocide of and land removal from American Indians, and the Christian enslavement of millions of Africans and African Americans in North America. These movements were marked by their color-coded aesthetics and power. Consequently, every single American, as well as those who visit the United States, receives a racial status within the anthropological hierarchy. And in the historical definition of the God-human interaction, race seeps in and out of the doctrine of theological anthropology."

introduction of affirmative action. He grounded his beliefs about humanity in the claim that "everybody is God's somebody."[6] This idea summarizes his complex response to racism and its consequences in American public life. As Proctor saw it, a "spurious anthropology" plagued the United States. He fought the racist practices that stemmed from that anthropology with a public faith that reflected a Social Gospel that was preached and practiced by numerous black Christians in the United States.

The basis of Proctor's claim was simple: all human beings are the children of God. This basic tenet of Christianity was foundational in the liberal theology of his age, but it also had meaning among African American Christians dating back to the eighteenth century—even earlier. Proctor was an integrationist who fought for equality in America. He was an activist who fought against racism with the power of persuasion. He believed that racism was at the root of many of the problems that adversely affected African Americans. He wanted to increase the opportunities that would create greater prospects for children of all races to achieve educational success and for persons who were in poverty to achieve a reasonable standard of living. He wanted to eradicate racism. His fight for equality also displayed advocacy of a black middle-class ethic of self-help by way of thrift, piety, education, and political participation. This notion is indicative of a longstanding tradition of African American Christianity as well, one that has concerned itself with social ethics and the problem of racism in American life.[7] Proctor was a part of that tradition and arrived at his conclusions after years of formation that nurtured his perspective on American life.

---

[6] See Samuel DeWitt Proctor's sermon, "Everybody Is God's Somebody," in *Sermons from the Black Pulpit, Samuel DeWitt Proctor and William D. Watley* (Valley Forge, PA: Judson Press, 1984).

[7] Richard W. Wills Sr., "Civil Rights and the Idea of Imago Dei: A Theological Reconsideration of Martin Luther King Jr." (Unpublished PhD dissertation, University of Virginia, 2005). He states a similar thesis for the public witness of Martin Luther King Jr. Wills also argues that King's concern for humanity and the pursuit of justice are informed by his religious beliefs about humanity. Wills claims that King was able to synthesize the positions of figures in Christian history, the Black Church, and voices from his formal theological education to establish his own ideas. Proctor and King are very similar when one considers their backgrounds and their views. Where they differ may be in their activism. King was a very vocal proponent of nonviolent protest. In addition, he led the demonstrations and marches that grew out of the notion.

A BLACK SOCIAL GOSPEL EDUCATION

Proctor was immersed in a theological network that promoted an engaged, Social Christianity. I will not describe the contributions of his family and church, the Bank Street Baptist Church of Norfolk, but they were integral in his upbringing and faith formation. Proctor was connected to theological institutions and communities that nurtured his Social Gospel inclinations. He had African American mentors who taught him the liberal ideas that he would affirm in his graduate education in Northern, predominantly white institutions. He embraced the idea that a very human Jesus was concerned about the plight and flourishing of humanity.

Proctor attended the Baptist-related Virginia Union University, a small historically black institution in Richmond, Virginia, and encountered religious intellectuals who would influence his vocational direction. Virginia Union established for itself a reputation for educating African American clergymen. The school started with the missionary efforts of the American Baptist Home Mission Society (later affiliated to the Northern Baptist Convention) and their desire to provide education for the "freedmen" during and after the Civil War.[8] The school is the product of the merger of Wayland Seminary (Washington, DC), the Richmond Theological Institute, and later, the Hartshorn Memorial College for women (all three schools were Baptist-related institutions). Ralph Reavis has observed that the goal of the school was to train leaders to teach, preach, and guide African American men and women of the Negro race. From its beginnings, the institution was dedicated to providing top-notch facilities and faculty members for its students. Proctor completed his studies at Virginia Union after transferring from Virginia State University in Petersburg. At Virginia Union, two prom-

[8] For more information on the history of Virginia Union University, see John M. Ellison, ed. "A Century of Service to Education and Religion," *Virginia Union Bulletin* 65 (June 1965): 4–107; *Virginia Union University and Some of Her Achievements: Twenty-Fifth Anniversary, 1899–1924*, ed. Miles Mark Fisher (Richmond: Virginia Union University, 1924); Cecil Raynard Taliaferro, "Virginia Union University: The First One Hundred Years, 1865–1965" (Unpublished PhD dissertation, University of Pittsburgh, 1975); and Ralph Reavis Sr., "Black Higher Education among American Baptists in Virginia: From the Slave Pen to the University," *American Baptist Quarterly* 11/4 (1992): 357–74. See also William H. Brackney, *Congregation and Campus: North American Baptists and Higher Education* (Macon: GA: Mercer University Press, 2008), 174–76.

inent scholar-practitioners invested in his journey. Richard I. McKinney (1906–2005), completing his PhD studies at Yale, had just taken on a faculty position at the university and would become the first dean of the School of Religion. And the most influential voice in Proctor's development as a religious intellectual would come from his relationship with the first African American president of the school, Dr. John Malcus Ellison (1889–1979).

Ellison was a teacher at heart, whose scholarship drew him little national acclaim in the larger academy. He completed his undergraduate studies at Virginia Union University (1917). He earned a master's degree from the Oberlin College Graduate School of Theology (1927) and his doctorate in sociology and Christian education at Drew University (1933). He was a churchman and educator, serving pastorates in Washington, DC, and in parts of Richmond, Virginia. During his professional career, Ellison founded and was the principal of a high school in his native Northumberland County, Virginia. His time in higher education included posts at Howard University, Virginia State College, and Virginia Union University. He succeeded William John Clark as the president of Virginia Union University in 1941. As the first African American alumnus to lead the school, Ellison's presidency generated enthusiasm within the student body and larger black community. Even after resigning the presidency, Ellison remained connected to the institution, settling into his post as professor and chancellor.

Ellison published several books and was adamant about preaching and writing. The list of his publications includes *Tensions and Destiny* (1953), *They Who Preach* (1956), and *They Sang through Crisis* (1961). He also published several pamphlets and books for local Baptist state conventions and ministerial organizations. Ellison credited his pastor, the Reverend Levi Reese Ball at the Shiloh Baptist Church in Reedville, Virginia, for setting a high example of ministry for him. Ball admonished Ellison not to emote during the sermon. (This lesson would stick with Ellison throughout his teaching and preaching career.) Ball prepared his sermons in manuscript form, and this practice rubbed off on Ellison. Concerning this, Ellison stated, "In my early ministry I began writing my sermons each week, endeavoring for correctness in composition and excellence in diction. My pastor, fortunately, was a man of fine education whose literary attainments appealed to me."[9] Seminary and graduate school probably cemented this prac-

---

[9] John Malcus Ellison to James H. Croushore, Archives and Special Collections, Douglas L. Wilder Library, Virginia Union University, Richmond, VA

tice for Ellison. The emphasis on writing translated well into his career as an administrator, preacher, and author. Many of his books consisted of his sermons. In his preaching manual, *They Who Preach*, Ellison dedicated a whole chapter to the idea of developing the sermon in written form. One needs to read only a brief portion of the chapter to understand Ellison's emphasis on writing and preaching. Ellison argued that writing challenges a preacher to be careful about his wording and intentional about the way she/he structures a sentence. This allows the preacher to produce a polished sermon with deeper insights and a "keener" interpretation.[10]

J. M. Ellison's sermons and writings were more than pious expressions of his evangelical faith. In an article entitled "The Problem of Community in America Today," Ellison argued that the race question was a pressing concern for black people. He stated, "The minority group for whom the phrase 'equal opportunity' has less meaning than any other is the American Negro."[11] In other sermons, Ellison included passages of famous literature and concepts from philosophy and psychology, and he combined his background in sociology with his understanding of God. He stated that the Apostle Paul's more excellent way (1 Cor. 12:31) requires the acknowledgment of "the dignity of human personality."[12] I am not sure if one can directly connect Ellison's emphasis on writing—and writing the sermon—to Proctor's practices and thoughts. The indirect influence is very clear, however. Reavis argues that Ellison had the ear of the preachers who sat in his classroom: "Dr. John M. Ellison influenced as many young ministers as any other clergyman of his day."[13] Proctor was within that sphere of influence.

Samuel Proctor's relationship with Ellison began early in Proctor's professional development. Bessie T. Proctor, Proctor's wife, observed that he and Ellison had a wonderful relationship dating back to Samuel Proctor's

---

(VUU); and John W. Kinney, "John Malcus Ellison: Narrated and Interpreted, 1980," photocopy, 7–8. Kinney interviewed Ellison for his research; the interview gives more detail about Ellison's relationship with Reverend Ball.

[10] John M. Ellison, *They Who Preach* (Nashville, TN: Broadman Press, 1956), 81.

[11] John M. Ellison, "The Problem of Community in America Today" *Journal of Religious Thought* 1 (1943): 13.

[12] John M. Ellison, *Tensions and Destiny* (Richmond, VA: John Knox Press, 1953), 126.

[13] Reavis, "Black Higher Education among American Baptists in Virginia," 370.

time in college. She noted that Proctor spent time with Ellison during those days. Proctor was Ellison's driver on many occasions.[14] Ellison was serious about the craft of preaching, and it is likely that Proctor looked to him for guidance. (Later correspondence between the two show that Proctor looked to Ellison for career advice and mentoring.)

Proctor was active on the campus of Virginia Union, and his extracurricular activities probably led Ellison to take note of this budding giant. In Proctor's senior year of college, he participated in a number of activities. A look through the school yearbook displays his busy itinerary. Proctor was band director, YMCA and NAACP advocate and participant, Pan-Hellenic Council member, president of the student government, vice president of the J. E. Jones Lyceum (the undergraduate ministers' group), honor student, and a member of the campus's Kappa Alpha Psi fraternity. He was not hard to notice on the small black college campus of Virginia Union University. Ellison, moreover, seemed to follow Proctor's academic and professional pursuits with interest. (Proctor sent Ellison regular updates on his progress in graduate school and at his church—the Pond Street Baptist Church in Providence, Rhode Island.) Between Ellison and Richard I. McKinney, Proctor had people who modeled the example of minister as scholar and practitioner. Both were proponents of the Social Gospel.

McKinney took time to mentor Proctor during his time as professor at Virginia Union. McKinney had also served as pastor of the Pond Street Baptist Church in Providence, Rhode Island, and would leave Virginia Union in 1944 to serve as president of Storer College in West Virginia. It is highly probable that Proctor's relationship with McKinney led to Proctor's nomination as the pastor of Pond Street in 1945.[15]

These prominent figures in Proctor's life were examples of educated black leadership and advocates of a social ministry. They exposed him to the possibilities that existed for persons to equip themselves intellectually in service to humanity. When the opportunity to attend seminary at Crozer Theological Seminary in Chester, Pennsylvania, was presented to Proctor,

---

[14] Mrs. Proctor shared this information in an informal telephone conversation with me on 21 March 2006.

[15] "Interrace Body Hears McKinney," *Providence Chronicle* (1 February 1947), 1. McKinney was also the biographer for Mordecai Wyatt Johnson, a champion of the Social Gospel and legendary president of Howard University.

theological education in the North was a logical step in his vocational development.

Similar to the educational journeys of Benjamin Mays, J. M. Ellison, and Howard Thurman, Proctor continued his education in schools that were influenced heavily by the liberal theological traditions of the late nineteenth and early twentieth centuries. Proctor completed his graduate professional studies at Crozer, pursued the PhD at Yale Divinity School, but transferred and graduated with a Doctor of Theology degree from Boston University School of Theology. Proctor left Virginia Union well equipped to enter the next phase of his academic career. With a solid intellectual foundation from Virginia Union and a strong social-spiritual foundation from home, Proctor was ready to engage the Social Gospel tradition, the historical-critical methods of biblical research, and racist attitudes at these formidable theological institutions.

In 1942 Proctor matriculated at Crozer Theological Seminary, a seminary affiliated with the Northern Baptist Convention. Although Proctor's education built upon his foundation at Virginia Union, it raised new questions for him about the Scriptures and his faith. In an article on Martin Luther King Jr.'s time at Crozer (1948–1951), Clayborne Carson has described some of the professors that Proctor would have encountered in his day. James B. Pritchard relied heavily on historical and archaeological findings when teaching his Old Testament course. Morton Scott Enslin, who taught New Testament courses, was a "Harvard-trained expert in the history of early Christianity." And George Washington Davis, a Northern Baptist educated in a Northern Baptist–sponsored seminary, was a disciple of Walter Rauschenbusch and the Social Gospel.[16] These men are some of the persons with whom Proctor spent time in dialogue. His description of the school may shed more light on the nature of its study of the Bible:

> The seminary was so radical in its approach to the Bible that it actually ruined the religious beliefs of some of my classmates. We were shocked to discover that Bible study included learning the history and geography of the Near East.... My professors taught that certain books of the Bible reflected different types of literature; some were written like poems or long parables to make a serious point. The teachers showed us how Bible stories had been revised by various

[16] Clayborne Carson, "Martin Luther King Jr.: The Crozer Seminary Years," *Journal of Blacks in Higher Education* 16 (Summer 1997): 124.

writers at different times, and taught us how to look at biblical events in a larger context. Indeed, by giving a deeper interpretation of the Bible, the Crozer theologians showed us how religion could have social and ethical application in the modern world.[17]

The theological path that Proctor traveled at Crozer presented some new challenges for him. The "Liberal" education at the seminary was different from his biblically conservative roots in the black Baptist tradition. He also had to deal with the issue of racism. Crozer may not have been as progressive on that issue as Proctor would have liked. Proctor, expecting the racial attitudes of educated Northern white theologians to be different from the ones he experienced from white persons in the South, learned that racist practices existed among the educated classes of the North as well. He was the only black student on the campus during his first year. One of his most memorable experiences was the new-student orientation. The students were given jobs to complete around the school, because the war (World War II) left Crozer short on staff. When the students gathered, the faculty supervisor, Dr. Reuben E. E. Harkness, announced all of the clerical and custodial assignments except for Proctor's work. He was the last person to receive a job. Proctor's responsibility was kitchen duty, and he "instantly aged ten years" when he learned of this task. Mrs. Moitz, the woman supervising food services, was ashamed of what had taken place and apologized to him. Proctor noted that it was then that he realized he was going to learn more about Jesus from the little old woman in the kitchen than he would from the professional theologians in the classroom. Mrs. Moitz and some other persons helped Proctor navigate the academic and social terrains of seminary life.[18]

---

[17] Proctor, *The Substance of Things Hoped For*, 47–48. See also Proctor, *My Moral Odyssey*, 64. In *My Moral Odyssey*, Proctor wrote, "The ultimate test of my freedom was the challenge to view the Bible differently. I was bound intellectually and spiritually, by loyalty to tradition and by emotional satisfaction, to cling to the Bible as the literal, inerrant word of God without further debate."

[18] Proctor, *The Substance of Things Hoped For*, 45; see also Samuel D. Proctor, "Turning the World Upside Down," sermon presented at the Trinity United Church of Christ, Chicago, IL, 1992, audiotape. See also Samuel D. Proctor, "Meeting the Challenge," *Selections* 14/3 (1998): 54–55.

An important person who must receive some attention when listing Proctor's intellectual mentors is the Reverend J. Pius Barbour.[19] Proctor sought refuge from and answers for the seminary experience in the Barbour home. Barbour, the pastor of the Calvary Baptist Church in Chester, Pennsylvania, from 1933 to 1974, was the first African American graduate of Crozer Seminary. Proctor spent time with Barbour, working through the "issues" he had during his years at the seminary. Proctor attended Calvary during his time at Crozer, and as Lewis V. Baldwin states, he became a "son" of the church.[20] (His service to the church probably included an occa-

---

[19] For more information on Barbour, see Lewis V. Baldwin, *There Is A Balm in Gilead* (Minneapolis, MN: Fortress Press, 1991); Richard Lischer, *The Preacher King: Martin Luther King, Jr. and the Word That Moved America* (New York: Oxford University Press, 1995), 67–71; Kirk Byron Jones, "King Had a Mentor in Chester" *Delaware County Daily Times* (Philadelphia area), 16 January 1989; Kirk Byron Jones, "The Activism of Interpretation: Black Pastors and Public Life," *Christian Century* 106/26 (1989): 817–18. We probably learn more about what took place during these visits from a survey of the research done on Martin Luther King Jr. As it relates to King studies, Barbour continues to appear as an important figure during King's time in Chester, Pennsylvania. Barbour worked with many of the African American students who came through the seminary. Proctor is among that group of students. He says little, however, in his writings about this experience. In Proctor's sermon "Taking Care of Unfinished Business," he mentioned that there were preachers who aided him in his journey. Moreover, he said that he asked the publisher of his book *Preaching about Crises in the Community* to list the names of those preachers—Joseph Pius Barbour, John Malcus Ellison, and John Bennett Henderson. See Samuel D. Proctor, "Taking Care of Unfinished Business," sermon presented at the Abyssinian Baptist Church, New York, 1987, audiotape.

Barbour and Proctor maintained a good relationship after Proctor's seminary days. Barbour was the editor of the *National Baptist Voice*, the official publication of the National Baptist Convention, USA. In a letter dated 1954, he invited Proctor to write an article for the periodical. Proctor dedicated his book on preaching about crisis in the community to Barbour. It is not clear how Proctor was introduced to Barbour. Based upon findings in the archives at Virginia Union University, it would not be a stretch to suggest that John M. Ellison alerted Barbour to Proctor's presence on the campus. Barbour and Ellison had a cordial relationship as well. In a letter to Ellison dated 1951, Barbour portended Proctor succeeding Ellison as the president of the Virginia Union. Barbour was about fifteen years off on his prediction.

[20] Baldwin, *There Is a Balm in Gilead*, 167.

sional Sunday-morning sermon and responsibility for one of its ministries.) In other words, the members adopted him as one of their own. Proctor described Barbour as a "scholarly man" who loved to participate in theological debates. Barbour was a conscientious person as it pertained to the matter of race in America, but his was not an activism of protest as much as it was mediation between the races. In examining Barbour, Richard Lischer notes that Martin Luther King Jr. appreciated the way in which he used the Hegelian dialectical method of preaching. Barbour was "skillful" with his use of the triadic movement of thesis, antithesis, and synthesis. Lischer argues that Barbour combined erudition with a folksy delivery.[21] The extent of Barbour's influence on Proctor is evident but immeasurable.

With Barbour as his mentor, Proctor remained immersed in the black church preaching tradition. Barbour later sought out opportunities for Proctor's voice to be heard among the members of the National Baptist Convention, USA. He wrote a letter to Proctor, inviting him to write an article for the *National Baptist Voice.* Barbour said he wanted to dig Proctor "out of oblivion."[22] In Barbour, Proctor remained connected to a person who understood preaching as a prophetic voice on matters of race. Proctor's relationship with Barbour was important during Proctor's Crozer period. Lischer acknowledges Proctor's place among the students Barbour mentored: "Of all the preachers who passed through the Barbour parlor over the years, Martin was the most promising, save perhaps for Sam Proctor, who would eventually succeed Adam Clayton Powell at Abyssinian Baptist Church in Harlem."[23] Proctor's time in Chester was important.

---

[21] Jones, "The Activism of Interpretation," 817; and Lischer, *The Preacher King,* 67–69. It is not clear if this was the preaching model that the Crozer preachers were taught. King is said to have been a practitioner as well. Proctor employs the same method and includes a "relevant question" to prepare listeners for the application of the truths that he presents in the thesis. Lischer interviewed Proctor for his section on Barbour's influence on King during the Crozer years. When reading this section, one cannot help but believe that Proctor describes some of the activities that took place during his time with Barbour.

[22] J. Pius Barbour to Samuel D. Proctor, 1 November 1951, Archives and Special Collections, VUU, Richmond, Virginia.

[23] Lischer, *The Preacher King,* 70. See also Proctor, *The Substance of Things Hoped For,* 49, 51. Two events from Proctor's time at Crozer should be acknowledged. In 1944, he married his college sweetheart, Bessie L. Tate, of Fredericksburg, Virginia. In that same year, they returned to Chester and accepted a job as

Proctor's formation within an incubator of Black Social Gospel thought prepared him for the education that he received in seminary and graduate school. Though he transferred from Yale, after spending a year with H. Richard Niebuhr (1894–1962) and Liston Pope (1909–1974), he landed at Boston University where its school of Personalism was on the ascent. Proctor balanced his pastorate and his studies, graduating with the Doctor of Theology degree in New Testament in 1950. To be sure, he never left the influence of the Liberal theological tradition. He could not avoid, nor did he choose to avoid, the ubiquitous conversations on Christian social ethics in the American Christianity of his day. This education shaped the way that Proctor understood the Jesus of his faith. He learned from these sources and voices to emphasize the historical Jesus as the example and model for Christian living. From this education, he learned the language that would make the Jesus of his childhood come alive in response to the social problems of the twentieth century.

Proctor saw in Jesus a cure to the human problem of sin. To solve this problem, Proctor argued, persons need a relationship with God. Christ accomplishes this objective. Proctor believed that Christ led the way for persons to live in relationship with God because of how Jesus lived and what he taught. Proctor summarized the matter in a tract on the ordinances of the Baptist church. In a section of the tract on the importance of the Lord's Supper, he reflected the basic belief that he held about the salvation that Christ offers: "This fellowship about the table is distinctive because we have not gathered around an idea, not around a book, not at a certain level of moral attainment, but we have gathered to remember a person who shared

---

live-in employees for the new president of the seminary, Dr. Edwin E. Aubrey (1896–1956) and his family. Aubrey succeeded Dr. James H. Franklin and kept Crozer entrenched in the Liberal theological tradition. Aubrey was a student of the University of Chicago and its empirical approach to theological studies. He earned the master of arts, bachelor of divinity, and doctor of philosophy degrees at the University of Chicago and taught at the school from 1929 until 1944. He served Crozer from 1944 to 1949. Proctor's interactions with Aubrey included theological discussions and studying the Aubreys "as though they were in a museum." Proctor kept in contact with Aubrey, seeking his guidance in revising his dissertation to submit to publishers.

our common humanity while at the same time pointed us to God."[24] He went on to write that the one who "seemest human and divine" exemplified the love of God to marginalized persons.

Proctor argued that the main aspects of Jesus's saving ministry were his teachings and his example. Jesus communicated the identity of God through his life and teachings. Proctor's view of Jesus was social and ethical. Jesus as Christ was the personality of God incarnate. He was the example and ethical paradigm of what God expects from humanity. These notions of Jesus were not new ideas in Proctor's world. Consider John M. Ellison's words about Jesus:

> Jesus had that kind of insight into the meaning of humanity. He had that profound awareness of God and man's relationship to God, and God's high purposes for all men. He wanted that conviction with His disciples and all of His followers in any age. Deep in His heart He carried the vision of what humanity could be if only the vital relationship between man and God could be established. And He had the profound conviction that it could be done. Toward that glorious ideal and goal all of His life's work and teachings were aimed.[25]

EDUCATION AND HUMANIZATION OF SOCIETY

For Proctor, all Americans should understand the consequences of racism in American life. In a 1985 sermon entitled "Jesus Christ, Prince of Peace," Proctor proclaimed:

> We are still fighting the civil war in so many places. We've not yet settled down and decided that blacks are free; that they are human; that they don't bite; that they don't go around all the time thinking of something violent to do; they do learn when they are taught; they can think; they can be responsible. Every day we are being nagged over and over again by this issue rising up to haunt us. It is practically impossible for us to spend the day thinking about things that everyone else would want to think about without having to pause at some time during the day and reckon with this strife that follows us on the basis of race in this country. We need to see this whole issue

[24] Samuel DeWitt Proctor, *The Christian Ordinances in Baptist Churches* (Richmond, VA: self-published, n.d.), 22–23. See also Samuel D. Proctor, "The Ministry of Reconciliation," L&S, *Providence Chronicle*, 2 October 1948.

[25] Ellison, *Tensions and Destiny*, 30.

> reconciled and the nation become one in freedom; and one in purpose; and one in fairness; one in justice; one in opportunity; one in the well-being of all her people.[26]

His early life in segregated Norfolk, Virginia, observing the racial codes of the South, displayed clearly for Proctor the problems of American society. It is fair to say that he saw racism as a primary cause of the moral crisis in the United States. At the root of racism was the devaluation of black personhood.

The racial problem in the United States concerned Proctor much more after his missionary tours in Europe and Asia. In 1954, Proctor reported his impressions of the world after returning from his missionary tour of 1953. He was a Baptist envoy along with several American Baptists who worked with local leaders in places such as India to turn over control of Baptist schools to the indigenous groups in those countries. During the trip, he reported that several residents questioned him about the nature of his relationship as a black person with the colonizers of the world. He was pressed to consider who he was as an American and as a citizen of the world. In one account, he recalled, "The bottom line was that I saw how many dark-skinned people lived in the world and that they all had been colonized by Europeans. This gave me an authentic identity with Third World people and their struggles for clean water, nutrition, food, health care, safe housing, basic education, and hope for a brighter future."[27] The report that Proctor submitted to the *National Baptist Voice* represents one of the earliest *written* statements that we have in which he presents his thoughts on matters of

---

[26] Samuel D. Proctor, "Jesus Christ, Prince of Peace," sermon presented at Abyssinian Baptist Church, New York, 1985, audiotape.

[27] Samuel D. Proctor, "Dean Proctor, Virginia, University, Reports on Trip to India," *National Baptist Voice* 26/10 (1954): 1, 13. I make the distinction "earliest written statements" because Proctor gave speeches at rallies during the Fair Employment Act movement in Providence, Rhode Island. At this time, there is no access to any written material that he produced during that time. He spoke on the radio and at a mass meeting to promote the cause, but these documents (if written) have not surfaced. In the weekly column for the *Providence Chronicle,* he said little to nothing about the racial problems in America. Proctor stated early in the 1954 article, "My discussion will be limited to the angle of a Negro, representing a foreign mission Board which has not succeeded in integrating Negroes into its work. I kept my eyes wide open and my ears to the ground for such overtones as only a Negro reared in the South and trained in Northern schools is capable of hearing."

race. Prompted by J. Pius Barbour, editor of the *Voice*, to recall his travels, Proctor shared stories about the way in which white missionaries raised questions about the ability of African Americans to proselytize persons in foreign countries. The sentiment affected the mood of the native residents, prompting them to look askance at Proctor until they conversed with him.

Proctor discerned the legacy of colonialism during that trip and realized the far-reaching influence of white supremacy. He saw, moreover, the extent to which European Americans, especially white Christians, were viewed with distrust in several locales. He stated, "One night I 'had it out' with 'leftist' students in Jamshedpur, India. They scolded me for being an American and a black person. They thought I should have fled my country or shot myself." But Proctor's response says much about his faith in America: "I explained that despite the injustices, I had accepted America as the place most likely to mature into a free, pluralistic society with individual liberties, a government by the consent of the governed, and an economy that could provide equal employment opportunities, housing, and education."[28] The trip alerted him to the urgency of the problems in the United States. He described the results of his travels by stating that his conscience underwent a "real metamorphosis."

Proctor witnessed an era of movements and changes in American society that kept him hopeful throughout his life. Yet he stated in one of his memoirs that he was awakened to the fact that integration was taking place "altogether too slow."[29] He believed that both whites and blacks in the United States were too comfortable with the state of race relations during the 1950s. That racism existed was not a question for Proctor. He was well aware of the existence of racism in the United States. He traced the effects of racism back to the origins of black/white relations at the founding of the American colonies. He wrote that racism "pervaded American culture since 1619." He argued that it arrived with the first enslaved Africans at Jamestown, Virginia. When whites realized that Africans could hold up under North American weather and diet, they made racial slavery an institution.

---

[28]Samuel D. Proctor, *My Moral Odyssey* (Valley Forge, PA: Judson, 1989), 89. I believe this first trip sensitized Proctor to the global experience of white supremacy.

[29]Proctor, *My Moral Odyssey*, 89.

He continued, "So today's Black minority condition is traceable to this incipient condition."[30]

Proctor saw in racial slavery the foundation of prejudice in American society. That prejudice contributed to the problems of black America was a given. The net result of it, he contended, was a "crisis in self-concept" among African Americans. In his memoir, he stated that some African Americans "grow to hate their identity," paralyzing any useful way of addressing the problems that they face. He observed, "An African American needs a healthy ego to shadowbox all day in a world not designed for her or his occupancy."[31]

Proctor believed that racism reached into most, if not all, aspects of American culture. He noted that white people maintained most systems of power in the United States. In the "religious right," he saw a threat to the rights of African Americans due to the fundamentalists' collusion with the state. Technology largely was limited to whites and minority populations were lacking in access. Wealth remained in the hands of an elite few. To be sure, he took issue with white backlash over programs such as affirmative action and the work of the Office of Economic Opportunity. He argued that many of the attacks against integration were made on specious grounds: "Whites who argue today that integration should not be forced and that groups should fall naturally into their own homogeneity freely and without interference have short memories. They have forgotten how segregation was invented and forced."[32] The late 1960s also proved to Proctor that African Americans who were vocal about gaining access to equal opportunity in the United States were treated poorly. As an integrationist, Proctor concerned himself with racism and the welfare of the nation. He was determined to see the nation live up to its pluralistic identity while embracing its national destiny and purpose. Within this framework, he contended, African Americans have historically represented the nation's great dilemma.

---

[30] Samuel D. Proctor, "Equity from a Racial/Ethnic Perspective," ERIC Document Research and Development Series No. 214J, National Center for Research in Vocational Education, 1981 ED215166, 4–5.

[31] See Samuel D. Proctor, *The Substance of Things Hoped For: A Memoir of African-American Faith* (New York: G. P. Putnam's Sons), 189.

[32] Proctor, *The Young Negro in America, 1960–1980* (New York: Association Press, 1966), 132.

The nation could hasten this embrace of its racial and ethnic pluralism through education. Proctor placed a large part of the burden on education. This meant, however, that the structures and content of the educational system and curriculum would need an intentional revision. The aim of education would be the humanization of society. He wrote, "Humanization refers to those conditions that encourage man to develop his unique and extraordinary capacities as a human being."[33] For Proctor, education needed some reworking to help society move in the direction of genuine community. The black population could no longer be content with the "favored and talented" black people representing the masses in "privileged positions" while impoverished members of the black community stayed locked into their positions in society. Too many resources reach privileged communities, and too many black and brown youth are marginalized in classrooms and in the work force due to the problems that stem from racism. Proctor saw education as the way to prepare people for inclusive community while stopping the cycle of poverty and futility in lower-income neighborhoods. He understood that people contribute to the larger systems that have calcified the racism in our institutions. Presenting at a conference at Duke University in 1965, Proctor placed the challenge to intelligent people of faith to help correct the wrongs of the past: "This is the wrong time for Christian, intelligent, concerned, dedicated people to be quiet and to allow the bigots and the superpatriots to misrepresent us, our country, and the cause of Christian idealism, which is still the dominant strain in our great American tradition."[34]

Employing the language of the Social Gospel, Proctor told the crowd that the kingdom of God invites people into a new moral standard for human existence and relationships.

AN ENGAGED PREACHER, A PUBLIC MINISTRY

A key component of Proctor's Social Gospel theology was the preacher's academic preparation. Proctor defined the preacher as that person who is "called by God, set apart, and acknowledged by the church as God's special

[33] Samuel D. Proctor, "Education and the Humanization of Society," *Educational Record* 57/4 (1977): 241.

[34] Samuel D. Proctor, "The Wrong Time to Be Silent," in *Christianity Amid Rising Men and Nations*, ed. Creighton Lacy (New York: Association Press, 1965), 173.

agent."[35] The preacher is authorized to preach the message because God "enters history" and gives people the assignment to preach. The calling that God places on one's life is the basis for one's ministry. Yet, Proctor argued, preachers should avail themselves of theological education. Proctor was adamant about the minister's preparation in some form of educational environment, preferably the seminary setting. On different occasions, he lamented the perils of the uneducated ministry. He called it sad when a pastor "has only a shallow preparation and is unable to teach."[36] He asked rhetorically about the consequences of a community that is "the victim of an untrained pastor." He implied that the result may be a community that must deal with a preacher who is a burden or embarrassment. Proctor saw education as the linchpin for the preaching ministry. The educated preacher receives the tools to engage the larger world and confront secular society.

Proctor had a particular vision for the education of church pastors and preachers. Understanding the traditional curriculum in the theological seminary, Proctor argued that its educational goals should be more practical. He desired a curriculum that moved away from theory and abstract concepts:

> It is a mistake, I believe, for preachers in training to focus more time and effort studying discursive, abstract, and analytical topics *about* Christianity than witnessing in detail the lives of those who followed Jesus in rare and creative *kingdom living*. It is also a mistake, I believe, for ministers in training to be exposed to many secondhand reports of discipleship at the expense of more hands-on practice in adventurous, selfless Christian and servant participation.[37]

A concept-focused education would not accomplish what Proctor felt ministers for this age required.

Proctor took a more earthy approach to the topic of ministry. He served congregations in his career and taught ministers in a seminary environment for a number of years as well. He wanted to mentor pastoral/practical theologians who would become public theologians—agents of change. At the heart of Proctor's thought was the idea that preachers should

---

[35] Samuel D. Proctor, *The Certain Sound of the Trumpet: Crafting a Sermon of Authority* (Valley Forge, PA: Judson, 1994), 6–7.

[36] Samuel D. Proctor, *We Have This Ministry: The Heart of the Pastor's Vocation* (Valley Forge, PA: Judson, 1996), 14.

[37] Samuel D. Proctor, "How Shall They Hear?" in *Effective Preaching for Vital Faith* (Valley Forge, PA: Judson, 1992), 85.

have a prophetic concern in their understanding of ministry. Yet his concern was holistic. He did not want a preacher to mount the pulpit forty Sundays in the year (or more), talking about social issues on each of those Sundays. He had a concern for caring for the church as a community and for the person as a child of God. Proctor understood that persons need counsel, and he cared for the soul. He understood that the sermon would reflect diverse concerns. His major issue, however, was for the preacher as a public theologian. He maintained that the preacher is positioned well to comment on all of the "crises" that arise in the community. It is the vocational responsibility of the preacher. Proctor argued that the preacher may not see a burning bush or feel led to liberate "enslaved sisters and brothers" in a hostile country. "But we are called by the crises of our times to be aware of the needs of people in our communities," Proctor insisted.[38]

Proctor charged the preacher to see society's ills as content for the sermon. He argued that social concerns are nonexistent in some sermons. This was problematic for him. He held that the Gospel of Christ is a response to the community's issues. Therefore, it is important that the preacher give meaning to the Gospel for the contemporary setting. The preacher must be equipped to "transpose" the message of the Gospel for the modern mind. The modern person does not live among sheep and goats, so preachers must give meaning to parables and environments that are foreign to their listeners. He stated, "Our first pulpit assignment is to make the congregation aware of the content, the body, the meaning of the gospel."[39] Proctor's book *Preaching about Crises in the Community* (1988) is the explicit product of his understanding of the Social Gospel. He used the book to alert primarily black preachers to the concerns at hand. Drugs, poverty, and education led the list of crises that plagued predominantly black communities, Proctor held. This book was an instruction manual, meant to raise for the preacher the battles that she or he should fight. Proctor figured out a purpose of ministry and used this book and others to bring attention to these topics.

Proctor argued that the preacher must have the type of prophetic insight to know that the community is amiss. The preacher connects to Christ and is sensitive to the problems in society. Preachers are in position to change the moral compass of society. For Proctor, the sermon is a primary

[38] Samuel D. Proctor, *Preaching about Crises in the Community* (Philadelphia, PA: Westminster Press, 1988), 12.

[39] Proctor, *Preaching about Crises in the Community*, 28.

vehicle to transmit the good news that Christ proclaimed. For example, Proctor went after "Christian academies" that functioned to keep white children from mixing with black children. But what did community mean for Proctor? It meant the full participation of black people—of every person of color—in every aspect of American life. It meant the affirmation of each person's worth as a child of God. Proctor envisioned a society in which that reality became the norm. He dedicated himself to preparing African Americans for that day.

A CULTURAL SYNTHESIS

Proctor wanted African Americans to move beyond living into stereotypes and embrace a self-understanding of blackness that would allow them to move freely among white people. This accommodation was his belief that black people had to compromise on some aspects of their cultural behaviors. He sought compromise by way of the visual presentation of African Americans. He was concerned that white people would misinterpret "pro-black" hairstyles (afros) and clothing (dashikis) of the 1960s. At the same time, he wanted white persons to see black militancy and a focus on black identity as a logical outgrowth of the social circumstances in the United States. In a 1969 article, he was both an apologist and mediator. He argued, "Let the catharsis take place. Let the chants and the slogans continue. Let the new styles in dress and medallions do for these youngsters what guitars, long hair and short skirts do for others."[40] He believed that black militancy was an opportunity to direct the energy of black youth into education and job training. The affirmations of blackness by militant youth represented an opportunity to fulfill the promise of American pluralism. Proctor observed:

> Racism, then, which once fell before the legal and scientific pressures is revived on pragmatic grounds. The blacks don't want integration! Then the logic has gone full cycle: blacks rejected; blacks become difficult; whites retreat; blacks further rejected. That is the simplest form of the argument. The more highly developed logic goes this way: the blacks are forced into cultural insularity; while insulated, they are treated unequally. This insularity and unequal treatment breed a sub-culture. The sub-culture is so repulsive [to whites] that further insularity is encouraged. Then the young blacks add to the

---

[40] Samuel D. Proctor, "The College and the Urban Community," *Liberal Education* 55 (March 1969): 80–81.

> logic by averring that this is what they want, a world independent of "whitey."[41]

With this type of philosophical approach to matters of race, he navigated a fine line between integration and accommodation.

Proctor represented the precarious standing of a black leader whose approach to social uplift modeled a black "bourgeois" approach. As an integrationist, he advocated for opportunity, using his academic and government offices as well as his pulpit to shed light on the conditions that blocked paths to true integration and progress for African Americans. He sounds more accommodating, or Americanist, when he recommends on more than one occasion that African Americans should shed portions of black "soul culture" in order to mesh in a pluralistic society. This type of ambivalence or double consciousness is evident in several of his articles and sermons. For example, in a 1969 article on the African American contribution to the American experiment, Proctor celebrated the ethos of black life and its offerings to the United States. He noted that African Americans provided the labor to build the American empire, simple creature comforts, music and other artistic forms, and a style of oration that combines "moral exhortation and political protest." He stated that this sermonic contribution became a novel form of American literature that "appealed to the authority of religion and to the implicit ideal of political democracy." (He embraced this style as a preacher and educator.) Yet he concluded the article with an interesting challenge:

> Let the black man saturate himself in his own background. Let him hear from his past and learn who he is. Let him search out the African roots of the American black community. Let him overcome his alienation and his identity crisis. Then let us say to him, "All right, it's time now for all the Americans to bring their own peculiar gifts to the enrichment of the whole society. Go on and be yourself. But remember that part of yourself lies in the fact that this is *your* country. Come now and help to make it great."[42]

Proctor would probably consider this a cultural synthesis. He could accept racial pride to the extent that it did not interfere with American plural-

---

[41] Proctor, "The College and the Urban Community," 83.

[42] Samuel D. Proctor, "The Black Contribution to the American Experience," *National Elementary Principal* 49 (September 1969): 20–22.

ism. He was not a racial chauvinist, but he believed that African Americans could help redeem the soul of America.

Proctor would acknowledge that African Americans have made longstanding contributions to society. He would also argue that African Americans have qualities from which a larger culture of persons could learn. For example, he was quoted in a 1967 *Chicago Defender* article stating that the years of oppression had found African Americans turning to peaceful methods for a solution to the race crisis. In that same article, he reportedly said that blacks have displayed more than enough courage by remaining dedicated to the United States throughout the terrible ordeal they have experienced.[43] A primary reason for blacks' peaceful approach to American racism, Proctor believed, has been the influence of Christianity. In later years, he wrote, "One reason why black people have clung so tenaciously to Jesus, despite the apostasy and failure of Christians in acknowledging our human kinship and despite Christians' exploitation of one another through slavery, colonialism, and rank racism, is that blacks have found in Jesus the authentic, transcendent God incarnate, above and beyond race and clan and class. In truth we are one human family."[44]

Nevertheless, Proctor did not allow his theological idealism to obstruct his view of reality. He understood that human beings would not change without some struggle. Proctor saw at different stages of his life that the collective moral will of the country did not unite on the issue of integration and racial harmony. He stated in a 1987 Christmas sermon that Americans have the brains to do it but not the heart for it.[45] One will find more examples of this line of thought in most of Proctor's sermons and writings.

Proctor spent the majority of his life arguing for an integrated, prejudice-free society that affirms persons of all races. The foundation of that genuine community was a belief in the inherent personhood of each individual. He sought to leverage the Social Gospel theology of his upbringing and intellectual formation, a *theopolitical* contribution to the public sphere, as a way of influencing education as a system and curriculum and the church to honor all humanity and create genuine community. Although he

---

[43] "Some Soul Culture Must Go if Integration Wins," *Chicago Defender*, 14 January 1967, 33.

[44] Samuel D. Proctor, "Everybody Is God's Somebody," 28.

[45] Samuel D. Proctor, "Jesus: The Prince of Peace," sermon presented at Abyssinian Baptist Church, New York, 20 December 1987, audiotape.

saw a great deal of progress on the matter, he was able to see the issues that remained at hand. Proctor lived long enough to witness several changes in society, but it is obvious from his sermon illustrations and writings that he was still combating racism during the twilight of his life. He fought for a racial progress that was real, validated by the moral and legislative support of the past. He celebrated legal victories but considered them hollow without the type of moral consensus and goodwill that is necessary for love to exist. Proctor saw integration as a step toward the kingdom's ethic of inclusiveness through genuine community.[46] But the fundamental starting point was the embrace of a belief in the personhood of all human beings. He preached and he taught a basic Black Social Gospel principle: "Everybody is God's somebody!"

---

[46] Proctor, *My Moral Odyssey*, 111.

Chapter 5

The Impact of Walter Rauschenbusch in Canada

Roger H. Prentice

In November 1889, many of the Baptist intelligentsia of North America met in the Jarvis Street Baptist Church, Toronto, Ontario. For three days, they intended to discuss the issues of "practical Christianity." In his welcoming address, Canadian clergyman B. D. Thomas[1] said, "You [American Baptists] have been an example and an inspiration to us in many ways. We rejoice in your missionary, educational and philanthropic enterprises. Your proximity has been a wonderful help to us in our activities here."[2]

Not very long after, Walter Rauschenbusch spoke to this assembly. He had already been ministering three years in New York, and he was deeply affected by the surroundings of his own congregation. His introduction was straightforward:

> It is certainly true that it is one of the main objectives of Christianity to change the individual life, and to implant in the heart of man the truth and love of the Lord Jesus Christ. But I claim that that is only one-half of the object of Christianity, that the other half is to bring in the Kingdom of God, and that the effort of the Christian Church ought to be directed in a like measure...by changing the individual

---

[1] *Souvenir, Ten Years Pastorate: Rev. B. D. Thomas, Jarvis St. Baptist Church, Toronto* (Toronto, ON: Davis & Henderson, October 1892). This includes a sermon, "The Harp of Ten Strings," pp. 5–16. Benjamin Daniel Thomas (1849–1917) was born near Narberth, Wales, and after training, the English Baptist Church of Neath became his first pastorate. He emigrated to the United States, held several church pulpits prominent, and in 1882 assumed the pulpit of Jarvis Street Baptist Church, Toronto, where he held forth on this occasion. His long, pointed beard and well-groomed mustache commanded an imposing figure.

[2] Proceedings of the Eighth Baptist Congress, held in the City of Toronto, Ont., November 1889. (New York: Baptist Congress Publishing Co., 1890), 3.

> and gradually having the influence emanate from him, but directly, and then having the influence of society re-act upon that individual.[3]

His speech revealed the opening reaches of his ministry, and this would soon affect church thought in the United States, and, soon after, the nation in which he was then speaking.

Canada was not unfamiliar to Walter Rauschenbusch, at least the populated area of central Ontario. His father, August, in his earliest ministry, helped to establish German Baptist congregations around "Berlin" in that province.[4] Later, his young family returned to that area and, tragically, their first son, Winfred, passed away of dysentery, bringing understandable grief to the Rauschenbusch kinfolk. Winfred was buried there, but his father kept a jar of earth from his grave all the while he lived in Rochester.[5] Walther, who later Anglicized his name to Walter, was born two years later.

Ontario was a special place for Walter and his family, it seems, for the final draft of his first well-known work, *Christianity and the Social Crisis*, was written at a natural woodland near where he would later build a cottage.[6] This was an area near Sturgeon Lake and Bobcaygeon, Ontario. Summer after summer the family would later return to that cottage for a restorative time, and it became a favorite refuge for Walter Rauschenbusch.

---

[3] Eighth Baptist Congress, 55.

[4] Harry A. Renfree, *Heritage and Horizon: The Baptist Story in Canada* (Mississauga, ON: Canadian Baptist Federation, 1988), 204: Dating back to 1851, when a church was founded at Bridgeport (Ontario) following a visit by August Rauschenbusch, twelve German Baptist churches were established. A number of them cooperated as members of Ontario and Quebec associations, although they were still members of the Eastern Conference of the United States. Renfree, 285, cited E. R. Fitch (ed.) *The Baptists of Canada* (Toronto, ON: Standard Publishing Co., 1911), 176–77, 194–95: "The [Bridgeport] church resulted from special services held among the predominantly Mennonite and Lutheran population of Waterloo County." In the nationalization frenzy during World War I, "Berlin," Ontario, was changed to the name of the British hero and become "Kitchener."

[5] Paul M. Minus, *Walter Rauschenbusch: American Reformer* (New York: The Macmillan Co., 1988), 7. Winfrid died on 28 August 1858, sixteen months old.

[6] Minus, *American Reformer*, 157, 158. In 1905, at Canandaigua Lake, just south of Rochester, Rauschenbusch rewrote his text. Minus wrote, "The following summer [i.e., 1906] was spent with his family in Ontario (near the spot on which he built a cottage in 1908), he returned to the manuscript and finally brought it to the point that he was ready to submit it to a publisher."

It would be here, in 1919, diplomatically after the end of World War I, where Rauschenbusch's ashes were brought and scattered on the lake.

All was not tranquil at the cottage, unfortunately, for after 1914, and with the hysteria of the Great War, the cottage was threatened with burning by those who did not understand the sympathies of Rauschenbusch for his father's native Germany and the higher ideals he identified there. Canada was at war with Germany on August 4, 1914, and the population was mobilized, armed forces sent, and they were soon dying for the cause.

For an understanding of the influence of Walter Rauschenbusch on Canada, and in particular the Canadian Baptists, it should be remembered that the nation was only one-tenth the size in population of the nation to the south, but the second largest national landmass (next to Russia) in the world. It was made up of many small towns and villages as well as a half dozen larger cities. Toronto was one, where Rauschenbusch was speaking the above words. The two North American countries look deceptively similar, but Canada is made of a subtly different fabric than the United States.[7]

When Rauschenbusch and his friend Leighton Williams travelled to the Baptist Congress in Toronto, Canada was only twenty-two years old, a collection of British colonies brought together in 1867 for mutual protection from the less-than-subtle hints from the south of forcible annexation. It was, and is, a constitutional monarchy and an integral part of the British Empire, highly influenced by British culture and polity. It also has a French heritage that was largely left intact after 1759 and the conquering of Quebec by "Wolfe, the dauntless hero." This political unity would assist those Canadians influenced by Rauschenbusch's mission. A sovereign is the protector of the people and even, in the extreme, from the government.

There are several main geographical areas of Canada: the East, Central Canada, the West, and the North, with the population inhabiting a fairly narrow band all along the border with the United States. The Eastern seaboard is the oldest part of Canada, of course, wrestled from the French in 1710 and 1759. The Maritime Provinces (Nova Scotia, New Brunswick, and Prince Edward Island), because of their closeness to the sea and its easy transportation opportunities, have had a familiar and usually cordial relationship with "the Boston States." Families, friends, and even church relationships between them have been close. It is in the Maritimes where the

---

[7] Minus, *American Reformer*, 136, 194; Dores Robinson Sharpe, *Walter Rauschenbusch* (New York: The Macmillan Co., 1942), 74–75

Baptists are most populous in relation to the Central and Western provinces.

OPENING CLOSED DOORS: THE MAIN CANADIAN BAPTIST EDUCATIONAL INSTITUTIONS

Baptists in Canada, as in the United States, established educational institutions. One of the more significant is Acadia University in Wolfville, Nova Scotia, founded first as Horton Academy in 1828, and a parallel college in 1838. One of the significant aspects of this founding was the charter that proclaimed that there be no religious tests for faculty, fellows, or students. It was open to all regardless of their station in life. Indeed, because other colleges demanded denominational loyalties, this was a breakthrough and perhaps a beginning of the socially caring approach the university was to take throughout its history.

For Acadia University, a second somewhat prophetic sign was the need to construct a college building during a financial depression occurring in Nova Scotia at that time. A young professor, Isaac Chipman, travelled the Maritimes to raise support. Instead of coin, he asked for building supplies that people might have had on hand. The social need was plain. In three years the building was accomplished—a social response of the people.[8] It was the same Isaac Chipman who convinced Acadia graduate Silas Rand[9] that work should be started amongst the Maritime Aboriginal people. This resulted in Rand's schools, missions, writings, hymns, and his developing an alphabet and translation of the Scriptures in the local aboriginal tongue.[10]

There were other Baptist seminaries and colleges founded in Canada: Montreal, Quebec; Fredericton, New Brunswick; St. Martins, New Brunswick; Toronto, which would move to Hamilton, Ontario; Woodstock, Ontario; Grande Ligne, Quebec; Okanagan (British Columbia); Brandon, Manitoba; and Edmonton, Alberta. Each would have distinctive characteris-

---

[8] Ronald Stewart Longley, Acadia University, 1838–1938 (Wolfville, NS: Acadia University, 1939), 45 ff. This was a sign that the local Baptists were convinced that the children of farmers, fishermen, and craftspeople should be able to improve their situations through a good education equally with the elite.

[9] Dorothy May Lovesey, *To Be a Pilgrim: A Biography of Silas Tertius Rand 1810–1889, Nineteenth Century Protestant Missionary to the Micmac* (Hantsport, NS.: Lancelot Press, 1992), 36.

[10] Longley, *Acadia University*, 40, n. 12.

tics, but they all manifested a populist (in the best sense) care for education. Smaller but more sectarian efforts would open and close along the way.

The most important institutions, Acadia, McMaster, and Brandon, would become the influential academies with regards to the Social Gospel in Canada. Each served the Baptists of their area. Each had significant leaders and professors who supported the ideals of the Social Gospel and graduated people who held these ideals for their own professional ministry. By a survey of these people it is possible to reconstruct the story of the Social Gospel and its success in Canada.

THE SOCIAL GOSPEL IN CANADA

The intellectual soil in Canada was fertile for the message of Rauschenbusch. The early pioneer society of Canada taught colonialists the importance of helping each other and of asking for help from the aboriginals who were long used to the land and its ways. The government was also expected to be a protector and helper to which a subject of the politically neutral king or queen may appeal.[11] It has been the pioneer culture of Canada where mutual help and support came naturally to Canadians as social norms.

Church congregations, too, were well acquainted with the teachings of Jesus and his approach to helping those in need and correcting social wrongs. Although the influence of Victorian Evangelicalism was holding some sway, the mainline churches were beginning to awaken to the agonies which industrialization was introducing to their neighborhoods.

By the turn into the twentieth century, significant Baptist leaders arose, amongst those of other Protestant denominations, who were beginning to sound the alarm bells of an impending social crisis. Mines in Nova Scotia, lumber mills in New Brunswick, factories in Ontario, farms in the prairies, railway construction through the Rockies, and gold prospecting in the Yukon all presented labor difficulties, dreadful accommodations, major health issues, and abject poverty. Like First Baptist Church, Amherst, Nova Scotia, people living under these conditions mixed freely with well-to-do management and factory owners, so the congregations often were aware of

---

[11] People knew the lines of another stanza of "God Save the Queen": "May she defend our laws and ever give us cause to sing with heart and voice 'God save the Queen.'"

their situations. This normally depended on their ministers at the time to raise the clarion call to social action.

The ministers, of course, were highly influenced by the training that they received at theological seminaries, and each of the main three universities maintained a slightly restrained emphasis on the Social Gospel. Those who attended more conservative schools in the United States, of course, were much less enthusiastic. The three main universities: Acadia, McMaster, and Brandon, were well aware of Walter Rauschenbusch during his lifetime and were influenced by him through their own faculties' training either at Rochester or Colgate seminaries, or through their own inclinations.

These universities were also not blind to the needs of the society in Canada around them, and in the world. In the Maritimes, for example, John Howard MacDonald, then only thirty-four years of age, but a rising star in his Maritime Baptist denomination, spoke at a missionary conference held at Truro, Nova Scotia. His speech was recorded, including, "The votaries of science and education sometimes say as they see the works of these agencies that have been used of God for the betterment of mankind. 'These are the gods which have brought us out of Egypt, and these are the gods that will lead us to the Canaan of social prosperity.' But these things left alone and unsanctified will curse and not bless us."[12]

In the same speech MacDonald went on to quote the American poet James Russell Lowell: "Show me a place ten miles square where a decent man can live decently, supporting and educating his children, unspoiled and unpolluted, a place where age is revered, infancy respected, and womanhood held in true regard, and I will show you a place where the gospel of Christ has gone and cleared the way and made decency and security possible."[13]

---

[12] *Messenger and Visitor* (predecessor of *The Maritime Baptist*) (5 May 1897): 1, "The Training of Young People in World-Wide Evangelism." MacDonald did not likely know of Rauschenbusch at this time of his presentation in Truro—Rauschenbusch had not started teaching at Rochester until later that year—but was growing in the same direction as Rauschenbusch. MacDonald would later become professor of church history at Acadia University.

[13] *Messenger and Visitor*. James Russell Lowell was an American poet, educationalist, and diplomat. He opposed slavery and other social ills. He was ambassador to the Court of St. James later in life. MacDonald was known for his own love of literature. When he was in his graduating year at Acadia in 1891—a distin-

At Acadia University, for instance, war veteran and hero Dr. Clarence Basil Lumsden, professor of Biblical Literature and vice president of the university,[14] wrote in 1927 the instruction to "Our Young People" column of *The Maritime Baptist* about "The Christian Citizen": "With the patriot and the Christian, welfare of country must take precedence over personal considerations.... He must support those agencies looking for betterment of social conditions."[15]

Also on the same faculty at Acadia, coincidentally, was William Norman Hutchins, professor of Old Testament and religious education. He was, as well, the Maritime Convention's first chair of their Social Service Board (1921–1923) and member of the Advisory Board of the Revised Standard Version of the Old Testament.[16] He wrote a textbook, *Graded Social Service for the Sunday School*, in 1914.[17] His opening sentence introduced his topic, "It is fairly well accepted that education is a social process and needs to be interpreted and promoted by established facts regarding the interactions of mind with mind."[18] He continued a little later, "If, then, social service is to contribute to the social banishment of class-consciousness and to take its place in the Sunday School as a socializing force, it must be

---

guished class in itself—MacDonald was chief editor of the student literary and news magazine, *The Acadia Athenaeum*.

[15.] Morris R. B. Lovesey, *Called to Serve: A Mini-biography of Clarence Basil Lumsden 1895–1970* (Wolfville, NS: Manning Memorial Chapel, Acadia University Chaplaincy, 1996, Chapel Booklet no. 4), 12. Lumsden lost an arm to a sniper while rescuing fellow soldiers during the Battle of Ancre Heights and the assault on Regina Trench, 1 October 1916.

[15] *The Maritime Baptist*, 22 June 1927, 10, "The Christian Citizen."

[16] Kirkconnell, *Maritime Baptist*, 40. The R.S.V. was an attempt to return the Scriptures to a recognizable vernacular.

[17] William Norman Hutchins, Graded Social Service for the Sunday School (Chicago, IL: University of Chicago Press, 1914, 4th impression 1920). Hutchins was born in Halifax, NS, 12 March 1869, a graduate of Acadia (BA 1891; MA 1894), Rochester Seminary (BD 1905), and University of Chicago (PhD 1913). Acadia honored him with a DD in 1932. In his early career, he was minister of several rural Nova Scotian congregations, First Baptist Church, Truro, NS (1902–1909) and Middleton, N.S. (1916–1922). He was president of the Maritime Baptist Convention for 1907–1908. This book referenced here undoubtedly sprang from his PhD dissertation.

[18] Hutchins, *Graded Social Service*, 1.

accompanied by an interplay of life that issues in establishing full human relations with other groups. Education is essentially a social process."[19]

Hutchins quotes at length Jane Addams, *New Ideals of Peace*, and C. H. Cooley, "Human Nature and the Social Order."[20] At the end of chapter 1, Hutchins writes, "In making the complete socialization of the individual its end, religious education has set itself no light or easy task, for when that end is realized and every individual is living in reciprocal relations of sympathy with every other individual we shall no longer need to wait for that ideal kingdom which Jesus called the kingdom of God."[21]

Canada was then relying on informal welfare care provided by those who would volunteer individual assistance or through church-related programs. Nonetheless, the people were beginning to request of the government its assistance for their communal need. The Liberal Party, then Her Majesty's Loyal Opposition,[22] talked about a national health service in 1916 and placed it in their official party program in 1919. Unfortunately, the Tories[23] were in power under Sir Robert Borden, and with the costs of the Great War pressing, the idea gathered dust until 1961.[24]

CENTRAL SQUIRES: THE ONTARIO AND QUEBEC CONVENTION

Central Canada had its own Baptist convention in fraternal relation with the Maritime and Western conventions. This convention was early in its interest in the Social Gospel. The Baptist Congress of 1889 in Toronto would have helped to promote this interest.[25] Colleges were established in

---

[19] Ibid., 8.

[20] Ibid., 5.

[21] Ibid., 11.

[22] There is an important distinction contained in this term: "Her Majesty's Loyal Opposition" are not part of the government and oppose any wrong governing but are loyal, at the same time, to the Queen (i.e., the State).

[23] Tories: a political nickname for the Conservative Party of Canada.

[24] Walter Stewart, *The Life and Political Times of Tommy Douglas* (Toronto, ON: McArthur & Company, 2003), 6.; Vincent Lam, *Tommy Douglas* (Toronto, ON: Penguin Canada, 2011), 155. The Liberals campaigned on this platform in 1945 and although forming the government at the time, they failed to enact any legislation that worked.

[25] Eighth Baptist Congress, 5–6. There were no discernable Maritime Baptist representatives at this Congress. v. pp. 5–6, "Officers of the Toronto Meeting."

Montreal[26] (which eventually failed in 1849) and Toronto, founded in 1881. An educated ministry was one of the priorities for Canadian Baptists.

By the turn of the century, Canadian Baptists were aware of a social crisis that was developing around them because of the vast influx of immigrants, mainly from the United Kingdom and Europe, growth of an industrial economy, labor unrest, and urban blight. Along with these unsettling features there was the frustration of farmers pioneering in the West and disquiet in British Columbia. Historian John S. Moir has written of "the acknowledgement by Canadian historians that the movement called the Social Gospel was and is one of the most important formative influences on our national development."[27]

The Canadian Baptist was the newspaper of the Ontario and Quebec Baptists and it became an early supporter of the Social Gospel, as John Moir reported:

> While *The Canadian Baptist* was still the property of William Muir [until 1882], its editorial column frequently expressed Social Gospel ideas. On one occasion Muir called on Baptists to bear witness to the "practical Christianity" in everyday life, because the secular and the religious worlds in fact are inseparable. On other occasions he commented on the need for purity in politics, on the church's responsibility to meet the temptation besetting youth in an urban environment, on the need for systematic care of the deserving poor, and on the urgency of combatting pornography and prostitution. For Muir the simple cure for fraud, dishonesty, avarice, strikes, lockouts and even wars, was to love your neighbour as yourself.[28]

E. W. Dadson became editor of *The Canadian Baptist* when ownership changed in 1882. He, too, held a constructive opinion about specific social problems. In 1887, he declared that the law of supply and demand was

---

[26] William H. Brackney, *Congregation and Campus: Baptists in High Education* (Macon, GA: Mercer University Press, 2008), 135–36. Brackney states that Canada Baptist College was founded in Montreal in 1838.

[27] John S. Moir, "The Canadian Baptist and the Social Gospel Movement, 1879–1914," in *Baptists in Canada: Search for Identity Amidst Diversity*, ed. Jarold K. Zeman (Burlington, ON: G. R. Welch Co., 1980), 47–159.

[28] Moir, *Social Gospel Movement*, 148–49. These would be precisely the issues of the Social Concerns Congress held in Ottawa in 1914 and for the Maritime Baptist Convention's Social Service Board in 1921.

"unchristian."[29] This followed up an earlier comment that the churches should offer leadership "for the solution of all these great social problems."[30] All this was an outspoken call for social justice, including in business life: "Too often capitalism divorced morality from business practice—the truly Christian industrialist would ensure that his worker got such a share in the profits as justly belonged to him."[31]

Dadson also called for reform for native rights,[32] which became an ongoing theme in the latter 1880s. It is an issue still being confronted by the present Canadian government. All this, of course, came before Rauschenbusch taught at Rochester and arose to be widely known in Canada through his publications. It indicates the "fertile soil" for the Social Gospel that was prepared for Rauschenbusch to reach out to his northern neighbors.

Dadson resigned as editor of *The Canadian Baptist* in 1889 and was succeeded by J. E. Wells, who would have been acquainted with Rauschenbusch since, at least, 1889, for he too spoke at the Baptist Congress in Toronto.[33] In editorials, Moir has pointed out that Wells criticized the churches for alienating the working class by always supporting the capitalists' cause.[34] In 1894 when the "Industrial Army" marched on Washington demanding work in the United States, Wells commented at length on the "cruel inequality" in the distribution of wealth.[35]

At the turn of the century, however, this enlightenment began to dim for about a decade within *The Canadian Baptist*, with a change of editors. It would revive again about the time of outbreak of the Great War in 1914,

---

[29] *The Canadian Baptist*, 24 November 1889. The author is indebted to the late John Moir for the references to this journal.

[30] Ibid., 18 September 1884.

[31] Ibid., 12 March 1885.

[32] Ibid., 14 May 1885.

[33] Baptist Congress, Toronto, 1889, 193–206, "What Hinders International Arbitration?" Wells began, "Why should not every boy and girl in the United States and Canada go to school and college until twenty-one years of age? Why should not every man and woman over twenty-one, in either country, have a work to do for the good of the community, and be placed under such conditions as would ensure that that should be the exact work for which the individual was best adapted, and that it should be done cheerfully, energetically, ungrudgingly?" Wells endorses the Social Gospel intentions fully as a Canadian. Wells was a respected lay journalist.

[34] *The Canadian Baptist*, 4 September 1890.

[35] Moir, *Social Gospel*, 152.

and by 1916 social concern reasserted itself in the newspaper's pages. A Social Welfare Board of the Quebec and Ontario Convention was formed and initiatives were begun after the achievement of the Armistice.

ECHOES FROM THE MARITIME PROVINCES

With the turn of the century, there were signs that the industrial base of the Maritimes was beginning to crumble in the face of an assault from Central Canadian commercial expansionism, taking over and closing down factories, banks, and other firms. In Cape Breton, there were strikes breaking out into violence around its coal and steel economy.

Interest in this social upheaval was indicated by *The Maritime Baptist*, reporting what the Ontario and Quebec Convention was discussing by mid-October of 1915:

> Social Services had a large place on the program. Five addresses were given on "The Social Message of the Prophets"; "Social Aspects of Christ's Ministry"; "Social Movement in the Early Church"; "Christianity and Modern Social Problems"; "Social Aspects on Modern Missions." The speakers included one pastor, one missionary secretary, the Chancellor of McMaster University,[36] and two professors, and no part of the proceedings awakened keener interest.[37]

The urban churches of the Maritimes, especially Nova Scotia, began to increase their awareness, as well. Henry Francis Adams, who preached at First Baptist Church, Truro, Nova Scotia, on Sunday, August 4, 1918—the fourth anniversary of the British Empire entering World War I—began by speaking against "militarism" and for economic stewardship. He proclaimed, "This brings the profound doctrine of Divine Ownership and Human Stewardship home to us very personally, for as we have carried out or repudiated it, so will our destiny be.... Live nobly: a splendid character is the best legacy you can leave behind. Love humanity, for without it your service will not reach God's books. Think little of self, for your deeds for others will be self-sacrifice."[38]

---

[36] Dr. Abraham McCrimmon (Chancellor, 1911–1922) v; Nancy Christie; Michael Gauvreau, *A Full-Orbed Christianity: The Protestant Churches and Social Welfare in Canada* (Montreal, PQ: McGill-Queen's University Press, 1996), 214.

[37] *The Maritime Baptist*, 10 November 1915, 5, "Ontario Letter."

[38] Ibid., 28 August 1918, 2–3. By this time Adams was ministering in Philadelphia but previously had been minister of First Baptist Church (later known as

A PECULIAR CASE STUDY: NOVA SCOTIA

The Great Depression (1929–1939), with 27 percent unemployment in Canada, and the Great Drought of the 1930s, which devastated the prairie provinces of Manitoba, Saskatchewan, and Alberta, pressed home national needs and suffering. Central Canada and its industrial core were similarly severely damaged. It was natural, then, for Canadians to take an interest in the words of Dr. Rauschenbusch from across the border. The Maritimes were similarly hit, especially in the industrial and urban centers. This manifested itself, at first, through the "Temperance Movement," in which alcohol was considered the "understudy" of much of the social unease and unrest. It took some time for the Baptists to realize that this was a symptom rather than the cause. It was really after the Great War when a greater general social concern appears in the convention's Eastern Canadian reports.[39]

Nova Scotians are generally more cautious, culturally, than other Canadians, perhaps due to their older and more interesting history. It was to the United States, however, that many of their promising and leading theology students migrated for their graduate training—a goodly number never to return. Newton was their favorite school, followed by Chicago and Rochester as the main educational places of resort for students graduating from Acadia University. An examination of Watson Kirkconnell's *The Acadia Record 1838–1953* reveals this.[40]

By the turn of the century, industrialization was creating a myriad of problems in Nova Scotia, where mines, steel plants, foundries, construction companies, quarries, and manufacturing plants had grown up in the 1880s. Michael S. Boudreau has studied the churches' response to this develop-

---

Zion Baptist), Yarmouth, NS, and for a short time (5 December 1890 to 31 May 1892) of First Baptist Church, Halifax: v. Edwin D. King; J. Gordon Quigley, *One Hundred and Fifty Years of the First Baptist Church Halifax, NS* (Halifax, NS: First Baptist Church, Halifax, 1977), 50.

[39] This is plainly evident in the annual reports in the Year Books of the Maritime Baptist Convention.

[40] Watson Kirkconnell, *The Acadia Record 1838–1953* (Wolfville, NS: Acadia University, 1953). A sample: forty-three graduated from Acadia in 1891: twenty-one were theology students with five going to Rochester, seven to Newton, one to Colgate, one to Chicago. The others served with just their BA, not uncommon at the time.

ment.[41] He came to the conclusion that "of the three denominations examined in this study, the Baptists possessed the richest tradition of social concern."[42] He particularly noted two Maritime Baptist clergy, Perry James Stackhouse and Henry Fish Waring. As it happens, they were well known to each other and the Maritime Baptist churches.

Boudreau pointed out that the Baptists concerned with the social crisis at the end of the nineteenth century did not separate the sacred from the secular: the church should speak out against the outrageous conditions of housing, alcoholism, low wages, child labor, and so forth through the clear (to them) message of the Christian Gospel. The Baptists were also the second largest Protestant denomination in the province at that time.[43]

"Social Reform" was first formally recognized as a committee by the Maritime Baptist Convention in 1911, long after the Ontario and Quebec Baptists were discussing it in Central Canada.[44] It is in this 1911 report that we find suggested "aids" for the "much needed" reforms:

1. supervised public playgrounds in every community,
2. establishment of Juvenile Courts and an Industrial University,[45]
3. proper classification and registration of offenders,
4. establishment of a farm where alcoholics could "redeem" themselves,
5. rigid enforcement of laws regulating sale of cigarettes, tobacco, houses "of ill fame," gambling dens, and "against the sale of

---

[41] Michael S. Boudreau, *The Emergence of the Social Gospel in Nova Scotia: The Presbyterian, Methodist and Baptist Churches with the Working Class 1880–1914* (Unpublished MA thesis, Queen's University, 1991).

[42] Boudreau, *Social Gospel*, 156.

[43] Ibid., 157.

[44] *Maritime United Baptist Year Book 1911*, ed. John Howard MacDonald, 110. Their report's title was changed to "Report of Temperance and Moral and Social Reform." It declared, "We believe, that as Baptists, ours is a golden opportunity, we must 'lengthen our cords and strengthen our stakes' and enter the field of practical sociology." This is, of course, an analogy to setting up tents in prospect of a storm—and portrays MacDonald's literary prowess.

[45] This suggestion continues, "For the protection, education and salvation of young offenders and would-be offenders against society. This method of dealing with young offenders has passed beyond the experimental stage in many places. Thus one is absolutely useless without the other."

immoral, obscene or suggestive post or picture cards, books or publications,"
6. deal with entertainment that was unbecoming,
7. concern for "the great influx of foreigners" with conflicting ideals, habits, and ethical standards.

At least it was a start. The moralistic language probably was for the benefit of the more conservative folk. In 1913, the convention added another concern, "the white slave traffic."[46]

By this time, the Maritime Baptists were still not a part of the Social Service Council of Canada.[47] By 1917, with World War I three years old as a major concern, the Maritime Baptists were recording, "The social problems of the people are being studied today with a new intensity as well as with a larger outlook."[48] It went on, "Your committee deeply regrets that our denomination is not giving to these questions the consideration that is their due, and that in the great nation-wide movement for social and moral betterment our denomination has no official representative through whom we can co-operate with the other great communions of our Dominion."

The frustration of the committee was brought to the fore with this proposal: "We recommend that the name of your committee be changed to that of Social Service. We further recommend that the pastors of our churches place greater emphasis on these great social issues; and that the Baptist people of our constituency may attain an intelligent grasp of present social conditions."[49]

The Social Gospel was beginning to pick up speed within the consciences of the churches. In the following year the name of the committee was changed to that of "Social and Moral Reform"—likely another compromise with the more conservative brothers and sisters—and the question of interdenominational cooperation proposed: "This matter had been discussed by several members of the Committee and from information gleaned from leaders of the other denominations they beg to submit that the ten-

---

[46] *The Maritime United Baptist Year Book* 1913, 138.

[47] The Social Service Council was formed in 1911 and held its first national conference in 1914.

[48] *Maritime United Baptist Year Book* 1917, ed. Robert J. Colpitts, 128, "Temperance and Moral Reform."

[49] Ibid., 1917, 129.

dency at the present time is to have the work of the Social and Moral Reform carried on along inter-denominational lines."[50]

As it happened, in the same year, the "Five-Year Program Committee," amongst its own recommendations, suggested that the fourth goal for the Maritime Convention would be "Social Service" and to have the Social Service Committee review the social conditions "within Convention," especially family life.[51] Finally, by 1919, the Social Service Committee, as it became known, in a report prepared by W. N. Hutchins, recommended that the Social Service Committee become a full board with departments for various activities and that members be appointed as such by the convention. In fact, the Five Year Program Committee did recommend, "That the Social Service Committee of the convention be changed into a Board of Social Services, appointed as the other Boards of Convention, with organized departments in Temperance, Child Welfare, Industrial Relations, Dependents, Defections, Delinquents, and any others that may be necessary."[52]

Finally, at the war's end, the Maritime Baptists moved into a program that Rauschenbusch could echo.[53] In its communication to the convention, the board of Social Service submitted its first annual report. It presented a platform for action including child welfare where "every child has the right to be well born, well nourished, and well protected." Several other key recommendations were:

> 7. The resources of the earth being the heritage of the people should not be monopolized by the few to the disadvantage of the many.
> 9. Work should be done under proper conditions with respect to hours, wages, health, management and morals.

---

[50] Ibid., 1918, ed. Robert J. Colpitts, 137.

[51] Ibid., 1918, 127, 128.

[52] Ibid., 1919, ed. Robert J. Colpitts, 141.

[53] Christie and Gavreau, *A Full-Orbed Christianity*, 20, reports on a similar slowness of the Methodists: "Generally speaking, the Methodist Church [of Canada] lagged behind the Presbyterians both in offering a critique of industrial capitalism and in seizing the opportunity to enlist the sympathies of labour. Only after World War I did the Methodists regularly support an agenda of democratizing industry...and concede the important principle that labour unrest resulted not from a failure of individual morality but was a symptom of a dehumanized capitalist system."

11. Women who toil should have equal pay with men for equal work.
13. Employers and employees are partners in industry and should be partners in the enterprise.
17. The bond of brotherhood is the final and fundamental fact and men are called to organize all life, ecclesiastical, civic, social, industrial, on the basis of brotherhood.

Mention was also made regarding domestic relations (and divorce), cooperating with other denominations in establishing a Maritime Home for Women (incarcerated by the courts) and a Maritime Home for Girls. [54] Rauschenbusch had come home in Canada.

E. R. Forbes has written about the seeming obsession with prohibition of alcohol by the denominations in the Maritimes, and the Baptists would be a prime example.[55] In his own article, Boudreau notes, "Identifying prohibition the "mid-wife" of the Social Gospel in Nova Scotia, Forbes does not probe beyond the issue to discuss the broader range of concerns associated with the new religious [postwar] perspectives."[56]

Rauschenbusch's influence in Canada obviously did not vanish with his death on July 25, 1918. Only a few months before that event, R. Osgood Morse, a prominent Maritime Baptist minister, wrote a book review about *A Theology for the Social Gospel.*[57] With usual Maritime reserve, he praised the work:

> There are those who will misunderstand, and misinterpret, and regret that publication of this book. Those who will do this are those who have given little thought and less life to the consideration and solution of Social Problems. Those who have become used to looking at Social Problems in their religious implications will warmly welcome this book. They will welcome it not because they accept all that the author teaches, but because they recognize in it an honest

---

[54] *Maritime United Baptist Year Book* 1921, ed. F. H. Beals, 112; also, Social Service Board Minutes, beginning 1921, A. J. Prosser, secretary (chair: W. N. Hutchins).

[55] E. R. Forbes, "Prohibition and the Social Gospel in Nova Scotia," *Acadiensis* 1/1 (Autumn 1971): 11–36.

[56] Boudreau, *Social Gospel*, 6.

[57] Walter Rauschenbusch, *A Theology for the Social Gospel* (New York: Macmillan Co., 1917; repr. 1918).

> realm of religious thought and life now opening to us. The work is frankly that of a pioneer blazing the trail. I am glad that this task has fallen to one so strong, so brave, so in sympathy with the masses of men as is Walter Rauschenbusch.[58]

Another example of the continuing influence of Rauschenbusch is evident when the whole front page of *The Maritime Baptist*, November 23, 1927, was headlined and presented with the article "A Social Gospel for Today," by Leland Foster Wood, professor of English Bible and Christian Sociology at Rochester Theological Seminary. The article, significantly reprinted for Maritime Baptist eyes, was made up of extracts from an address delivered at the annual opening of the seminary and published in their *Bulletin*.

Wood's piece is an incisive proclamation of the social unity sought by the Social Gospel. It began, "The Social Gospel is a response of Christianity to the fact that men live their lives in groups.... The recovery of the hope of a kingdom of heaven that should come much closer to the place where men dwell seemed like the recovery of a long-lost chord of Christianity."[59] Wood invoked Rauschenbusch, "prophet of God and herald of the Kingdom."

> The idea of the redemption of the social organism is nothing alien. It is simply proper part of the Christian faith in the redemption from sin and evil. As soon as the desire for salvation becomes strong and intelligent enough to look beyond the personal bias of the individual, and to discern how our personality in its intake and output is connected with the social groups to which we belong, the problem of social redemption is before us and we can never forget it.[60]

The significance of this not only remains in its very words, but that it was published in a Canadian, especially a Maritime, Baptist weekly newspaper on the front page and long after Rauschenbusch's death. Many other Social Gospel proponents had been forgotten, but apparently Dr. Rauschenbusch still rang clear to the paper's readership.

Like all nations, Canada was traumatized by the Great War, with a loss of 60,000, one tenth of its population. Naturally, most were its young peo-

---

[58] *Maritime Baptist*, ed. Robert Colpitts, 20 February 1918, 16.

[59] *Maritime Baptist*, 23 November 1927, 1, 5, Leland Foster Wood, "A Social Gospel for To-day."

[60] *Maritime Baptist*, 23 November 1927.

ple upon whom the future seemed to depend. Conversely, it was also believed that it was "the war to end all war," so the 1920s became a hopeful and determined era for peace and prosperity. The Social Gospel began to shine through in those days in Canada and did more so after 1929, when events reversed dramatically.

Illustrative of the hopes of the 1920s would be a paper given at the Baptist World Congress held in Toronto in 1928. Dr. J. H. MacDonald spoke on the topic of "militarism." He said, "You may employ blacksmiths to beat her bayonets into plowshares, but a nation's real armament is in her ideals, her industry and her spirit.... It is no use to put off the armour of Caesar without putting on the armour of God." He went on to say,

> The religion needed is not one swathed in dogmas formulated in the dim light of Mediaevalism, but the untrammelled religion of the Prince of Peace—a religion so social that it will not stand for leaving vast ranges of human conduct outside the realm of justice; a religion so rational as to make one see that a neighbour's hurt is your hurt and a neighbour's gain is your gain; a religion so spiritual that it will lay the axe at the root of the trees of militarism and not be satisfied to lop off its menacing branches.[61]

THE "DIRTY" THIRTIES

These optimistic economic and political observations begin to wane with an abrupt Napoleonic Waterloo. The stock markets collapsed in London, then New York, in September 1929. This affected the economies of the world precipitously. Worse, in the Prairie Provinces, the Great Drought began. Properties were lost, savings vanished, work ceased. This was not what the kingdom of God was supposed to resemble. Churches lost income; welfare requests rose astronomically. Worse, hints of trouble in Europe arose and the Nazis took power in Germany. For Canada, the abdication of King Edward VIII, who was adored by Canadians, shook political sensibilities. The King had property in Alberta and maintained the Canadians' unfailing af-

[61] Fourth Baptist World Congress, Toronto, Canada, 23–29 June 1928: Record of Proceedings, ed. W. T. Whitley (London: Kingsgate Press, 1928), 268, 269; "Militarism," Professor J. H. MacDonald, BA, DD, CBE, F.R.G.S. Dr. MacDonald was professor of church history at Acadia University at that time. Significantly, he was deputy director of the Canadian Armed Forces Chaplains Service in London after serving about two years as a chaplain in the trenches, during World War I.

fection, and losing the King so abruptly and thoughtlessly awakened concern about governmental authority. Finally, the royal tour of King George VI (who succeeded King Edward) and Queen Elizabeth, his consort, in May and June of 1939 alerted Canadians to the real dangers of a conflict looming ahead. This fear became a reality on September 10th of that same year.[62]

After World War II, there could be no return to any naïve belief that human failure could be obliterated without a reconsideration of theology and social concern. Furthermore, it may not have been possible to avoid another tumultuous time which the church endured during the Cold War, or the 1960s aftermath of Vatican II, and the emergence of the revolting "Flower Power" generation.

Ironically, as William Brackney has pointed out recently, the conservative evangelicals finally grasped the importance of a Christian commitment to the tenets of the Social Gospel.[63] It is likely that American conservative evangelicals, of most stripes, have more influence in Canada than the mainline denominations. Radio, television, the Internet, to say nothing of reoccurring "revivals," spread their message not only to churches but also to the listening nonchurchgoers in Canada.[64] Brackney offers a persuasive argument that this group has reassessed Rauschenbusch and his thoughts more positively after World War II. The impact of their adoption of the social-concern action events certainly is alive in the northern nation as a result of, but mostly separate from, the government's involvement.[65] Indeed, the government, sometimes a source of finances to these groups of "Christian charities," is beginning its own backlash. In 2018, groups seeking government aid for student summer employment have to check off a box that states that they are not against various government policies such as abortion, medically assisted death, and legalization of marijuana. This is a conundrum for many

---

[62] Canada declared war on Germany one week after Great Britain. It required a vote in the House of Commons and the Senate, as well as royal assent, and it took some time to summon members of Parliament from the far reaches of the nation to Ottawa. There was one vote against: J. S. Woodworth, member of the Coöperative Commonwealth Federation (CCF). He took his stand as a private member rather than as the leader of his party.

[63] William H. Brackney, "Walter Rauschenbusch: Then and Now," *Baptist Quarterly* 48/1 (January 2017): 23–46.

[64] Almost all of the networks of the United States are available in Canada via the ubiquitous "cable" upon which Canadian viewers depend.

[65] Brackney, *Congregation and Campus*, 40–45.

Christian charities, particularly the conservative ones. It is interesting to see "separation of church and state" promoted by the state.

THE SOCIAL GOSPEL ARISES IN CANADIAN POLITICS

> We have heard here the ultimate statement of the Baptist doctrine—complete separation of Church and State. But I read a short time ago the life of that great and noble man, Thomas Arnold of Rugby,[66] and also that of Frederick Dennison Maurice[67]; and I remember that they held the view that the Church and State are necessarily, and in their nature, one.... Would you accept the formula, that there must be complete division in the *organization* of religion and State, but that there must be an inter-penetration of the *life* of Church and State?[68]

These are early words of Walter Rauschenbusch, uttered in Canada, and almost prophetic in their application to the Dominion. It would take fifty-five years after the Baptist Congress proceedings before a government was elected in one province, Saskatchewan, which was led by a Baptist minister who was devoted to the Social Gospel and introduced the first stages of public medical insurance. It would be seventy-two years after the congress before a Progressive Conservative Party government would promise it to the whole nation in 1961.

Canada proved to be well-ploughed legislative soil into which the speeches and writings of Walter Rauschenbusch could be planted for a national harvesting. It has flourished increasingly ever since.

Remembering the "Roaring Twenties," one easily realizes the shock of the collapse of the economy with the Great Depression. In fact, the economy of Canada was beginning to fade by the late 1920s, and studies like that of Samuel Alexander Saunders explored in depth the economic welfare, in his case, the Maritime Provinces.[69]

---

[66] Thomas Arnold (1795–1842) was a reformist headmaster of Rugby School, and father of Matthew Arnold.

[67] Frederick Dennison Maurice (1805–1872) was an English Anglican theologian and one of the founders of the Christian Socialism movement.

[68] Walter Rauschenbusch, Baptist Congress Proceedings, Toronto, 1889, 139. Italics are in the original text.

[69] S. A. Saunders, *The Economic Welfare of the Maritime Provinces* (Wolfville, NS: Acadia University, 1932).

There was great concern about the depression of 1929, of course, but little was done, almost perpetuated by a state of denial. The Cape Breton coal industry was beginning to recover from serious labor disturbances by 1939. As far as the churches were concerned, it was just awakening to a new crisis. There were church leaders who were actually taught by, or at least aware of, Walter Rauschenbusch. They were, by the end of the Great War, beginning to exercise their own influence. Church leaders in Canada such as J. S. Woodsworth (1874–1942), M. J. Coldwell (1888–1974), and Stanley Knowles (1908–1997) were Canadian prairie churchmen who would proclaim the need for a Social Gospel both in the church and in politics in the 1930s and 1940s.[70]

In the Central Provinces, leaders such as Howard Primrose Whidden, Carl Addington Dawson, and E. W. Dadson propelled social concern amongst listening Baptists, and in the Maritimes, people like Perry James Stackhouse, Henry Fish Waring, Ross Chipman Eaton, and John Howard MacDonald were wise proponents of social care. From their native Canada also went significant leaders to the United States to add their influence there: Dores Robinson Sharpe, Shirley Jackson Case, and even, after significant ministries in the Maritimes, Perry Stackhouse. They discovered that they could add their voices for the Social Gospel there.

In Canada, it can be argued that Thomas Clement Douglas had the greatest impact on the Social Gospel. Douglas was a Baptist minister of the rural town of Weyburn, Saskatchewan. From this unlikely circumstance, he would lead a new Socialist political party, be elected a member of the provincial legislative assembly, become the premier, and lead for almost twenty years a government that would establish Social Gospel legislation that would eventually advance into the rest of the country. After twenty years in

---

[70] James Shaver Woodsworth was a Methodist minister who worked with the poor, left the church, and became first leader of the Coöperative Commonwealth Federation (CCF) in 1932. Major James Coldwell, educationalist, succeeded Woodsworth in 1942 as leader of the CCF. In 1961, he continued with the New Democratic Party (NDP) and was known for promoting the welfare state to Canada. Stanley Howard Knowles was a Brandon College graduate and United Church of Canada minister. His father was Nova Scotian and his mother from New Brunswick. He represented the CCF and NDP in Parliament and was an expert on parliamentary procedure in Canada. He is recognized for introducing the Canada Pension Plan and other features of the welfare state, and as an advocate of social justice.

Regina and provincial politics, Douglas left for the federal seat of government in Ottawa, and, in due course, became party leader in Ottawa. In 2004, he would be voted by Canadian citizens the "Greatest Canadian of the Century."

The governments in Canada, provincial and federal, are parliamentary, in the British tradition, and this is important to recall when regarding the influence of the Social Gospel in the nation. Tommy Douglas's convictions about the Social Gospel were the main reason this rural Baptist minister helped to form a third main political party in his province and in the Dominion.

The third party was first named the Cooperative Commonwealth Federation (CCF), a familiar term for Social Gospel followers, and, after 1961, this was dissolved to join as a New Democratic Party (NDP).[71] Since then, the party has been the government in five of the ten provinces.[72] It has never been in power in Ottawa, but in 2011 a federal general election elected the NDP as Her Majesty's Loyal Opposition, the party in Opposition with the most seats on that side of the House of Commons.[73]

Rauschenbusch was not unfamiliar with political dynamics, especially with early experiences with Henry George. At the 1889 Toronto Baptist Congress, Rauschenbusch asserted, "I have read Mr. George's book [and] I revere and honor him as my teacher to some extent in these [political] things."[74] Dores Sharpe has also related how Rauschenbusch apparently ad-

---

[71] It is tempting to note some significance in the loss of the old Social Gospel terminology which could indicate some loss of the religious side of the political movement. It probably was inevitable.

[72] Saskatchewan, British Columbia, Alberta, Ontario, and Nova Scotia.

[73] The election was held on 2 May 2011. The results: Conservative Party of Canada: 166; New Democratic Party: 103; Liberal Party of Canada: 34; Bloc Quebecois: 4. The Right Honourable Steven Harper was asked by the governor-general to form a government and become prime minister of it. The NDP lost this distinction about four years later, in 2015, when the Liberal Party became the government with a sweeping victory with the Right Honourable Justin Trudeau as prime minister winning 184 seats. The Tories came in second (99 seats), becoming the Official Opposition. The NDP slipped back to third-party status (44 seats) and the Bloc Quebecois rose to 10 seats. The Bloc Quebecois stands only in the Province of Quebec and is a separatist party.

[74] The Baptist Congress Proceedings, 1889, 55. Just before, he explained, "For the last three years I have been working in New York City, and by reason of

vocated in March 1890 for ballot reform and the establishment of an independent party to stand for election.[75]

It is interesting to note that an attempt was made to form a Christian Socialist society in New York and its manifesto stated, "The natural movement of society seems to us towards some sort of *coöperative commonwealth*." Sharpe used the italics and inserts his own comment that "coöperative commonwealth" was a favorite expression of Social Gospel followers. This term and the goals of Rauschenbusch were almost exactly parallel to the Regina Manifesto,[76] which was signed a year after the CCF was born in July 1932.[77] Needing "a flashy finish" to the text of the manifesto, Frank Underhill added to the long-debated document "No C.C.F. Government will rest content until it has eradicated capitalism and put into operation the full programme of socialized planning which will lead to the establishment in Canada of the Co-operative Commonwealth."[78]

This last sentence would not have been Rauschenbusch's choice if he were alive, but it originated from some of the more stringent Socialists in Britain who were just as influential in Canada.

---

the pity and sympathy which the Lord Jesus Christ has implanted in my heart, I have not been able to look on the things I see about me there unmoved, or without thinking on the causes of those sad appearances." Then he continued, "I am glad to say, for the information of the gentlemen who questioned the accuracy of the preceding speaker's [his friend and also a Baptist minister in New York City, Leighton Williams] statement of the principles laid down by Henry George, that I have read Mr. George's book, that I revere and honor him as my teacher to some extent in these things."

[75] Sharpe, *Walter Rauschenbusch*, 91.

[76] Lam, *Tommy Douglas*, 56–59. In part, it stated, "We believe that these evils [speculators, profiteers, and economic depressions] can be removed only in a planned and socialized economy." Lam observes, "Many parts of the Regina Manifesto, though decidedly idealistic in 1933, now occupy the mainstream of Canadian values" (57).

[77] The CCF was born in Calgary, July 1932, with delegates from the Labour Party, United Farm representatives, and the rail unions.

[78] Stewart, *Tommy Douglas*, 103. Stewart adds, "This sentence would later become, in [M. J.] Coldwell's words, a 'millstone around the party's neck,' although that was not the reaction when it was read to the cheering convention in Regina."

THE TOMMY DOUGLAS STORY

It was no accident that Tommy Douglas (1904–1986) was voted the Greatest Canadian of the Century.[79]

The Canadian ecclesiastical establishment was already alert to the impact of Walter Rauschenbusch ever since the Toronto meeting of the Baptist Congress.[80] Tommy Douglas was eight years old when he arrived with his mother and sister to join his father in Winnipeg.[81] Unknown then, of course, but "Tommy," as he has always been known, would become the best-known Social Gospel advocate in his adopted nation. In Winnipeg, he became well aware of social needs, particularly in the Western Provinces of Canada. He would be the powerhouse that propelled those who created the "Regina Manifesto" into a main political party of Saskatchewan, and then a strong third party of the nation. It re-echoed the Social Gospel language by finally choosing the name, "Cooperative Commonwealth Federation," becoming, after 1961, the New Democratic Party.[82]

Perhaps the party is best known for establishing the first government Medicare program when it came to power in Saskatchewan after an election on June 15, 1944[83]—first in Saskatchewan, and then persuading an always-hesitating minority liberal government to do it nationally.[84] Finally, a na-

---

[79] Lam, *Tommy Douglas,* 3. The voting took place across Canada under the auspices of the Canadian Broadcasting Corporation (CBC), one of a number of Crown Corporations owned by the state. It was modeled after the British Broadcasting Corporation (BBC). Independent of the popularly elected House of Commons, the CBC officially comes under the Crown.

[80] Eighth Baptist Congress Proceedings 1889, op. cit., p. 55. Rauschenbusch opened his first speech including this statement: "I have done some reading and some thinking upon the matter [social needs], but very little speaking." This is likely the first real exposure that Canadian church people had of Walter Rauschenbusch.

[81] Lam, *Tommy Douglas,* 11.

[82] Stewart, *Tommy Douglas,* 7–8.

[83] Ibid., 161. The party won an astounding 53% of the vote and 47 of the 53 seats in the legislature, upsetting the long-ruling Liberals.

[84] Ibid., 222–36. In the 1965 federal election, the results: Liberals 131 seats, Tories 97, NDP 21, Social Credit Party 5, and the French Social Credit Party, Ralliement Créditiste, 9. Stewart commented, "If the Liberals had dumped, or even delayed, the promise to bring in medicare, their hold on power would not have lasted long." They would have lost a vote in the House of Commons and would

tional Medicare came into effect July 1, 1968, forty-nine years after Saskatchewan.

This was not the only victory for the CCF/NDP, for they put political pressure, usually on the liberals, to pass other universal social welfare legislation, including the "Baby Bonus," maternal and paternal leave, minimum wages, income assistance for low incomes, Old Age Security Plan, Canada Pension plan, Unemployment Insurance, Retired Registered Savings Plan (RRSP: a tax shelter), Economic Development Agencies, Universal Child Care benefit, and a host of other social welfare programs.

Douglas was a Baptist minister accredited until his dying day by the Baptist Union of Western Canada.[85] He was educated at Brandon College, McMaster University, and was a doctoral student at the University of Chicago with Arthur Erastus Holt, a Social Gospel champion. It was about this time that Douglas began serious reading about the Social Gospel, as in Fred Henderson's *The Case for Socialism*, Rauschenbusch's *Christianity and the Social Crisis*, and Canadian J. S. Woodsworth—whom Douglas would admire for the rest of his life.[86]

It was Holt's method to teach by sending his students to collect information through their own circulation amongst the "hobo jungle" near the railway tracks of Chicago.[87] This had a profound effect on Douglas and, suggests Scott Pittendrigh, likely edged him nearer the Christian Realism of Reinhold Niebuhr, but "rooted him in the language of Rauschenbusch's Social Gospel theology."[88]

Congruent with this, there was another member of the clergy prominent in the Canadian public eye, a Methodist, J. S. Woodsworth. James Shaver Woodsworth moved to Brandon in 1892 and was ordained in 1896. While studying at Oxford University in 1899, he became interested in social welfare work. Returning to Manitoba in 1902, Woodsworth soon became involved working with poor immigrants lured to the prairies by land

---

have had to recommend to the governor-general, the Queen's representative in Canada, to call another election which they would have almost surely lost.

[85] Ibid., 125.

[86] Ibid., 84.

[87] Scott Michael Pittendrigh, "The Religious Perspective of T. C. Douglas: Social Gospel Theology and Pragmatism" (Unpublished MA thesis, University of Regina, 1997), 31.

[88] Pittendrigh, "Religious Perspective," 18, 102.

grants and rich soil. He preached a Social Gospel that called for the kingdom of God, "here and now." It was not long before his relations with the Methodists became difficult, and he resigned from the church in 1918 because of his denomination's support for the Great War.[89]

It was the pastoral ministry that attracted Douglas, and he and his new wife settled at the Calvary Baptist Church in Weyburn, Saskatchewan, in 1930. The stock markets had crashed, and the Great Drought of the 1930s was just beginning. Douglas had his work cut out for him. He became involved with the social welfare of the community and developed quickly into a very popular minister in the small town. He began, with these rather ordinary steps, a Social Gospel revolution in Canada.

The story of his almost falling into politics because of the destitution of the people around him is well told. He stood for Parliament in the 1935 federal election, and he often told the story:

> I got a visit from the superintendent of the Baptist Church for the West.... I said, "Many people here have been pressing me to run again. I don't want to run. On the other hand, I've seen the party build up and I hate to walk out and leave it." He said, "Leave it." Then he made the great mistake, saying, "If you don't leave it, and if you don't stay out of politics, you'll never get another church in Canada, and I'll see to it. The board has given me authority." I replied, "You've just given the CCF a candidate."[90]

Tommy won his constituency and marched on to be a member of Parliament. On February 11, 1936, he gave his maiden speech in that august chamber in Ottawa.[91] He described the abject poverty he had seen in Sas-

---

[89] Nancy Christie and Michael Gauvreau, *A Full-Orbed Christianity: The Protestant Churches and Social Welfare in Canada 1900–1940* (Montreal, PQ: McGill-Queen's University Press, 1996), 12. The authors successfully argue that Woodsworth left the Methodist church not because he lost his faith but that "Woodsworth maintained that the measure of one's religiosity was measured by participation in practical social service and that this meaningful behaviour of social responsibility was not limited to the institutional church."

[90] Lam, *Tommy Douglas*, 47. Citation: Tommy Douglas, 1958, on his decision to run for Parliament in 1935.

[91] J. E. Harris, *The Baptist Union of Western Canada: A Centennial History 1873–1973* (Saint John, NB: Lingley Printing Co., 1976), 137. Apparently, time moderates views. Almost forty years later Harris wrote condescendingly as a part of

katchewan and concluded, "The people of Canada look to us; the people of Canada trust in us; the people of Canada are counting on us; in heaven's name let us not fail them."[92]

Back in Saskatchewan, the need for good political leadership called, and Tommy responded. There was a provincial election called in 1944. He left Ottawa, won the premiership, and a new light began to glow from the premier's office in Regina—a Social Gospel-inspired government was born. It continued to grow through the decades, metamorphosing in 1961 into the New Democratic Party (although it never was a government in Ottawa). They played their political hand well, mainly through the Liberal Party, and their policies carried the votes in the House of Commons for the welfare state in Canada—so it was finally established, much to the joy of Tommy Douglas.

As Lam has concluded,

> [Tommy] might not have grasped for small glories, but NDP policies clearly migrated into Liberal platforms in many areas. The political lineage of initiatives such as nationally owned central banking, a bill of rights, a progressive income tax system that favoured lower-income earners, unemployment insurance, a contributory pensions plan, old-age pension, and universal health insurance can all be traced directly back to the Social Gospellers, the CCF and the NDP. A surprising number of these innovations bear the handprint of a certain Baptist minister, either through his pioneering initiatives in Saskatchewan or in his role as first leader of the NDP.[93]

An observer might note that as the years progressed and advancement was made, the Gospel part of social concern faded from view. To Canadians today, it is less Christian, but, rather, "civilized" to have a well-run and socially concerned government. The Canadian government is becoming more and more inclusive, which admits other religious faiths at its borders. The day of Tommy Douglas is, perhaps lamentably, over, but this might have

---

Western Baptist history, "We see no unworthy motive in Tommy Douglas. We agree with Jack Scott of the Vancouver Sun who said of Mr. Douglas, 'He was motivated entirely by an ideal.' To call him a politician is an insult to him. He was and is a dreamer and humanitarian, genuine and intellectually honest."

[92] Lam, *Tommy Douglas*, 71. Source: *Hansard*, 11 February 1936.

[93] Ibid., 209–10.

been the inevitable result of a broadening society rejoicing in a welfare state. It is an honorable inheritance for Tommy to leave all Canadians.

Lam has summed it up:

> A Social Gospeller from start to finish, Douglas was pleased that social activism enjoyed a resurgence in the mainstream of Christian churches late in his life. At that time, he reflected, "The universe isn't made up of a great cruel God who tells everyone what to do, or of a great organization called the Church that steps with relentless heel on anyone who doesn't do what it tells them to do.... Jesus was in his day, and he hasn't been surpassed since, a great moral teacher who recognized man's place in society...that the great motivating force in society is love for your fellow man...and that there is something that for want of a better term they call the Kingdom of God, which is simply an association of people who have certain ideas in common."[94]

Tommy Douglas died on Monday, February 24, 1986, at his home in Ottawa, of cancer. Walter Rauschenbusch contributed much to Tommy Douglas and Canada—to the place where his ashes still rest at the bottom of Sturgeon Lake.

Some Modest Conclusions

Upon reflection, it is difficult not to see through much of the anecdotal evidence (it is still being written) that Canadians, certainly within the churches, and even outside of it, were greatly influenced by Walter Rauschenbusch's writings. His influence was transmitted, sometimes directly, but, more probably, indirectly. The people mentioned above, and many others, transmitted the grand concepts of the kingdom of God to the Canadian public. That public, up to at least the 1960s, was basically "church orientated" and accorded to the church respect and leadership. It might be claimed, mainly through Tommy Douglas and his colleagues, J. S. Woodsworth, M. J. Colwell, and Stanley Knowles—all of whom were members of Parliament—that Rauschenbusch and his cause may have had more influence upon his Northern Neighbor than in his own native land.

---

[94] Ibid., 213.

It might be noted that in the shared 1936 hymnbook of the United Church of Canada and Canadian Baptist churches, William Blake's hymn was regularly and enthusiastically sung by congregations:

And did those feet in ancient time
Walk upon England's mountain green?
And was the Holy Lamb of God
On England's pleasant pastures seen?
And did the countenance divine
Shine forth upon our clouded hills?
And was Jerusalem builded here
Among these dark satanic mills?

And with determination, they would sing forth from the pews,

Bring me my bow of burning gold!
Bring me my arrows of desire!
Bring me my spear! O clouds unfold!
Bring me my chariot of fire!
I will not cease from mental fight,
Nor shall my sword sleep in my hand,
Till we have built Jerusalem
In England's green and pleasant land.

Archaic as these words might sound in the ears of people today, they held great meaning for Canadians. No longer do Canadians think in terms of the ever-arching beneficent British Empire, but rather in the human fellowship of a Commonwealth of Nations. The three main Baptist universities—Acadia, McMaster, and Brandon—in the post-World War I era, often honoring Rauschenbusch's works, educated even more leaders for a Gospel welfare society. Many Canadian Armed Forces chaplains encouraged veterans to return with Rauschenbusch's Gospel illuminations.[95] This was indeed

[95] Duff Crerar, *Padres in No Man's Land: Canadian Chaplains and the Great War* (Montreal, PQ: McGill-Queen's University Press, 1995), 179–80. "Chaplains such as George Fallis preached that, while Jesus was known as the Prince of Peace, he should also be recognized as the 'Prince of Justice and Righteousness.' Similarly, Walter Rauschenbusch's *The Social Principles of Jesus* and Harry Emerson Fosdick's *The Manhood of the Master* became the basis of many a Canadian chaplain's Bible

the leaven in the lump upon which Tommy Douglas and his usually happy band of Social Gospel siblings planted the beginning of the rising loaf of a socially caring state. Perhaps Walter Rauschenbusch would have nodded with approval.

The "Moral and Social Reform Council of Canada" developed in December 1911, and in early March of 1914, the council held a Social Service Congress in Ottawa with many speakers, including the church, addressing social concerns. Council members included the Church of England in Canada (the Anglican Church of Canada), the Methodists, Presbyterians, Baptists, Congregationalist churches, the Trades and Labour Congress of Canada, the Dominion Grange and Farmers' Association, the Salvation Army, the Canadian Purity Education Association, the Evangelical Association of North America, and the Dominion Women's Christian Temperance Union.[96]

J. W. Aitkens, minister of the Metropolitan Methodist Church of Toronto, presented a paper titled "Jesus Christ and Industry." Rauschenbusch's thoughts were prominent in the assembly, and in discussing the relationship between the "boss" and the laborer, Aitkens said, "In this connection, Prof. Rauschenbusch says: 'The community of true men is a community of labour, and when a man gets outside of the common work of mankind, he gets outside of the Kingdom of God.' Evidently Jesus Christ has very little sympathy with the man whose chief objective is to make a pile of money and settle down."[97]

---

study or discussion group. After the Armistice both books became part of the curriculum of the joint Chaplain Service—YMCA Citizenship Campaign, which was intended to indoctrinate returning veterans with the ideals of the Kingdom of God....

As Allied victory drew nearer, however, Walter Rauschenbusch's work gave timely emphasis to Jesus' social crusade. Despite his emphatic rejection of war as a method of realizing the kingdom, chaplains eagerly drew upon his method of realizing the Kingdom, chaplains eagerly drew upon his portrait of Jesus's zeal for the highest ethical, economic, and political principles of brotherhood."

[96] "Social Service Congress: Ottawa 1914: Report of Addresses and Proceedings" (Toronto, ON: The Social Service Council of Canada, 1914) p. iii. The president was the Rev'd. Albert Carman, Methodist, and the treasurer was the Rev'd Prof. E. M. Kierstead, DD (Baptist).

[97] "Social Service Congress," 44–45.

In all, there were sixty-two speakers, twenty of whom were clergy, seven were members of Parliament, eight were women (including two female medical doctors), several judges and lawyers, and one governor-general, His Royal Highness the Duke of Connaught.[98]

It must be admitted, naturally, that there always has been a conservative element in the warp and woof of the Canadian fabric. In Rauschenbusch's day, the "mainline denominations" were far more open to the Social Gospel than the more sectarian ones. Discussions within conferences and conventions were often convoluted and intricate.

An interesting possible illustration of the change in Canadian Baptists just after 1900 might be the adoption of the British Baptist *Hymnary* with two Canadian supplements in 1904. One Supplement was integrated at the end of the book, but another, much smaller and half-sized, was labeled an "Extra Supplement." It was obviously a last-minute inclusion, and it was bound within the midst of the volume. In it we find the likes of Frank Mason North's hymn first published the year previous, 1903.[99]

---

[98] "Social Service Congress," vii–viii. The Duke of Connaught was the third son of Queen Victoria and brother of King Edward VII. In 1914, he was the uncle of the reigning king, George V (1910–1936). It is significant that the King's Representative was present.

[99] *An Annotated Anthology of Hymns*, ed. J. R. Watson (Oxford: Oxford University Press, 2002), 279–80. The hymn was "A Prayer for the Multitudes," first published in North's magazine, *The Christian City* (June 1903). North (1850–1935), a Methodist minister, was greatly involved with inner-city work of New York and well known to Rauschenbusch and in Social Gospel circles. This hymn was included in every subsequent Canadian Baptist hymnbook and is well loved. In recent years, it has been "modernized" to be inclusive of gender sensitivities. The 1904 "extra supplement" contained only the first and fifth stanzas, but the following hymnaries included all six (tune: Walton):

1. Where cross the crowded ways of life,
Where sound the cries of race and clan,
Above the noise of selfish strife,
We hear Thy voice, O Son of Man.

2. In haunts of wretchedness and greed,
On shadowed thresholds, dark with fears,
From paths where hide the lure of greed,
We catch the vision of Thy tears.

4. The cup of water given for Thee
Still holds the freshness of Thy grace;
Yet long these multitudes to see
The sweet compassion of Thy face.

5. O Master, from the mountain side
Make haste to heal these hearts of pain;
Among these restless throngs abide,
O tread the city's streets again;

When Walter Rauschenbusch passed away on July 25, 1918, he was mourned in Canada as elsewhere, and the editor of *The Maritime Baptist* wrote with great feeling:

> Last week we published the statement from Dr. Walter Rauschenbusch in respect to his attitude to the present war.[100] Since then news has reached us that this eminent Christian teacher and scholar has been suddenly called to the home eternal. It is scarcely too much to say that Dr. Rauschenbusch was the most widely known and one of the most influential Baptists in [North] America. For many years he has left his impress upon the succeeding classes at the Rochester Theological Seminary, and that institution has sustained a heavy loss in his death. But his greatness and most enduring work was undoubtedly rendered through his books by which he made a valuable contribution to the thought of the age and to the solution of the social problems created by our modern civilization. He will be lovingly and gratefully remembered even by many who never came into direct touch with his magnetic personality.[101]

B. D. Thomas was right when he said to the Baptist Congress in 1889, especially to the visiting American Baptists, and, unknowingly, to Walter Rauschenbusch himself, "You have been an example and an inspiration to us in many ways. We rejoice in your missionary, educational and philanthropic enterprises. Your proximity has been a wonderful help to us in our activities here."[102]

The legacy of Walter Rauschenbusch continually enriches Canadians to this day.

---

3. From tender childhood's helplessness,
From woman's grief, man's burdened toil,
From famished souls, from sorrow's stress,
Thy heart has never known recoil.

6. Till sons of men shall learn Thy love,
And follow where Thy feet have trod;
Till glorious from Thy heaven above
Shall come the city of our God. Amen.

[100] *Maritime Baptist*, ed. the Rev'd Robert J. Colpitts, 31 July 1918, 3.

[101] *Maritime Baptist*, 7 August 1918, 4, "Notes and Commentary." The editor Robert J. Colpitts had been a student of Rauschenbusch himself.

[102] Eighth Baptist Congress, 1889 in *Maritime Baptist*, 3. Dr. Thomas was born in Wales, emigrated to the United States, and held prominent churches there until he assumed the pulpit of Jarvis Street Baptist Church in Toronto in 1882.

Chapter 6

The Social Gospel of the Orient: The Story of the Telugu Church

Chakravarthy R. Zadda

During the nineteenth century among the Baptist churches in the United States, the story of founding the church among the Telugu-speaking Dalits in India was told several times for its significant accomplishments in foreign missions. That story of the Telugu Church is again narrated here for two reasons. First, to show how the foundation of the Telugu Church had an impact upon and intersected with the life of Walter Rauschenbusch and his work for the Social Gospel movement, and second, to make the case that missionary endeavor is not a one-way process from donor to the receiver, but always a two-way process which benefits both the sending agency, the mission society, and the receiving agent, the mission field.

THE STORY OF THE TELUGU MISSION

"Gone are the days when India was seen as a country of snake charmers, rope tricks and pompous maharajas; it is now being seen as a country producing entrepreneurs, efficient doctors and engineers of Information Technology," notes Smarak Swain, writer for a leading business magazine.[1] India has come a long way with its technological acumen in the global scene over the past seven decades. Swain further writes, "[The] 19th century, it is said, was the best time to be a British and [the] 20th century to be an American, no doubt, [the] 21st century is the best period to be an Indian."[2] While the making of modern India is definitely an achievement of great leaders of the nation, one should not lose sight of the nineteenth-century modern missionary movement, which laid the foundations for the great Indian renais-

---

[1] Smarak Swain, *21st century: Best time for an Indian* (http://www.rediff.com/money/2006/dec/11iit2.htm). Accessed 2 April 2018.

[2] Ibid.

sance and for empowering the outcaste communities, the Dalits, in building this strong nation.

The English missionary "Serampore Trio," Joshua Marshman and William Ward under the leadership of William Carey, laid the underpinnings of the missionary movement in India during the 1790s. Eventually, by the turn of the century, several Protestant missionary agencies from the West established their mission stations in India. Of them, the American Baptist Foreign Missionary Society (ABFMS), is known for its significant work among the Telugu-speaking Dalits (belonging to Madiga and Mala communities) in the current states of Andhra Pradesh and Telangana in South India.

Presently there are nearly 640,000 Telugu Baptist Christians worshiping every Sunday in more than a thousand congregations.[3] James Taneti has defined Telugu Baptists' social location as belonging to "an ethnic group at the bottom of the caste hierarchy and considered 'untouchable' by the dominant Telugu society."[4] These Madigas and Malas, along with several other outcaste communities (untouchable), identify themselves as Dalits.

Dalits are "outcastes" falling outside the traditional four-fold caste system consisting of Brahmin (priest), Kshatriya (warrior), Vaishya (merchant), and Shudra (servant) castes.[5] They are considered "untouchable" because of the extreme impurity and pollution connected with their traditional menial occupations, and they are therefore physically and socially excluded and isolated from the rest of the society. Dalits were given derogatory names such as chandalas (those who deal with disposal of corpses), untouchables, outcastes, depressed classes, and harijans, down through the centuries. However, Dalits today are increasingly adopting the term "Dalit" as a name for themselves because they have found their identity in the word. The word Dalit comes from the Sanskrit root *dal-* meaning "burst, split, broken or torn asunder, downtrodden, scattered, crushed, destroyed."[6]

---

[3] James Elisha Taneti, "Telugu Baptist Christianity: A Religion of the Marginalized" *American Baptist Quarterly* 29/1, 2 (Spring–Summer 2010): 63.

[4] Taneti, "Telugu Baptist Christianity," 63.

[5] Chakravarthy R. Zadda, "Shoemaker and Missionary: A Dalit Christian Perspective", in *Expect Great Things, Attempt Great Things: William Carey and Adoniram Judson, Missionary Pioneers*, eds. Allen Yeh and Chris Chun, (Eugene, OR: Wipf & Stock, 2013), 28.

[6] James Massey, *Dalits in India* (New Delhi: Manohar Publication, 1995), 15.

Thus, these indigenous communities choose to be identified with the word Dalit. It reflects their identity by embracing their experiences of discrimination with affirmation.

Based on the 2011 India census, it is estimated that there are 260 million Dalits around the world, more than 166 million of whom live in India.[7] Of the 27.8 million Christians in India,[8] Dalits constitute about 16 million, mostly living in the southern states of Andhra Pradesh, Telangana, Karnataka, Kerala, and Tamil Nadu. It is important to note that 95 percent of Christians in Andhra Pradesh and Telangana come from the two Madiga and Mala outcaste communities, whose traditional caste professions were weaving and leather tanning.

As a group, Dalit Christians are thrice discriminated in the Indian society—first, within the church, second, in society, and finally by the state. Dalits embraced Christianity, seeking a better life with dignity, but they continue to experience discrimination even within the church. The dominant caste converts, though few in number, hold the leadership of the church. They do not accept the people of lower castes as their equals. Unchristian and discriminatory practices are being continued within the church even today. Whether Christian or Hindu, the dominant caste people in society treat Dalit Christians with the same contempt and subject them to the same ill treatment as their Hindu Dalit counterparts. The state itself discriminates against Christian Dalits on the basis of religion, denying their privileges as granted through the Presidential Order.[9] Further, currently

---

[7] "Overcoming Violence: Churches Seeking Reconciliation and Peace," (http://www.overcomingviolence.org/en/resources/campaigns/women-against-violence/now-we-are-fearless/dalit-fact-sheet.html). Accessed on 2 April 2018.

[8] "India has 79.8% Hindus, 14.2% Muslims, says 2011 census data on religion, First Post," (https://www.firstpost.com/india/india-has-79-8-percent-hindus-14-2-percent-muslims-2011-census-data-on-religion-2407708.html). Accessed on 2 April 2018.

[9] The third paragraph of the Constitution (Scheduled Castes) Order 1950, popularly known as the Presidential Order, stipulates "no person who professes a religion different from Hinduism shall be deemed to be a member of Scheduled Caste." By restricting the Constitution benefits to a particular religion, the Order has divided the entire Dalit community on the basis of religion. Dalits professing Christian faith were deprived of the reservations provided as backward community which was sanctioned through Constitution of India. "The Constitution (Sched-

there are anti-conversion laws enacted by a few states that marginalize the Dalits for choosing a religion other than the one into which they were born. The interview of John R. Mott with Gandhi on December 19, 1939, indicates the general opinion of the caste Hindus about the Dalit's conversion movements, which unfortunately remains the same even today. Gandhi said, "Would you, Dr. Mott, preach the Gospel to a cow? Well, some of the untouchables are worse than cows in understanding. I mean they can no more distinguish between the relative merits of Islam and Hinduism and Christianity than a cow."[10] The social status of the Dalits in the minds of caste communities remains much the same, even after seventy-one years of independence. In spite of these challenges, Indian Christians (among whom Telugu Christians are a significantly sizable group) are faithfully following their Christian commitments. The mass movements of Madigas speak for their own spiritual aspirations for socio-religious liberation in a caste-ridden Indian society.

ORIGIN OF THE TELUGU MISSION

The mission to the Telugus was initiated by several missionary agencies from the West, with the United States and Canada at the top of the list. The congregations that are affiliated with American Baptist Foreign Mission Society are now organized as the Samavesam (Fellowship/Federation) of Telugu Baptist Churches (STBC).

The American Baptist mission to the Telugus was initiated through the American Baptist Foreign Mission Society in 1835 when the Revs. Samuel S. Day and E. L. Abbott, accompanied by their wives, were appointed in response to the request made by Adoniram Judson, the American Baptist missionary to Burma, seventeen years previously. Initially, Judson and his wife, Ann Hasseltine, were commissioned by the American Board of Commissioners for Foreign Missions as Congregationalist missionaries to

---

uled Castes) Order," 1950 (http://socialjustice.nic.in/writereaddata/UploadFile/scorders-updated-30062016.pdf). Accessed on 2 April 2018.

[10] Arundhati Roy, *The Doctor and the Saint: Caste, Race, and Annihilation of Caste the Debate Between B. R. Ambedkar and M. K. Gandhi* (Chicago, IL: Haymarket Books, 2017), 102; *The Collected Works of Mahatma Gandhi, Vol. 70*, 76–77.

the East. Judson arrived in Calcutta on June 17, 1812. It was during his voyage to India that he became a Baptist.[11]

The story of the introduction of the Gospel to the Telugus is coincidentally connected with Judson's missionary work. In 1818 on a voyage to South India, Judson accidentally spent some weeks among the Telugus. While sailing from Rangoon to visit a distant part of the Arakan coast, unfavorable winds changed the course of his plans.[12] The boat, beaten by the storm, eventually landed at "Machilipatanam," to the south of the river Godavari in Andhra Pradesh. They had no food for days and the people on board were sick and afflicted with diarrhea. Two English people got Judson and others ashore and helped Judson recover his health. He utilized the recuperation time by sharing the Gospel with the Telugu people. After his strength was restored, Judson travelled to Rangoon by road through Madras (currently called Chennai). The humble hospitality he received motivated Judson to request of the ABFMS that a missionary be sent to work among Telugus.[13] Judson's unplanned missionary journey introduced the Telugu people's need for the Gospel message among their communities to the outside world. However, the Telugu Mission did not receive missionaries for another seventeen years. Amos Sutton, a missionary for General Baptists of England, who was working among the Oriya-speaking people of Orissa state, northeast of Andhra Pradesh, visited the United States in 1835. During that visit Sutton addressed the Baptist General Association of Virginia and appealed for work among Telugus.[14] In response to his passionate plea,

---

[11] Gregory A. Wills, "From Congregationalist to Baptist: Judson and Baptist", in *Adoniram Judson: A Bicentennial Appreciation of the Pioneer American Missionary*, ed. Jason G. Duesing (Nashville, TN: B&H Publishing Group, 2001), 154; also the classic Courtney Anderson, *To the Golden Shore: The Life of Adoniram Judson* (Valley Forge, PA: Judson Press, 1987), 126–42.

[12] Robert G. Torbet, *Venture of Faith: The Story of the American Baptist Foreign Mission Society and the Woman's American Foreign Mission Society 1814–1954* (Philadelphia, PA: The Judson Press, 1955), 34.

[13] E. B. Bromley, *They Were Sent from God: A Centenary Record 1836–1936 of Gospel Work in India Amongst Telugus in the Godavari Delta and Neighbouring Parts* (Bangalore: Scripture Literature Press, 1947), 8.

[14] Taneti, "Telugu Baptist Christianity," 64.

Samuel S. Day and E. L. Abbott were appointed to start the Telugu Mission.[15]

INITIAL CHALLENGES

The Telugu Mission was a challenging field. The missionaries reached out to all the communities, but focused primarily on the caste Telugus in hope that if they were reached by the Gospel, eventually the downtrodden would follow. However, efforts to reach out to the caste Telugus for the most part ended up in futility. Several times during the foundational years the missionary society wanted to abandon the mission.

Disappointment began as early as the appointment of their first missionaries. Though both the Days and Abbotts were appointed to the Telugu Mission, when they arrived in Calcutta 1836 it was decided that only Rev. Day and his wife, Roenna Clark, should go to the Telugu people of South India, while the Abbotts should work among the Karens of Burma in the east.[16] The two men received divergent responses in their respective mission fields. Abbott sent home reports of an enthusiastic welcome for his message, while Day experienced nothing but hostility or indifference. Day made several trips across the cities on the coast between Vishakapatam and Madras and finally established the mission station for the Telugus in Nellore city in 1840.[17] After nearly five years of hard work, Day had his first convert in Venkappah from Nellore, who accepted the Gospel and was baptized on September 27, 1841. Venkappah's conversion was the inauguration of the greater mission yet to unfold among the out-caste Telugus.

Again in 1853, during the annual meeting of the newly formed American Baptist Missionary Union (ABMU) in Albany, New York,[18] it was pro-

[15] "The Telugu Mission: Jubilee Exercise," *The Baptist Missionary Magazine* 66/2 (February 1886): 50–52.

[16] James M. Baker, *Contending the Grade in India* (Ashville, NC: The Biltmore Press, 1947), 59. David Downie, *The Lone Star: The History of the Telugu Mission* (Philadelphia, PA: American Baptist Publication Society, 1893), 26.

[17] John Craig, *Forty Years Among the Telugus: A History of the Mission of the Baptists of Ontario and Quebec, Canada to the Telugu, South India 1867–1907* (Toronto, ON: J. Craig, 1908), 13.

[18] In 1845 the Baptist community in the United States divided over slavery issues into the Southern Baptist Convention and affiliation with the societies supported by Baptists in the northern and western states. In 1846, the American Bap-

posed that the Telugu Mission be closed for the lack of positive response among the Telugus and Mr. and Mrs. Jewett, then stationed missionaries, be moved to Burma.[19] Dr. Edward Bright, the home secretary of the ABMU, turned to the mission map where the American Baptist Foreign Mission Society had originally pinned stars for their mission stations, pointed to Nellore (the Telugu Mission), called it the "Lone Star," and said, "There are many to care for the brilliant constellation in Burma, but who will care for the Lone Star?"[20] Glaringly, one star stood alone in South India against the cluster of stars on Burma, on the east of India.

The Telugu Mission identified by one star on the map got the attention of all the members in the meeting, including Dr. Samuel Francis Smith, author of the famed American patriotic hymn "My Country, 'Tis of Thee." Caught up with the words "lone star," he wrote the following poem as his dream for the Telugu Mission:

"THE Lone STAR"

Shine on, "Lone Star!" Thy radiance bright
Shall spread o'er all the eastern sky;
Morn breaks apace from gloom and night;
Shine on, and bless the pilgrim's eye.

Shine on, "Lone Star!" I would not dim
The light that gleams with dubious ray;
The lonely Star of Bethlehem
Led on a bright and glorious day.

Shine on, "Lone Star!" in grief and tears,
And sad reverses oft baptized;
Shine on amid thy sister spheres;
Lone stars in heaven are not despised.

---

tist Foreign Mission Society was reorganized as the American Baptist Missionary Union. See Torbet, *Venture of Faith*, 114.

[19] John E. Clough, *Social Christianity in the Orient* (New York: The Macmillan Co., 1914), 64.

[20] Grace Mitchell Everts, *One Purpose True* (Philadelphia, PA: American Baptist Publication Society, 1903), 127.

Shine on, "Lone Star!" Who lifts his hand
To dash to earth so bright a gem,
A new "lost pleiad" from the band
That sparkles in night's diadem?

Shine on, "Lone Star!" The day draws near
When none shall shine more fair than thou;
Thou, born and nursed in doubt and fear,
Wilt glitter on Immanuel's brow.

Shine on, "Lone Star!" till earth redeemed,
In dust shall did its idols fall;
And thousands, where thy radiance beamed,
Shall "crown the Saviour Lord of all."

The next morning Dr. Smith gave the poem to Judge Harris, the chair of the meeting, who in turn read it to the board. The poem moved their hearts, and they offered a second chance for the Telugu Mission.[21] However, in India it was not easy for the missionaries to make much progress among the caste Telugus.

The question "Shall the Telugu mission be abandoned?" came up again at the annual meeting of 1862 held in Providence, Rhode Island. Lyman Jewett's hopeful response to the ABMU executive committee provided the Telugu Mission not just a third chance, but also more resources. The Rev. John E. Clough and his wife, Harriet Sundarland, were appointed as missionaries to the Telugu Mission. The Cloughs joined the mission on April 22, 1865,[22] and with a mass conversions of the Dalits, brought a paradigm shift in Baptist missions. The Telugu Mission, which had been on the list to be shut down, came to live up to the dream of Samuel Smith. John Clough continued his missionary work among the Telugus until he retired in 1906.

CLOUGH AND MASS CONVERSIONS

John E. Clough was ahead of his time in several ways, and his missionary methods were severely criticized both by the home board and the political

---

[21] Clough, *Social Christianity*, 65.

[22] Clough, Ibid., 60.

nationalists of the country. Initially, Clough, like his predecessors, started his work among the caste people in Ongole, a town nearly eighty miles from Nellore. The resistance of the caste people towards the Gospel and their minimal response pushed Clough to reflect critically on his missionary theology. The Indian culture taught him how to live in a multireligious society. His inclusive missiological approach can be seen when he challenged the exclusivistic missionary theology of the West. He wrote, "Christian people took it for granted that the older religious were wholly bad, and that their scriptures contained nothing but evil. There was no sympathetic approach, no feeling that perhaps God had not left himself unrevealed to the heathen world."[23] This approach opened a new avenue to understanding the context of not just finding faults with the native religion, but identifying the positive aspects to be used as connecting points. He was radical for his time and became more tolerant towards the Hindu religion. Seeing that the Christian movement among the Telugus was limited to Madigas conversion, he wrote, "As the years passed I grew tolerant and often told the caste people, if they could not, or would not, receive Jesus Christ as their Saviour, to serve their own gods faithfully."[24] Furthermore, Clough was convinced that the caste Hindus were in some respects better than the Americans. He even challenged the American audiences during his visits home to be true Christians. He wrote, "I told them to wake up, and be true Christians, or else the Hindus would come over to America and try to convert the Americans."[25] The new approach of inclusivism certainly had an impact on the creation of new converts among the Telugus. In 1866 there was a remarkable shift in the life of the "lone star mission." A group of nearly thirty people from "Madiga" community, led by their leader, Yerraguntla Perriah, approached Clough, seeking to be baptized to join the Christian faith.

One can note at this point the sharp distinction in the approaches towards the Gospel of the outcastes versus the caste people. While missionaries were reaching out to the caste people and spending their resources to convert them, the outcastes were inviting the missionaries to come to their villages to offer them baptism. The Madiga leaders heard about the Gospel of Jesus Christ and found a kind of social liberation in the conversion movement. They, in turn, motivated the community to embrace the Chris-

---

[23] Clough, Ibid., 73.

[24] Clough, Ibid.

[25] Clough, Ibid.

tian faith as a liberation from caste discrimination. Sometimes they would walk miles to Ongole to receive baptism from the missionary. This set in motion a great awakening among the Dalits, leading to mass movements to Christian faith.

The shift in Clough's missionary model can also be seen during the years of famine in the Telugu land. He shifted the focus of the mission work during 1877 and 1878 to famine relief to provide food for work to all the famine victims. Using his civil engineering background,[26] Clough took the contract from the government to build Buckingham Canal, which provided employment to the poor. People found work and were able to feed their families during the famine. Clough resisted the baptisms for those who wanted to become Christian during this period, though preachers were allowed to share the Gospel with the workers.

After the relief work ended, people from the Madigas and Malas through their community leaders created pressure on Clough to offer them Christian baptism. Talking about the mass conversions and what these meant to the Dalit communities, Clough quoted the words of Yerraguntla Perraih: "His request to me was practically that I should let this Christian movement go in the channels formed by Indian movements of spiritual significance."[27] Clough could now see not just the social liberation from the caste oppression, but also the spiritual empowerment of the Dalits in the conversion movements.

When Clough allowed the baptisms, large numbers of people were initiated into the ordinance of baptism, and 9,606 Madigas were baptized and became members of Ongole church. The movement continued and spread across the two Telugu-speaking states, drawing national and international attention. By the end of 1883, with more than 20,000 members, the Ongole church became the largest Baptist congregation in the world.[28] Clough embraced as his new task "[providing] the vision and the means for socially

---

[26] Wilbur B. Stover, *India a Problem: Present Conditions* (Elgin, IL: Brethren Publishing House, 1903), 203.

[27] Taneti, "Telugu Baptist Christianity," 93.

[28] Paul William Harris, "The Social Dimensions of Foreign Missions: Emma Rauschenbusch Clough and Social Gospel Ideology," in *Gender and the Social Gospel*, eds. Wendy J. Deichmann Edwards and Carolyn De Swarte Gifford. (Urbana, IL: University of Illinois Press, 2003), 89.

uplifting the Untouchable converts and making the movement a real force for social change in caste-ridden India."[29]

The story of the mass conversions among the Telugu Dalits was shared among the churches in United States, and Clough became a prominent, yet controversial, figure for his missionary methods. With his bold move from individual conversion to mass conversions of the communities, Clough thus became the pioneer of Social Christianity. With this approach, new believers are freed from the potential isolation from their own society by mass conversion, and they continue to belong in the community even after becoming Christian.

THE TELUGU MISSION AND WALTER RAUSCHENBUSCH

Walter Rauschenbusch's connection to the Telugu Mission comes primarily from his sister Emma Rauschenbusch, a missionary to the Telugus and later, wife to John E. Clough. Different phases of Emma's work with the Telugu Mission constantly informed and transformed Rauschenbusch's theological formation.

Throughout their lives, foreign mission work was part of Walter and Emma Rauschenbusch's lives. They were children of a missionary, August Rauschenbusch, who was sent to work among the German immigrants in the United States in 1846. As a missionary's children, their early years were spent in both Germany and Rochester, New York. In their formative years, Emma and Walter were introduced to the socioeconomic challenges of life in the poor neighborhoods of cities in the United States.

As young students, both Walter and his sister were from a generation thoroughly influenced by the modern missionary movement of the nineteenth century. Foreign missions always had a significant impact on Walter Rauschenbusch's spiritual formation, though he did not personally serve any mission field. After finishing his seminary education in 1885 at Rochester Theological Seminary, Rauschenbusch felt a call to foreign missions: "I ought to be a preacher, and help to save souls. I wanted to go out as a foreign missionary—I wanted to do hard work for God. Indeed, one of the great thoughts that came upon me was that I ought to follow Jesus Christ in

---

[29] Harris, "The Social Dimensions," 93.

my personal life and die over again his death."[30] He longed to be a missionary overseas but also had a heart for mission in his native land. He even appealed to those who did not have a call to foreign missions that they should "bind themselves to give some term of their youth at least to social work in the trenches."[31] Informed by foreign missions, Rauschenbusch saw the need for mission work on American soil to provide economic and social justice to new immigrants.

Rauschenbusch was inspired by the Telugu Mission and its social dimension of the Gospel initially through his sister, Emma Rauschenbusch, who accepted a call to be a missionary to India, in 1882.[32] It was through her work of empowering the women of India for social change that Walter was informed of the social dimension of mission. This empowerment of caste women in the mission field was an outcome of the woman missionaries in the West seeking their own missionary enterprise "women's work for women."[33] As Paul W. Harris has commented, "Woman missionaries in this era worked to forge a separate sphere for themselves within the missionary enterprise, and in so doing they added a social dimension to conceptions of 'heathenism.'"[34] For Rauschenbusch the social issues of the women both in the home country and on the mission field were right before him because of his sister.

After her initial weeks of work among the women in Madras (Chennai), Emma was transferred to Ongole in August 1883 to join the social movement of the Madigas alongside of Clough. This brought Rauschenbusch direct knowledge of the social transformation of Dalits in the Telugu Mission. It was the personal connection to the social change through the mass conversions of Telugu mission that motivated the young seminarian towards the social dimension of the Gospel.

---

[30] Walter Rauschenbusch, "The Kingdom of God" (1913), in *The Social Gospel in America, 1870–1920: Gladden, Ely, Rauschenbusch*, ed. Robert T. Handy (New York: Oxford University Press, 1966), 265.

[31] Barbara A. Lundsten, "The Legacy of Walter Rauschenbusch: A Life Informed by Mission," *International Bulletin of Missionary Research* 28/2 (April 2004): 75.

[32] Dores Robinson Sharpe, *Walter Rauschenbusch* (New York: Macmillian Co., 1942), 39, 48.

[33] Harris, "The Social Dimensions," 88.

[34] Ibid.

Walter's second connection to the Telugu Mission came through his personal interactions with John E. Clough. In her article titled "The Legacy of Walter Rauschenbusch: A Life Informed by Mission," Barbara A. Lundsten has identified the story of the Telugu Mission as the first and by far the most lasting impression of his education and spiritual formation. Clough's speech during the commencement service of Rochester Theological Seminary in 1884 informed the young seminarians (including Walter) of the exponential growth of the Telugu church among the Madigas through the mass conversions. He then impressed upon them the need for more workers to serve as evangelists and pastors to serve in the Telugu Mission.

The mass conversions not only made Clough famous but also gained critics who questioned his mission method of baptizing in groups. Because Clough supervised the relief work, the converts were suspected as "rice Christians" who were converted through force or inducement.

While Emma was shouldering the mission responsibilities in India, John Clough returned to the United States in 1884 on a furlough. It was during this time Clough was engaged in clarifying to the Western audience the spiritual quest of Madigas through the mass conversions to Christian faith. One principal critic of Clough's mission methods was the president of Rochester Theological Seminary, Augustus H. Strong. Clough visited Strong during his trip to engage with him personally. It was these constructive conversations that eventually paved the way for Clough to receive an invitation to speak at the Rochester Seminary commencement service.

Hospitality during his trip to Rochester came through Emma, who invited Clough to stay with her brother, Walter, as his guest. The personal interactions with Clough about the social transformation of Madigas as Christians inspired Walter's theological thinking towards the need of a Social Gospel in the United States. With his strong advocacy for the social movement of Madigas, Clough made a lasting impression on Walter's theological thinking.

The third connection of Walter Rauschenbusch to the Telugu Mission clearly demonstrates his love for foreign missions and desire to be a missionary to the Telugus. In 1886 Walter was invited to consider the position of the president of Telugu Theological Seminary in Ramapatnam. Unfortunately, although Rauschenbusch was open to the possibility, God did not open that door for him and it did not happen. Despite that, his willingness to be open to such a possibility speaks of Clough's influence and the fact that Rauschenbusch loved the Telugu Mission and was certainly passionate to work among the Telugus.

Finally, Rauschenbusch has played a significant role in telling the Telugu story to the world. He walked alongside of Emma as she published her works about the Telugu Mission. Following her initial time with the mission, and after Clough returned from his furlough, Emma suspended her mission work to deal with depression and ill health. Eventually she travelled to Europe to pursue her studies, and she received a doctorate from the University of Bern in 1894. The same year Emma married Clough (who had lost his wife, Harriet, the year before) and joined the Telugu Mission again, as her second missionary journey among the Telugus.

As an academician, this time Emma took up the task of researching the Madiga conversion movement. She published the book *While Sewing Sandals: Tales of a Telugu Pariah Tribe* in 1899. It is a classic work and unusual for the time. She used sociological and ethnographic analyses that acknowledged the Madigas themselves as the real agency of the origins of the movement. A second book, *Social Christianity in the Orient*, published in 1912, though written in first person as an autobiography of John E Clough, was authored by Emma. This work highlighted the outcaste's opposition to the caste system, providing a social dimension to becoming Christian before the rise of the Social Gospel movement in the West.

CONCLUSION

The Telugu Mission, which at one time had been considered one of the least significant operations on the mission map of the ABMU, with its continued challenges to even survive, has become a beacon of hope for Dalits. Like most of the Western missionaries who were sent to India by different missionary agencies, in his initial phase of missionary work, Clough tried to reach out to the caste Brahmins with the Gospel of salvation. The assumption was that if the Brahmins, as the highest in the caste system, were converted, then the people in the lower castes would eventually follow. The practice of this downward filtration theory blinded the missionaries to the social transformation that the Dalits (outcaste communities) were proactively seeking. Emma Clough, being a woman, could see the aspirations of the Dalits more vividly than her husband, John. It is through her work that Emma introduced Walter to the theological framework for the Social Gospel movement. Her book *While Sewing Sandals* has provided the voice for the Dalit liberation story.

Contrary to the expectations of the missionaries, the Gospel as a way of socially transforming power reached out to the Dalits as an agent of both spiritual and social change. Clough and his team's invitation by the leaders of the Madiga community to offer them baptism was an act of social transformation that broke the age-old caste system that had deprived them of their basic human dignity. It was these mass conversions of the Madigas into the Christian fold that made John Clough a pioneer for a Social Gospel understanding of mission. His defense of the Madigas' conversions and his subsequent missionary methods for social empowerment raised concerns about his work both by the ABMU in the United States and by the local caste leadership in India. However, the bold commitment of Clough in spearheading the advocacy of the mass movements among the Telugus for a social transformation of Madigas has inspired several young minds in the United States to embrace a call to overseas mission. The fact that 80 percent of the contemporary Indian church is Dalit has nullified the allegation of "rice Christians" and loudly speaks for the credibility of the mass conversions and social transformation of the Dalit communities.

The story of the Telugu Baptists, told to inspire the young and "best men" of America, in the words of John E. Clough, motivated not just twenty-five men for overseas missionaries to Telugu land, but also several others to embrace a missionary call to be apostles of the Social Gospel in America, Walter Rauschenbusch among them.

Today Walter Rauschenbusch is known for his contribution to the Social Gospel movement of the late nineteenth and early twentieth centuries. He has inspired many global leaders such as Dr. Martin Luther King Jr., Bishop Desmond Tutu, and others to seek social justice. However, it is humbling to know that through their Christianization, an outcaste community of Madigas, who for centuries suffered the social oppression of being denied basic human dignity as Untouchables, inspired Walter Rauschenbusch in his work. Once again, we see affirmation that the Christian Gospel mission is always beneficial to both the sending and the receiving agencies. Each will have their transforming moments, but in their own way.

Part III

Specific Aspects of the Rauschenbusch Legacy

Chapter 7

"Love a good girl, marry her as soon as conditions permit"[1]:

Walter Rauschenbusch, Gender, Family, and the Social Gospel

Wendy J. Deichmann

> The simplest and most familiar social organization is the family. It is also the most Christian. It is so Christian that the word "Father" has become the most satisfactory symbol of a loving God, and the word "child" the most trustful expression of our relation to him.... As for the word "mother"—that carries a mystic breath of religious sweetness to which we all do homage.[2]
>
> —Walter Rauschenbusch,
> *Christianizing the Social Order*, 1912

The boy, Walter Rauschenbusch, became a man in the context of Victorian America. He eventually composed an influential theology informed by his personal history, ecclesial tradition, and white middle-class American culture. His resolve to overcome both personal and broader social crises in ways that would lead to a much better future helped to shape not only his own life, but also that of his family and his professional work, including his contribution to the Social Gospel movement. This essay will examine Walter Rauschenbusch's views on gender and family, especially as expressed in several of his speeches and publications.

It is no secret that Walter Rauschenbusch grew up in a tragically dysfunctional home. Historian Klaus Juergen Jaehn depicted his parents' mar-

---

[1] Walter Rauschenbusch, "What about the Woman?" Handwritten Lecture Notes, 1902–1912, 1–3 (Rauschenbusch Family Collections, American Baptist Historical Society, Atlanta, Georgia).

[2] Walter Rauschenbusch, *Christianizing the Social Order* (New York: Macmillan Co., 1912), 128.

riage as having begun "under an ill star."[3] Paul Minus described this relationship as afflicted by "marital bitterness,"[4] and Susan Curtis styled it "bitter and unsatisfying."[5] More recently, biographer Christopher Evans noted that in addition to his father's "harsh authoritarianism," Walter "lived in a house torn apart by August's violent verbal confrontations with his wife." By the time Walter was only four years old, his parents' relationship "had reached a point of irreconcilability," and his father "increasingly viewed his relationship with [his wife] Caroline as a curse." August even admitted to one family member praying at times for her speedy demise.[6] His parents' estrangement, Walter later wrote, was one of "the great sorrows in my life."[7] His early home environment galvanized the younger Rauschenbusch's determination "not to repeat the sins of his own father" in the family he hoped someday to raise.[8]

While the son, Walter, eventually grew to respect his father's academic and professional accomplishments, the ongoing tension between his parents contributed to permanent emotional distance between him and his father.[9] The saving grace for young Walter's social and emotional development was his mother, Caroline Rauschenbusch. Despite her husband's excessive, angry tirades and long absences, Mrs. Rauschenbusch attempted to provide a loving, supportive environment for the couple's three children.[10] For example, beginning in 1865, the mother and children spent three years with extended family in Germany apart from the children's father. Shortly after

---

[3] Klaus Juergen Jaehn, *Rauschenbusch: The Formative Years* (Valley Forge, PA: Judson Press, 1976) 13.

[4] Paul M. Minus, *Walter Rauschenbusch: American Reformer* (New York: Macmillan Co., 1988) 14.

[5] Susan Curtis, *A Consuming Faith: The Social Gospel and Modern American Culture* (Columbia, MO: University of Missouri Press, 2001) 105.

[6] Minus, *American Reformer*, 15.

[7] Christopher H. Evans, *The Kingdom Is Always but Coming: A Life of Walter Rauschenbusch* (Grand Rapids, MI: William B. Eerdmans Publishing Company, 2004) 13–14, 18.

[8] Christopher H. Evans, "Gender and the Kingdom of God: The Family Values of Walter Rauschenbusch," in *The Social Gospel Today*, ed. Christopher H. Evans (Louisville, KY: Westminster John Knox Press, 2001), 57.

[9] Evans, *The Kingdom Is Always but Coming*, 17, 35; Jaehn, *The Formative Years*, 13; Curtis, *Consuming Faith*, 106.

[10] Curtis, *Consuming Faith*, 107.

Walter moved to New York City in 1886 to begin his first pastoral assignment, Caroline Rauschenbusch moved in with him. She lived four years in the apartment from which he conducted his ministry, supporting him in his work.[11]

The Rauschenbusch marital woes occurred against a cultural backdrop of enormously high expectations for the American family, including expectations for a loving, harmonious relationship between husband and wife. Middle-class Victorian culture in the United States during the late nineteenth century honored family life as the cornerstone of a successful democracy. As Janet Fishburn put it, "the middle-class Victorian family was quite literally the 'building block' of society. The spirit of love and brotherhood learned in a stable, loving family was expected to flow naturally through the family into society."[12] The dissonance is striking, to say the least, between August and Caroline Rauschenbusch's anything-but-loving spousal relationship and the prescribed standards of their wider cultural context.

Apart from their marital conflicts, Walter Rauschenbusch's parents adhered devotedly to Victorian culture's prescribed, separate spheres of work for women and men, and they educated their children to do the same. Everyone was expected to marry and raise a family to help build the moral and relational infrastructure of society. Husbands were to provide financially for their families through successful employment in the outside world of business, industry, and politics. Wives were to fill complementary roles in the home sphere characterized by religious piety, moral purity, and submissiveness to the husband. Thus, while men continued to rule and run the outside Victorian world, their wives would labor to prepare the next generation of well-cultured, Christian, male leadership, as well as the next generation of submissive, home-loving, pious women to support their husbands in the prescribed, happy, moral, family environment.

It was one of Walter Rauschenbusch's goals in life to fulfill this Victorian vision of the family to a much greater degree than what his incompati-

---

[11] Caroline Rauschenbusch spent her final years in Germany, living near her daughter until her death in 1913. Evans, *The Kingdom Is Always but Coming*, 61, 131; Jaehn, *The Formative Years*, 13; Brackney, "Historical Introduction," *Walter Rauschenbusch: Published Works and Selected Writings*, Vol. I, xiii.

[12] Janet Forsythe Fishburn, *The Fatherhood of God and the Victorian Family: The Social Gospel in America* (Philadelphia, PA: Fortress Press, 1981) 23; Evans, *The Kingdom Is Always but Coming*, 183–84.

ble parents had been able to do. His commitment to classic Victorian gender roles was demonstrated, and quite possibly deepened, by his remarkably happy marriage with Pauline Rother Rauschenbusch. Pauline, who was born in Germany and became a successfully employed school teacher in Milwaukee, was three years Walter's junior.[13] The couple met in 1889, became engaged three years later, and were married in 1893. As was culturally expected upon marriage, Pauline relinquished her teaching position to join Walter in New York City and to support him in his pastoral ministry.

Pauline Rauschenbusch is depicted as a "partner" in his ministry, hosting ladies' society meetings and other social gatherings "as well as managing the duties of cook and housekeeper." In an 1894 letter to Walter she wrote, "You must pray for your little girl dear one that she may always help you and never keep you back from your duty. That is my earnest desire to be a real helpmeet to you."[14] When she became ill from exhaustion in 1912, Pauline expressed a sense of inadequacy in fulfilling her role as wife and mother, as if she believed she could never do enough to support her husband. While convalescing, she wrote to their son, Paul, "We must all help father—he has no easy task in life. But if everything goes well at home it helps him very much indeed."[15] It is not surprising, then, that Pauline was Walter's favorite image of "the ideal American woman." Not only did she cheerfully sacrifice her own professional opportunities for the sake of their marriage; she ably and consistently supported him in his work, birthed and raised five successful children, maintained the family home, and loved and cherished him until his death.[16]

Walter Rauschenbusch was determined that his children would experience the same kind of happy life that he and Pauline enjoyed as hardworking, successful family members and contributors to society. In 1898, he updated his will to include his parental concerns for the children. He specified that if anything happened to him, he wanted Pauline to ensure that their sons engaged in sports and prepared to earn a livelihood in which they could serve humanity, God, and "the Kingdom." The desire he expressed for their daughters was that they would become good wives and mothers. While he wanted all his children to become well educated, the

---

[13] Evans, *The Kingdom Is Always but Coming*, 86.

[14] Ibid., 112–13.

[15] Ibid., 228–29.

[16] Ibid., 135–37, 315.

focus of the boys' education was for success in business, industry, and politics. For the girls, "Let them learn to cook well and rationally; to make their own dresses and trim their own hats; and to get manual skill in every way," he wrote. He was concerned, further, that "the high intellectual and moral tone of the family life which we have tried to maintain" not "be merged in anything common or base."[17]

What Rauschenbusch taught and wrote in his public work quite naturally cohered with his ideals for his own family. In his manuscript for *The Righteousness of the Kingdom*, which he began writing in the 1890s,[18] Rauschenbusch examined biblical teachings of Jesus and the Apostle Paul regarding "Sex and the Family." Significantly, his views about biblical counsel on these subjects did not tend to change over time. Rather, he blended what he interpreted from Scripture with a culturally conditioned understanding of proper spheres and practices for men and women and held on to these for dear life. The implications he drew from Scripture early in his career were woven into subsequent work and reiterated time and again in his speeches and publications.

In *The Righteousness of the Kingdom* (originally *Christianity Revolutionary*) Rauschenbusch noted that both Jesus and Paul despised sexual impurity and Jesus "advocated and represented a higher standard of purity than his times." Yet Jesus consistently showed respect for women, challenged double standards that were oppressive to women, and championed women who transgressed conventions to serve and worship him.[19] He observed that "a voluntary renunciation of marriage for the sake of the Kingdom of God" was for Jesus a higher standard even than marriage. Jesus upheld, however, not only the holiness of marriage as a bond that ideally "does not admit of dissolution," but one that should not be meddled with or broken "to gratify a fit of anger, a new lust, or a desire of profit." He noted that "interference with marriage sows the seed of every trouble," a theme he would repeat frequently in his social commentary. Here he emphasized the connection between the family and the larger society, stating that "the damage done by

---

[17] Ibid., 137–38.

[18] The original manuscript title was "Christianity Revolutionary," later retitled and published by Max Stackhouse as *The Righteousness of the Kingdom*.

[19] Walter Rauschenbusch, "The Righteousness of the Kingdom," in *The Righteousness of the Kingdom*, ed. Max Stackhouse (Nashville, TN: Abingdon Press, 1968), 236–37.

dissolving the family life is in exact proportion to the fundamental social importance of the family and to its blessings when good." Interestingly, he commented that even in his own time, "divorced women furnish far more than their proportion of criminality," but stopped short of commenting about the relative criminality of divorced men.[20]

The implications Rauschenbusch drew from his study of New Testament teachings on sex and the family were three-fold. First, Jesus set a standard "in the direction of the permanence of marriage" rather than its dissolution. This, he argued, meant anything that endangered marriage should be speedily resolved, including the looming social problems of scarcity and "industrial anxiety." Second, the fact that Jesus stood up for women against cruel and unfair treatment meant that "the letter of Christ's teaching" should never be used against women. Third, the difficult issue of marriage and divorce should be resolved with and among couples prior to marriage as a preventative measure against divorce. For Rauschenbusch, this included surrounding young people with communities made up of persons of similar "rank and wealth" to prevent the interference of monetary considerations in the formation of relationships, along with provision of an ample, healthy social life in which young people could meet eligible prospects. It also meant increasing the "education and independent position" for girls and women so they could approach marriage prospects as equals rather than "waiting for somebody to support them."[21]

Rauschenbusch commented in "Christianity Revolutionary" not only upon the enormous challenges that threatened the ideal marriage in large cities, but also upon the unhealthy expectations and double standards that faced women and men as marriage prospects. "It is notorious," he stated, "that women are not on an equal footing with men in view of marriage." He decried "how girls are forced out of their natural modesty," that they had to "study to be attractive" and use "means of attraction" that gave "a less permanent basis to love." Further, girls were often pressured by mothers to settle for a man "whom they respect little and love less" because he may represent their only chance. Meanwhile, bachelorhood was on the rise because single men increasingly wanted and could afford a higher standard of living than could married men. Also, single men believed they could "have the enjoyment of women's society without its burdens." A rise in the num-

[20] Ibid., 238.

[21] Ibid., 240–42.

ber of single men, Rauschenbusch declared, is "always a sign of a rotting civilization."[22]

The relationship between healthy families and healthy society was reciprocal for Rauschenbusch. Healthy families generated healthy societies and "only a healthy society, in which life is simple and a living certain, makes the formation of families safe and desirable for the men and makes woman for her own sake a treasure to be sought after, a helpmate and not a burden, a giver of comfort and not a despoiler of it." Conversely, he wrote, "everything that hinders the ready formation of marriages is a cause of social corruption," including and especially money.[23]

In a speech entitled "What about the Woman?" Rauschenbusch addressed young men, specifically, in an effort to turn their hearts and lives toward marriage. This speech, which he gave on at least twenty occasions between 1902 and 1912, mostly to YMCA groups, was a passionate plea to young men entering adulthood. Rauschenbusch wanted them to uphold biblical standards of sexual morality and to aspire for genuine love and mutual respect in a happy marriage and idyllic family life. Having not married, himself, until his early thirties, Rauschenbusch knew well the terrain of single, young adulthood. He expected, based upon his firsthand experience, that every young male would be faced with decisions about how to respond to women in the world and in intimate relationships. Clearly, he wished to steer young men away from paths that would lead to the immorality he detested and the kind of unhappiness that had gripped his own family of origin.

In "What about the Woman?," Rauschenbusch argued that fundamental to manhood itself was the life process of forsaking father and mother and assuming "the burden of family cares [and] yoke of life-long labor." This matter was no less important for womanhood, he pointed out, for the woman entering marriage and family life "braves sickness, travail, [and] knocks at the gates of death [in pregnancy for the] sake of love." In true Victorian fashion, Rauschenbusch asserted that "a pure woman" would give her body and whole personality as wife to a man expecting "life-long love [and] protection of the man in return." At the same time, it was a husband's right to expect his wife would take care of his "needs of body and soul." The

---

[22] Ibid., 243.

[23] Ibid., 243–44. See also *Christianizing the Social Order*, 136.

fulfillment of these expectations by a married couple, Rauschenbusch opined, would translate into happiness and "fulfillment of life."[24]

To arrive at an ideal relationship with a woman, however, Rauschenbusch advised his audiences there were things they needed to know about both their own, and women's, sexual "instincts." He warned that the combination of self-interested sexual excess and the "corroding contagion of sinful women" would lead to the "sapping of physical [and] mental strength and self-pollution." He noted, also, that the physical aspect of sexual life was more serious, more dangerous, and more painful for women than for men. This was because for women it included monthly menstruation, nine months for each pregnancy, additional months of nursing, and years of rearing children. Moreover, he asserted, there was a corresponding influence of sexuality upon the "mental and moral life" of young women. He attested to "the transformation of a young girl when happily married; still more if [a] happy mother." He continued, "No woman comes to perfection of womanhood without these experiences."[25]

It did not take much imagination for an honorable young man to know what Rauschenbusch thought he should do. He did not want to leave any room for doubt, however. The largest part of "What about the Woman?" was a detailed description of the horrible outcomes for women when men took advantage of them sexually, a violation that undermined both personal and social morality. Consequences of such actions, as he described them, included personal degradation, shame, loneliness, unwanted pregnancy, suicide, social condemnation, elimination of happy marriage potential, and possibly the low life of prostitution. What kind of chivalrous American male, duty bound "to protect a woman at all costs," would stoop to such "supreme wrong and harm" so that he could experience a "few minutes of highly-wrought physical pleasure and the woman a life-time of suffering?" he asked. Rauschenbusch offered scathing comments, as well, on the "murder of the social institution of the family" through adultery, divorce, and participation in prostitution.

"Never wrong woman," Rauschenbusch admonished the young men. Rather, he advised, they should practice "habits of decency and modesty," think "nobly of women," and give a woman the benefit of the doubt if they think she is acting too boldly. He wanted his listeners to cast their influence

[24] Rauschenbusch, "What about the Woman?", 1–3.
[25] Ibid., 6–7.

"on the side of chastity," to stand against and break down "evil tendencies" such as smutty stories, bold looks, and "low estimate of women." Doing so would make a difference in the world by improving standards for the following generation. Those plagued by wrongful temptations he directed to seek help and to pray for willpower. Prayer, he encouraged, would help temptation "grow pale and vanish like an evil dream." His concluding guidance was to "love a good girl, marry her as soon as conditions permit, then be faithful to her as you expect her to be."[26]

In a 1909 speech entitled "Social Value of Women," Rauschenbusch stated his belief that there had been an evolution of the family through human history and compared earlier human behavior with that of animals. He noted that "mother-love developed before father-love," as it was the mother, primarily, who cared for and protected the young. From this he concluded that "woman [was the] first nucleus of [the] family," connecting naturally with children and their welfare, modeling this behavior so children would also learn to love each other. With the beginning of agriculture, while men continued to hunt and fish, women learned skills of planning and patience, tending the fields and the family hut. Eventually men began to help women by lending their brawn to clear land and assist with field work. When this happened, it freed woman for the "finer work of [the] house," which in turn allowed her to develop her aesthetic side, the "love of beauty, desire of adornment and [the] beginnings of art."[27]

As humans migrated "northward," Rauschenbusch continued, they took with them the Promethean gift of fire to maintain warmth, as well as for cooking and fashioning tools. Woman then became the guardian of the family fire, and the "house grew up about [the] fireplace." As she tended the hearth, the woman nourished her children and provided "comfort for man." There were "long nights, at [the] hearth-fire," he noted, and eventually "artificial light [became the] condition of highest civilization." However, with the emergence soon thereafter of the "patriarchal" family, the status of woman was diminished to the extent that she became viewed as property by man, her freedom was circumscribed by his jealousy, her face was covered,

[26] Ibid., 30.

[27] Walter Rauschenbusch, "Social Value of Woman": American Baptist Historical Society, Handwritten Lecture Notes, Atlanta, Georgia, 1–4. See also *Christianizing the Social Order*, 128–34.

she became an object of polygamy, and she was bought and sold and used as a worker to support man and to bear his children.[28]

According to Rauschenbusch, a "slow rise to equality" was initiated in the era of the Roman Empire, which was characterized by prosperity, improved housing, democracy, and the rise of Christianity. Family life became gentler and more refined, preparing the way for the "spirit of equality and of moral relations" that, he believed, typified the ideal family arrangement.[29] For Rauschenbusch, the spirit of equality was not synonymous with sameness. Rather, the spirit of equality in the modern family was expressed, as he put it, in a "division of work." That is, while the man was employed in "outside work," the woman's domain of work and place of rest was the home. The man was employed so he could make the "economic contribution" to the family, without which he was viewed as exploiting the woman, who accomplished her sphere of work tending the home. The man's rightful reward was to find "rest, harmony, [and] happiness at home." While woman's work in the home may not be easy, she was able to experience the benefit of independence in the oversight of her domain. That domain encompassed things that "girls prefer," he explained, and listed tasks such as caring for sickness, hygiene, cleaning, repairs, ordering, dusting, making things last and making things "go farther."[30]

Although he believed modern society had reached the pinnacle of development in home and family life, Rauschenbusch perceived serious social threats to this ideal. In notes for his speech were concerns about the home being neglected and "stripped of [its] economic function" as a consequence of more women working outside the home. He also worried about women competing with men in the workplace, resulting in lower wages for all, a high price to pay for women's love of greater independence and their "own purse," he added. He commented also upon "hurtful influences" he had observed amongst modern women, such as interference with others' marriages, flirtatious teasing, female rivalry, jealousy, and the "economic waste" associated with silly fashions and ornaments. His address about woman's "social value" concluded with an assessment of her value to a baby boy, a growing boy, a young man, a husband, and a father. To these, her values were as mother, comforter, teacher of manners and dress, provider of faith-

---

[28] Ibid., 5–6.

[29] Ibid., 8–9.

[30] Ibid., 9.

ful love, and bearer of children. In summary, her value was assessed by her capacity to offer "happiness, contentment, nobler life, and religious influence" to her family. Ultimately, such a woman, a "happy mother" had a "better lot than man," he concluded.[31]

In subsequent years, Rauschenbusch expressed these and related views in a growing number of publications, including *Christianity and the Social Crisis* (1907), *Prayers of the Social Awakening* (1910), *Christianizing the Social Order* (1912), and *Dare We Be Christians?* (1914).

In *Christianity and the Social Crisis*, he returned to his earlier examination of scriptural teachings and their implications for the social problems of his own time. In doing so, he sympathized with the "emancipating sense of equality" experienced by Corinthian women in the Apostle Paul's letter, but pointed out that he also understood Paul's "vexation and distress" when he heard that expression of their newfound freedom resulted in disorder. Echoing his own disapproval of sexually suggestive women's attire, he emphatically agreed with Paul's "prudence in bidding them keep within the bounds of customary modesty and restraint."[32] Further, in New Testament times, the strain over the emancipation of women coupled with Corinthian contention over marriage, Rauschenbusch argued, anticipated the modern view that "marriage should rest on spiritual affinity and sympathy and not on physical or conventional grounds."[33]

In addressing the social crises of his own time, Rauschenbusch decried numerous ways the ideal family was being undermined. These included a "downward curve in the percentage of marriages" and, among those who were married, fewer children. Both facts were caused by economic fear, he reasoned, because "the attraction between men and women" had not changed. He worried about the impact of a growing "class of involuntary celibates" in society, which he saw as more dangerous even than the increasing divorce rate. He feared that "the unmarried thousands in the freedom of modern life" would not be able to "maintain their own purity [or] respect the purity of others,"[34] which would bring about the horrible consequences of impurity he had enumerated in his lecture "What about the Woman?"

---

[31] Ibid., 10–12; see also *Christianity and the Social Crisis*, 276–77.

[32] Rauschenbusch, *Christianity and the Social Crisis*, 134–35. Rauschenbusch quoted 1 Corinthians 2:2–16.

[33] Ibid., 135. Here Rauschenbusch footnoted 1 Corinthians 7.

[34] Ibid., 272–73.

With fewer marriages and fewer children born to those who prudently refrained from taking on commitments they might not be able to fulfill, Rauschenbusch was also concerned that "the reproduction of the race [was] left to the poor and ignorant," who were far from able to raise up the moral offspring needed to oversee an improved future for the human race.[35] He believed that children were necessary, especially among the "able and educated," not only to populate future generations, but also to cement relationships and give familial quality to life. As for those who married but refrained from bearing children, he wrote that "the absence of children decreases the cohesive power of the married relation, the blitheness and youthfulness of life, the unselfishness of character, the insight into human nature; in short, it blights much of what is really fine and high in the souls and relations of men."[36]

Rauschenbusch expressed concern here, as well, about the impact of adverse economic conditions upon the purity and well-being of women. With fewer men pursuing marriage, women would have to take what any willing man offered or "go without." It was because of such "grim necessity" that women were driven to "new ways of getting bread and clothing," he wrote, when what the "great majority of girls heartily prefer [is] the independence and the satisfaction of the heart which are offered to a woman only in a comfortable and happy home." He allowed that "some educated girls think they prefer the practice of a profession because the dream of unusual success lures them," but, he predicted, "when they have had a taste of the wearing routine that prevails in most professions, they turn with longing to the thought of a home of their own." He lamented the entry of young girls in the workplace "at the very age when their developing body ought to be shielded from physical and mental strain," where they were required to remain standing long hours, and "pushed to exhaustion" during busy seasons. As a result, "many of them enter marriage with organic troubles" that appeared later in life. Further, "girls pass from school to shop or store and never learn housekeeping well," he complained. If they are left to learn these skills later on during childbearing years, "the strain is immense, and is likely to affect the temper and the happiness of the home," he warned.[37]

---

[35] Ibid., 273–74.
[36] Ibid., 274.
[37] Ibid., 276–77.

In the conclusion to his chapter on "The Present Crisis" in *Christianity and the Social Crisis,* Rauschenbusch reiterated the same fears about sexual impurity he had expressed in "What about the Woman?" He followed his own advice about giving women the benefit of the doubt, praising the "unstained virtue and nobility of the great majority of working girls" with whom he had made acquaintance, and explained that most had to choose between suffering want or supplementing their earnings another way. The wages of many were insufficient to "support themselves in comfort and to dress as the requirements of their position and of modern taste demand," he explained. Women in this situation were in danger of falling prey to "numbers of unmarried and married men about them looking for transient love." With few if any marriage prospects in sight, their "womanly desire for the company and love of men" combined with craving for "the clothing, the trinkets, the pleasures that glitter about them" could readily tempt women down immoral pathways. Some of the more naïve and unsuspecting women might accept promising employments that were in fact traps into prostitution. Rauschenbusch's greatest fear was not prostitution, however, which carried shame as a deterrent to its rapid spread. Rather, it was that "the standard of purity for [women] may drop and approximate the standard prevailing among men." He worried over what would be the outcome "if the unmarried multiply; if homes remain childless; if families are homeless; if girls do not know housework; and if men come to distrust the purity of women?"[38]

The key to the well-being of society and its future progress, Rauschenbusch believed, depended not only upon the family, but especially upon the purity of women. Purity was what suited women for the highest of all expressions of womanhood: motherhood within the context of family life. Family life without a pure, loving woman to hold it together was an impossibility from his vantage point. This view was expressed, for example, in his *Prayers for the Social Awakening* (1909), in which he offered to God "praise and benediction for the sweet ministries of motherhood in human life" and expressed gratitude for

> our own dear mothers who built up our lives by theirs; who bore us in travail and loved us the more for the pain we gave; who nourished us at their breast and hushed us to sleep in the warm security of their arms. We thank thee for their tireless love, for their voiceless prayers,

---

[38] Ibid., 278–79.

> for the agony with which they followed us through our sins and won us back, for the Christly power of sacrifice and redemption in mother-love.[39]

His prayer included a petition that God would expand the vision of mothers beyond their own children and see themselves "as the patriot women of their nation, who alone can build up the better future with fresh and purer life." Certainly, he included his own daughters, Winifred and Elizabeth, when he invoked "upon the girls of our people the awe of their future calling, that they may preserve their bodies and minds in purity and strength for the holy task to which the future may summon them." He prayed also for the women who desired to become mothers, but "whose lives are barren of its joys." Finally, he asked that "the protecting love of motherhood" would "set its tireless strength to lift humanity from the reign of brutal force and to found the larger family of men on the blessed might of love."[40] Such love, he wrote in *Dare We Be Christians?* was the "society-making force" upon which not only families, but social progress depended.[41]

If the role of mothers was central to the family and the family to society, fathers were also needed in support of mothers, for their protection, and in the proper socialization of children, especially boys. In the history of the family, the father figure had evolved from autocratic exploiter of women and children to kind, loving, stable, and responsible supporter of the family. Over time, what the father had "lost in power" he "gained in love." In earlier times, children became attached only to their mothers. In modern times, "when the father ceased functioning as a tyrant, he won his share of love."[42] Rauschenbusch modeled the role of loving and beloved husband, as well as a kind and attentive father, with substantial relationships with each of his children until his death.[43]

Rauschenbusch made clear in his writings that he was in favor of both women's education and woman's suffrage. However, he continued to be-

---

[39]Walter Rauschenbusch, "For All Mothers," in *Prayers of the Social Awakening* (1909, new edition, Boston, MA: The Jordan & More Press, 1925), 92.

[40] Ibid., 93.

[41] Walter Rauschenbusch, *Dare We Be Christians?* (1914, reprint, Cleveland, OH: Pilgrim Press, 1993), 30.

[42] Rauschenbusch, *Christianizing the Social Order*, 133; and *Christianizing the Social Order*, 131.

[43] Evans, "Gender and the Kingdom of God," 58.

lieve that the best and God-ordained primary roles for women were as wives and mothers. Women in these roles had been instrumental, to say the least, in his own life and in the fabric of society as he knew it. Moreover, despite his historical accounts of the downfall of patriarchy, Rauschenbusch continued to express a view of woman that clearly implied she needed man both to guide and protect her.

This patriarchal perspective appeared in an article he wrote for *The Biblical World* entitled "Some Moral Aspects of the Woman Movement." Rauschenbusch wrote with a tone of sarcasm that "women have arrived" in industry, education, and politics, and this signaled a revolution he was prepared to accept as inevitable. However, he warned that the results of the woman movement "will not be all to the good." In fact, with considerable passion he predicted that "concomitant evils" would come of it. He questioned whether women were morally capable of handling employment relations, spiritual matters, money and wealth, proper standards of modesty, and resisting a "slow landslide" toward the low sexual standards of men.[44]

"Some Moral Aspects of the Woman Movement" was published in October 1913, one year after Walter and Pauline Rauschenbusch's eldest daughter, Winifred, entered college. Perhaps the passion in this article, which almost reads like an angry tirade, is not unrelated to the friction that occurred during this period between Walter and Winifred. In his superb biography of Rauschenbusch, Christopher Evans has traced the correspondence between father and daughter, in which issues such as her own independence, future, and self-determination over clothing, sexuality, and other matters were openly discussed between them. Walter's efforts to steer his daughter in the direction of traditional roles and practices were consistently, passionately, and respectfully rebuffed. Her view of womanhood was her own, not her father's.

By 1917, when Rauschenbusch gave a commencement address for Simmons College, his tone toward the young women graduates was different. He spoke of the impact of the war on young women and men, whose destinies were "bound up together." He urged the women to live the lives God had given them—each to develop her own personality, but to do so

---

[44]Walter Rauschenbusch, "Some Moral Aspects of the 'Woman Movement,'" *Biblical World* 42 (October 1913), 195–99. Rauschenbusch also discussed what he believed was women's weakness for fashion, also their physical weakness and need for protection by men in *Christianizing the Social Order*, 255–57, 413–15.

with a concern for all humanity. He reflected aloud on all that women had gained in recent years, that many had "worked through to splendid self-possession and intelligent affirmation, not only of their rights in the family, in business and industry, and in the state, but to an affirmation of themselves, which is far more." He acknowledged that "outside of the home" used to be man's domain, but "today many women are quite capable of doing what men have done, and 'then some.'" He predicted that "women will never again vacate the place into which they stepped while the men were fighting." He affirmed their education, which would allow them to master their work, and wished for them "a work which will so finely express your best capacities and ideas that you can take an artistic and religious satisfaction in it and feel that you are fellow-workmen with God." He encouraged them to find love, and, in a moment of personal revelation, to give the love between fathers and daughters a chance. In closing, he urged them to save their own souls and the soul of the nation by "keeping supreme those higher purposes which we have proudly affirmed, but which will surely be swamped and submerged unless we hold them tenaciously. We shall love our country most truly when we see it as a servant of the Kingdom of God, of that true humanity in which God's will is completely done."[45]

It is not altogether clear why Walter Rauschenbusch's tone about women and their new roles beyond the home sphere changed so dramatically from one document to the other, with only four years between them. His death just over a year after his Simmons graduation address prevented further elaboration on his part. Did Winifred have something to do with it? Or the war? The onset of illness? Was he simply being polite and respectful to the young women graduating from college? One thing was clear. The world of his children and their peers had changed, and there would be no going back.

Several questions and conclusions may be drawn from this study of Walter Rauschenbusch's views on gender, family, and the Social Gospel. First, his thoughts on these matters were shaped by his life experience and can only be understood in the context of his personal experiences and Victorian cultural context, not to mention his German Baptist background and influences. Because of his own particular life experiences, in which he and his wife, Pauline, triumphed over the unpleasantness of his childhood

---

[45] Walter Rauschenbusch, "Issues of Life," *The Simmons Quarterly* 7 (July 1917): 1–9.

through their successful, if not salvific, traditional Victorian marriage, a desirable alternative to traditional roles may have been unimaginable to him, at least until late in life when he was forced by his own daughter to consider other possibilities.

Second, and building upon the previous assertion, Rauschenbusch was much more traditional on these subjects than some other Social Gospel figures, including one of his mentors, Josiah Strong, and many of the women in the movement, such as Frances Willard, Ida B. Wells-Barnett, and Jane Addams. The scope of this study does not permit in-depth comparisons.[46] Suffice it to say this is one of the many ways in which influential leaders of the Social Gospel movement differed from one another while championing a wide variety of social reform causes.[47]

Third, it should not surprise students of Rauschenbusch, when one looks at the cultural and ecclesial landscape of the time, that a middle-class, white, male, seminary professor adhered to traditional family and gender ideology and discouraged progress toward full equality of the sexes. Who gives up power willingly or without a fight? More than a century after Rauschenbusch's death most of the world and the vast majority of Christians still do not believe in or practice gender equality.

Fourth, Rauschenbusch's emphasis on family and its relationship to society and the kingdom of God was unrelenting and thoroughgoing. Such attention to human social relationships and their potential impact upon individuals, society, and the greater world is admirable. It points, a century later, to the continuing relationship between the family and social issues such as poverty, education, violence, obesity and other health concerns, domestic violence, and more. Are Jesus and the kingdom of God still as applicable to the subject of family and related social matters? How and why or why not?

---

[46] Janet Fishburn compared the views of several Social Gospel figures in *The Fatherhood of God and the Victorian Family* as did Susan Curtis in *A Consuming Faith*. See also Carolyn De Swarte Gifford, "The Woman's Cause Is Man's? Frances Willard and the Social Gospel"; Wendy J. Deichmann Edwards, "Women and Social Betterment in the Social Gospel Work of Josiah Strong"; and Janet Forsythe Fishburn, "Walter Rauschenbusch and 'The Woman Movement': A Gender Analysis," in *Gender and the Social Gospel*, eds. Wendy J. Deichmann Edwards and Carolyn De Swarte Gifford (Urbana, IL: University of Illinois Press, 2003).

[47] See "Introduction: Restoring Women and Reclaiming Gender in Social Gospel Studies," in Deichmann and Gifford, *Gender and the Social Gospel*, 4–5.

Finally, we are left to ponder, in our own time and circumstances, how the values and experiences of personal life are connected to families of origin, to culture and socialization, to the well-being of society, and, in Walter Rauschenbusch's words, to an "always but coming" kingdom of God.

Chapter 8

The Significance of Walter Rauschenbusch to the Black Church

Darryl M. Trimiew

It is my task to reflect on the significance of Walter Rauschenbusch's work for the black church. I have spent months pouring over historical materials to see whether there is any historical significance there—that is to say, to answer in the affirmative that Rauschenbusch's work significantly affected the African American church, within his lifetime or shortly thereafter. The clear short and unhappy answer is no. There has not been much significant effect that can be attributed solely and directly to Rauschenbusch. Nevertheless, I can say that Rauschenbusch has had a significant direct effect on the economic emphasis of modern theology, an issue in which I have specialized. But first I should explain my initial conclusions about the past. There are three reasons why Rauschenbusch's work was not and has not been more influential for the black church. Much can be explained by understanding African American religious history.

AFRICAN AMERICAN CHRISTIANITY: A NEW UNDERSTANDING OF GOD

Africans, my ancestors, were brought to the New World as property—that is, as slaves. While many Africans were Christians, these were not the groups who were brought over. Accordingly, African Americans were converted to Christianity by colonization and force; that is, the process of making them good slaves involved, as much as possible, the destruction of their traditional religious beliefs, which were primarily ancestor-reverencing and, in a small minority, Islam. This process took place over a lengthy time period.[1] Part of the process involved the imposition of colonial Christianity. Colonial Christianity emphasized the legitimation of slavery, the authority of the

---

[1] Albert J. Raboteau, *Slave Religion: "The Invisible Institution" in the Antebellum South* (New York: Oxford University Press, 1978), 204.

masters, and the duty of slaves to not think for themselves. Blacks in particular were instructed to have whites think and act for them. Traveling evangelists went to plantations and generated over time slave exhorters who developed slave religion. Over time, in hush arbors which were under the control of slaves, they redeveloped a Christianity more suitable to sustaining an oppressed people.

This black Christianity was spread primarily orally, as reading for slaves was discouraged, and, after slave rebellions, outlawed outright. So slaves became Christians but not in the same ways with the same ideas as whites. This then was a Christianity disinclined to have whites making all decisions in heaven or hell. African American slaves knew themselves to be equal to whites in stark contradiction to white Christianity. They understood their labor to be stolen and they embraced the God of the Hebrews who had led them out of slavery and Egypt into a promised land of freedom. So, their Christianity was not limited to being saved and blessed in heaven after serving faithfully and painfully on this Earth. Howard Thurman's grandmother exemplifies this religious identity as follows:

> "During the days of slavery," she said, "the master's minister would occasionally hold services for the slaves. Old man McGhee was so mean that he would not let a Negro minister preach to his slaves. Always the white minister used as his text something from Paul. At least three or four times a year he used as a text: 'Slaves, be obedient to them that are your masters...as unto Christ.' Then he would go on to show how it was God's will that we were slaves and how, if we were good and happy slaves, God would bless us. I promised my Maker that if I ever learned to read and if freedom ever came, I would not read that part of the Bible."[2]

This rejection of the white hermeneutic of inequality was not unique to the Thurman family but an immutable value in slave religion. This was the first reason why Walter Rauschenbusch would, later on, not be an attractive source.

Slave religion and its manifestation as African American Christianity after Reconstruction continued being a religion that was concerned with material sustainability and with commutative justice. Their God was con-

---

[2] Howard Thurman, *Jesus and the Disinherited* (Nashville, TN: Abingdon Press, 1970), 30–31.

cerned with justice and required people to be just in their relations with those around them. Thus, where possible, many escaped slavery. Some who could not run away frequently "stole" from their masters with clear consciences, understanding that they needed the stolen goods more than their masters, and, more importantly, that the goods, usually food, were produced by their stolen labor. Thus the "God's Trombones" understanding of God was a God of the Hebrew prophets who demanded that the wealthy quit oppressing the poor.[3] Thus their Christianity did not necessarily accept the fairness of the economic relations of slavery or, subsequently, sharecropping, or later unfair industrial-production wages. Blacks never freely accepted the rightness of the post-slavery condition of last hired, first fired—they did, however, learn to cope with it. As a result, African American Christianity always understood that religion and economics and politics are always connected and cannot be compartmentalized. This was the second reason they did not receive Rauschenbusch.

African American Christianity has always had a demand for justice that it understood was divinely sanctioned. It was primarily understood experientially through conversion by means of oral catechism, rather than theological doctrine. And that is the third limiting structure, the origination of black Christianity as a nonliterate religion.

Summing up, black Christianity has historically been the most powerful and the primary organizing institution in America for blacks—so far. But it has been a religion that has not required a learned clergy and has been ambivalent about the requirements of having a seminary degree in order to minister. This reality is a waning one, giving way to a preference for educated rather than jackleg ministers.

However, in 1861, when Walter Rauschenbusch was born, most blacks were still slaves. Later in his pastorate in Hell's Kitchen there were some blacks present, but not in the numbers of the later first Northern mass migration. This discussion on the nature of African American Christianity before and during the lifetime of Rauschenbusch explains why, though Rauschenbusch's book a *Theology for the Social Gospel* sold 50,000 copies,

---

[3] James Weldon Johnson, *God's Trombones: Seven Negro Sermons in Verse, Penguin Twentieth-Century Classics* (Uri) Http://Id.Loc.Gov/Authorities/Names/N88540505 (Uri) Http://Viaf.Org/Viaf/SourceID/LC|n88540505 (Uri) Https://Open-Na.Hosted.Exlibrisgroup.Com/Resolver/Wikidata/Lc/N88540505 (New York: Penguin Books, 1990).

few were read in all probability by black clergy. Such clergy were formed in an oral manner in the tradition of the black church. Further, even Howard Thurman, who actually graduated from Rochester Theological Seminary, did not do so until the twenties, well after the death of Rauschenbusch.

Accordingly, most black churches were not introduced to the White Social Gospel except by means of Black Social Gospeler Reverdy Ransom, who had a relationship with the liberal theologian Shailer Mathews. But Ransom's Social Gospel approach was his own and not dependent on Matthews. It grew, instead, out of the black church itself, which was an avatar of Social Gospel approaches prior to Gladden, Matthews, or Rauschenbusch. [4]

To repeat: African American Christianity believed in divinely sanctioned commutative justice and an intervening God who required it. It had a clear understanding of social sin and the need to redeem and reform American Christianity. It had followed this approach since its inception, well before Rauschenbusch, or even Reverdy Ransom. Ransom, like the later Martin Luther King Jr., was happy that some Social Gospelers confirmed what the black church had always preached. Why is Ransom important? He is important because he was a forerunner to M.L.K. Martin was, as is well documented, familiar with and in agreement with much of Rauschenbusch's work. But as other commentators have demonstrated, M.L.K. was not dependent upon Rauschenbusch's work for his own theology and the subsequent civil rights leadership. This is why it is difficult to assess the influence of Rauschenbusch on the black church. The black church had practiced its own Social Gospel for a long time. It is, accordingly, much easier to evaluate the influence of Rauschenbusch on a specific black leader, such as King. King approved of some aspects of Rauschenbusch's approach but rejected other aspects of it. In particular, King could not embrace Rauschenbusch's racism and commitment to the white supremacist American dream. So, it must be concluded that Rauschenbusch had little reception and influence in the African American church. We are now prepared finally to ask some fundamental questions about Rauschenbusch.

---

[4] Calvin S. Morris, *Reverdy C. Ransom: Black Advocate of the Social Gospel* (Lanham, MD.: University Press of America, 1990).

FUNDAMENTAL QUESTIONS ABOUT RAUSCHENBUSCH

First, did Walter Rauschenbusch's Social Gospel theology cause American Christianity to fundamentally question its prior commitment to oppressive, Constantinian religion? Did he radically and successfully criticize its participation in the conquest of North America, the destruction of first peoples, the enslavement of Africans, and, lastly, the ongoing development of managerial capitalism that continues to this day?

These are very serious questions. Rauschenbusch's failure to address them is not at all unique. With a few exceptions, white theology has rarely addressed such issues—especially in a critical manner. Here I am simply putting my oar in the water. I want these questions at least raised in order to avoid a robust adventure in revisionism. Why is revisionism such a threat? I believe it is such because of the current economic and moral crisis in modern America. Since much that Rauschenbusch wrote *correctly challenged* the historical continuation of a false attempt to separate religion, politics, and economics, and did so forcefully and clearly, he is not a theologian to be ignored or rejected. His work was and is important, his contribution to white theological discussion impressive.

That Rauschenbusch did not radically challenge the false narrative that the founding of this country was fulfilling a divine imperative, that he did not challenge the gross immorality of American exceptionalism, is both true and not at all unusual. Rauschenbusch was the son of a first-generation German immigrant who both celebrated America's welcoming of others and implicitly, and simultaneously, sacralized its representation of the doctrine of Manifest Destiny—a justification of the American conquest. [5] Being a beneficiary, he could not ask radical questions that undermined that doctrine. Simply put, Walter Rauschenbusch did not rise above the white supremacy of his era. Very few European Americans did. A century later, many are still struggling to do so. A nearly elected Senate candidate in Alabama has gone on record as stating that America was great during slavery. Such statements should energize and alarm all of us. Rauschenbusch's racism does not, however, allow us to dismiss him out of hand any more than we should dismiss Greek philosophy as of no value because they had slaves and patriarchy, or dismiss Lincoln as a political leader because he firmly

[5] Ben Sanders, "Walter Rauschenbusch on Society," in *Beyond the Pale: Reading Ethics from the Margins*, eds. Miguel De La Torre and Stacey Floyd Thomas (Louisville, KY: Westminster John Knox Press, 2011), 111–18.

believed in the inferiority of African Americans and desired my ancestors' repatriation to Africa.

Rauschenbusch's work should be understood and valued with a frank acknowledgement of its skewed worldview and mistaken theories of human inequality that remain foundational to his theology. We must, however, situate his worldview and his theology fairly in their historical context. I have published previously a review of Social Gospelers that clearly demonstrates their rejection of and refusal to cooperate with potential African American Social Gospel collaborators, such as Reverdy Ransom.[6] I have been criticized as overstating the case, and yet my critics failed to point out or explain any mistakes in my review, which I stand by. Since my earlier essay, others have borne out my position with reference to Rauschenbusch. One, Ben Sanders III, specifically addresses this concern. While Sanders documents Rauschenbusch's racism more fully and definitively than I do, he does not thereby dismiss him as a theological source. Sanders notes the potential for creation of a more just and equal political and economic order using the work of Rauschenbusch. He is correct that the potential is there and that a social and political theology that addresses economic justice more directly needs to be promulgated and instantiated in American Christianity.

However, this is a challenge for us the living to address, since it was not addressed fully in Rauschenbusch's era. And why, we may justifiably ask, was it not addressed? Most would say that the Zeitgeist was against it. The Socialist interventions of Henry George, which influenced Rauschenbusch more than any teachings of Marx and Engels, were swallowed up by the death of Progressivism ushered in by World War I and the Leninist Communism that followed. The Gilded Age that Rauschenbusch wrote against was also interrupted by world events. While the international capitalist economy, disrupted by the war, resumed in the Roaring Twenties, the impulse to attempt to usher in the kingdom of God was not. Any optimism that the West had that was not crushed by WWI was smashed by the Great Depression and subsequently by WWII. This is a very brief and partial account for the rise of neoorthodoxy and even the Christian realism of Reinhold Niebuhr.

---

[6] Darryl Trimiew, "The Social Gospel Movement and the Question of Race," in *The Social Gospel Today*, ed. Christopher Evans (Louisville, KY: Westminster John Knox Press, 2001), 17.

Yet neither the neoorthodoxy of Barth nor the realism of Niebuhr ever fully addressed or repented of the real problem of the West; namely its continued commitment to the conquest of nonwhite peoples, internally or internationally. This international imperialism inherently supported the organizing principles of fascism. Thus, the rise of Mussolini, Franco, Hitler, and Stalin was a logical outcome of a kind of reorganization of the world order under the continued control and exploitation of European powers on colonized soils. The overthrow of fascism did not discontinue the white impulse to dominate and exploit nonwhites. Rauschenbusch's call for the creation of a more socially just America, perhaps with more Socialist distributions, does not in any way reject and repent of Manifest Destiny and the so-called "white man's burden."

Accordingly, like an Old Testament prophet, Rauschenbusch and other Social Gospelers could call for a radical revolution of values that condemned the monopolies and corporate greed in America without ever addressing any calls for reparative justice or even any demands for the redistribution of wealth to African Americans or native peoples. If he had lived longer, Rauschenbusch would have celebrated Franklin Roosevelt's New Deal. It may even be said that Rauschenbusch's work laid a religious foundation for the same. But Rauschenbusch's kingdom of God, if realized, would have maintained segregation and Jim Crow, because American white supremacy required it. Thus, the history of liberal or progressive theology that succeeded the Social Gospel was just as racist as its practitioners.

When decades later the civil rights movement pushed for racial, economic, and political justice, white American Christians were as unprepared to respond justly as in Rauschenbusch's time. King's "Letter from a Birmingham Jail" is so powerful precisely because of the continued intransigence not just of Americans, but American Christianity. White America's white flight from urban centers to the suburbs has been led by the church, not resisted by it. King partially approved the call to social justice voiced by Rauschenbusch. He also partially approved the recognition of injustice made by Reinhold Niebuhr, without the gradual incrementalism that Niebuhr championed. King always had to push for more radical change than either theologian called for. Niebuhr's commitment to white supremacy and Western imperialism is most obvious in his push for tolerable justice, rather than liberation for African colonized peoples, particularly the ones under the heel of Great Britain. Noting these historical facts helps to explain why neither Democratic Socialism nor Rauschenbusch's kingdom of God flourished or persisted in America. Democratic Socialism was probably more easily established in Western Europe precisely because the wealth that helped legitimate the social safety nets needed there to soften managerial capitalism was made possible by the exploitation of nonwhites in colonies external to the colonizers. America was always a colony committed to the destruction of the first peoples of this land—initially by the hand of the British but finally and more vigorously by the former colony itself.

These facts and their reiteration are important in helping to explain why, in the twenty-first century, Americans are more divided than ever as to whether government should intervene on behalf of the truly disadvantaged and whether such intervention is required by the Gospel.[7]

Most economists now say that we are entering a new epoch in which economic inequality is greater than ever.[8] Accordingly, the problems that Rauschenbusch raised in the last Gilded Age are still with us. What has now changed is the "us" in question. The browning of America is now an ongoing existential reality and a unidirectional process. Therefore, the public policy distribution of the benefits and burdens of our society cannot be publicly justified with the characterization of the polis of decision makers as being solely white. When Trump's followers cry that they want their country back, what they are truly decrying is the loss of political, moral, economic, and spiritual decision-making monopolies. Other voices must now be heard—hence, those who do not champion the one-percenters that even Rauschenbusch took on must be discounted and dismissed by the protectors of the one-percenters.

In Rauschenbusch's era, African Americans were a subjugated people. Unable to be held in the bonds of slavery, we were nevertheless second-class citizens subject to lynching and oppression under Jim Crow. While full equality has yet to be achieved, de jure equality has been realized. That is to say no one in the public square (except Judge Roy Moore and Donald Trump) can explicitly call nonwhites second-class citizens and expect to get elected to national office. Doing so now smacks of Trumpism and other primitivisms. Vulgar white supremacy has been rejected by most white Americans—at least for now. Thus, the civil rights movement and subse-

---

[7] Darryl Trimiew, "Michael Novak on Capitalism," in *Beyond the Pale: Reading Ethics from the Margin*, eds. Miguel De La Torre and Stacy Floyd Thomas (Louisville, KY: Westminster John Knox Press), 189–98.

[8] Paul Krugman, "For Whom the Economy Grows: G.D.P. is only part of the story, and we need to know the rest." *New York Times*, 30 August 2018.

quent world events such as the overthrow of most European-controlled colonies have put us nonwhites in a place quite different than that of Rauschenbusch's era. The election of President Barack Obama did not usher in a postracial society, but it did present the possibility of the consensual creation of a non-racist America sometime in the future.

So now all of our churches could work together in serving the world and in trying to influence public policy such that even if the kingdom of God is not realized, at least significant safety nets that permit flourishing for all could be realized. This can be done and should be done, but the same problems that beset Rauschenbusch before WWI still beset us. The most important problem is a metanarrative known as the story of success.[9] The story of success is a cover story that is foundational to our sinful ethos and social identity and serves as a common goal for most Americans. In the story of success, self-made men celebrate their wealth and prestige without acknowledging the many gifts that God freely gives to some. The story of success is sinful because it holds up the self and the American Dream as idols to strive to serve. While it is true that anyone in America can succeed, it is not true that everyone can succeed in a capitalist free-market society. It is this latter truth that the story of success does not acknowledge.

Recently, I published an essay entitled "America Land of the Free, Home of the Poor: Inequality as a Way of Life."[10] There I gave one major reason for poverty and inequality in America: our irrefutable preference for the myth of meritocracy over calls for governmental intervention on behalf of the poor. [11] Also, I demonstrated why Americans resist ameliorative American public policy even in the face of widespread inequality and poverty. In another recent essay, entitled "Martin Luther King Jr., Economic Rights and Ecology: Can There Be a Beloved World Community?," [12] I referenced the problem of the story of success and our addiction to neoliberal consumerism. There I explained how our current way of living is not

[9] Roger G. Betsworth, *Social Ethics: An Examination of American Moral Traditions* (Louisville, KY: Westminster John Knox Press, 1990).

[10] Darryl M. Trimiew, "America Land of the Free and Home of the Poor: Inequality as a way of life," in *Spirit and Capital in an Age of Inequality*, eds. Robert P, Smith and Ted A. Jones (New York: Routledge, 2018), 258.

[11] Ibid., 258.

[12] Darryl Trimiew, "Martin Luther King, Jr.: "Wirtschaftliche Rechte und Okologie. Kann es eine Beloved World Community geben?," in *Zeitschrift Fur Theologie Und Gemeinde* 23 (2018): 177.

sustainable in an increasingly ecologically fragile world. I maintained that our only way out of the corner that we have painted ourselves into is to hold to a covenant like King's "Beloved Community." I maintained that we must come into solidarity with the poor and cut back on our consumption and spoilage of planet Earth. The Beloved Community is the kind of covenant that could be adopted globally that can address all our problems internationally and domestically. The racism of Rauschenbusch, though lessening over his lifetime, was always going to cripple movements towards the kingdom of God because it was based in the heresy of white supremacy and exclusiveness.[13] Indeed, Rauschenbusch's late nods to possible international connectedness never fully figured into his theology. His earlier call for more German immigrants was more than a preference for his own *volk*, or just a desire for more celebrants of German culture, of wiener schnitzel, Beethoven, Bach, and Brahms. It was also a cry for the firming up of the numerical dominance of white people in America. According to Gary Dorrien, Rauschenbusch once wrote, "Are the whites of this continent so sure of their possession against the blacks of the South and the seething yellow flocks beyond the Pacific that they need no reinforcement of men of their own blood while yet it is still time?"[14] On another occasion, Rauschenbusch warned his listeners that "Anglo-Saxons need to join with the princely stock to protect American democracy from the demands of 'alien strains' arriving from other parts of the world."[15] In these quotes Walter Rauschenbusch more closely presages the theology and racial animosity of President Donald Trump than Martin Luther King Jr.

This observation is, in fact, very important to this essay. For while it is true that Rauschenbusch never abandoned white supremacy, he was, of course, critical of American slavery. And after his 1911 investigation of black life in Nashville, he was aware of the suffering of Southern blacks under the system of Jim Crow. Nevertheless, he never made the leap of genuinely claiming all humans as being truly equal and never acknowledged that the struggle for a more just distribution of the benefits and burdens of social

---

[13] Rufus Burrows, *God and Human Dignity: The Personalism, Theology, and Ethics of Martin Luther King, Jr.* (Notre Dame, IN: University of Notre Dame Press, 2006), 40.

[14] Ibid., 50.

[15] Cited in Gary Dorrien, *Soul in Society: the Making and Renewal of Social Christianity* (Minneapolis, MN: Fortress Press), 43.

goods was morally compelling. His conversion to equality was more along the lines of "Jesus loves the little children, all the children of the world, red and yellow, black and white, they are precious in his sight, Jesus loves the little children of the world." He evolved into developing a relatively more humane, though still paternalistic, stance. Rufus Burrow, a noted Rauschenbusch scholar, observes him as follows:

> In time, in his own way, Rauschenbusch would come to reject the stance of southern whites and others who believed blacks to be less than human and were not of one blood with whites. In 1914 he espoused what he considered the Christian way toward solution; "However great the practical difficulties may be, the Christian way out is to take our belated black brother by the hand and urge him along the road of confidence, and of pride and joy in his race achievements...." His tone here is paternalistic, and he fails to acknowledge that blacks were autonomous moral agents.[16]

Here we can see why the black church, if indeed it was widely exposed to Rauschenbusch's work, would never have positively received it. Racist semi-benevolent paternalism is never attractive. But as previously mentioned, the limited historical reception and significance of Rauschenbusch by the black church does not preclude a modern, current appreciation of his work or its use as a foundation for a new Social Gospel.

RAUSCHENBUSCH AND KING: BRIDGES FOR OVERCOMING RACIAL POLARIZATION IN MODERN AMERICA

If we can hear with fresh ears Walter Rauschenbusch's enthusiasm for God we can benefit by it. He once wrote, "It is for us to see the Kingdom of God as always coming, always pressing in on the present, always big with possibility, and always inviting immediate action."[17] This is a genuine expression of God's sovereignty and a continued call to us to cooperate with God, regardless of the cost. Though Rauschenbusch was beset with the false expectations of Progressivism, we need not be. We can understand his call to be a reiteration of Christ's call to us to action on behalf of the downtrodden.

---

[16] Burrows, *God and Human Dignity*, 52–53.

[17] Walter Rauschenbusch, *A Gospel for the Social Awakening: Selections from the Writings of Walter Rauschenbusch* (Eugene, OR: Wipf and Stock Publishers, 2008), 45.

And the "us" that this commission commands is everyone—a point that escaped Rauschenbusch, just as "all men are created equal" was never rightly understood by Jefferson. In the twenty-first century every American should want equality for all, and every Christian should want to be a member of the kingdom of God. Indeed, we should want it to be in our midst, regardless of race, gender, sexual preference, or any other particularity.

Though Rauschenbusch may not have understood that this call was for all Christians, as well as the truth that all Christians are equal, we do not have to continue his error. We can understand the kingdom of God to be *inclusive* as a corrective of Rauschenbusch's historical utterances. We can, because Martin Luther King Jr. did: this is the bridge to the possible creation of a non-racist America. Following King we can try again to create the Beloved Community. In doing so we free this covenant and way of life from the limiting particularity of Christianity and open up the possibility of forging covenants with all partners who seek to further justice, equality, and love, without regard to their religion, creed, or philosophy. Even Rauschenbusch, more than one hundred years ago, understood the need for justice partners.[18] Disaffected whites from rust-belt states who will not hear Cone, King, or Cannon may well hear Rauschenbusch. It is with this wider coalition that true revolutionary change can take place. Rauschenbusch was a reformer, but he understood the true nature of Christianity. He once said, "Christianity is in its nature revolutionary."[19] Unlike current evangelical Christianity, which is not revolutionary or conservative, but rather reactionary, Rauschenbusch was in favor of the redistribution of wealth in the economically unjust context of his Gilded Age. He once wrote, "Wealth is to a nation what manure is to a farm. If the farmer spreads it evenly over the soil, it will enrich the whole. If he should leave it in heaps, the land would be impoverished." Here Rauschenbusch, despite his racism and naiveté, is in his own modest way a nascent liberation theologian and a precursor to those more commonly known to be liberation theologians like Gustavo Gutierrez, James Cone, and, of course, Martin Luther King Jr. But of what current importance is this recognition and characterization of Rauschenbusch?

---

[18] Rufus Burrows, *Extremist for Love: Martin Luther King Jr., Man of Ideas and Nonviolent Social Action* (Minneapolis, MN: Fortress Press, 2014), 52–53.

[19] Walter Rauschenbusch, https://www.brainyquote.com/quotes/walter_rauschenbusch_318291.

First, it is important in that it separates practitioners of liberation theology from the charge of being closet Communists, since Rauschenbusch clearly predates Communism. Gary Dorrien, a noted scholar of the Social Gospel, calls to our attention other Black Social Gospelers not dependent on Marxist thought, such as Reverdy Ransom, Ida B. Wells-Barnett, Nannie Helen Burroughs, Adam Clayton Powell Sr., and Mordecai Wyatt Johnson, among others.[20] Indeed, what recent scholarship reveals is the fact that the Black Social Gospel movement predates Rauschenbusch, Gladden, Shailer Mathews, and others as a wing of the African American church.[21] This again is a reason why the reception and significance of Rauschenbusch by the historic African American church is minimized.[22] Burrows has made it clear that King appreciated Rauschenbusch's work in part because it resonated with the Social Gospel movement of the black church, even though that movement did not originate with Rauschenbusch's work.[23] As previously mentioned, King appropriated and accepted some of Rauschenbusch's work while rejecting other aspects, which he did for very important reasons.

While being able to cite Rauschenbusch would not necessarily impress the African American church and community, it did evidence to whites, to whom King was also trying to communicate, that he was familiar with white theological sources and movements. It was a way for King to speak to white liberal Christians out of their own tradition. This facilitated his effort to show white liberals that the struggle for justice for blacks was also their duty. Further, Rauschenbusch's push for economic justice for impoverished whites was correctly understood by King as a possible historical source and support for his struggle for economic justice for blacks.

King modified and used Rauschenbusch's ideas, and so can we. The question is, should we? Walter Rauschenbusch was deeply flawed because of his white supremacy, so why bother? We bother because we know that no pastor, no theologian, no leader is perfect.[24] We all have clay feet. We con-

---

[20] Gary Dorrien, *The New Abolition: W. E. B. Du Bois and the Black Social Gospel* (New Haven, CT: Yale University Press, 2015), 483.

[21] Burrows, *Extremist for Love*, 52–53.

[22] Noel Leo Erskine, *King among the Theologians* (Cleveland, OH: Pilgrim Press, 1994), 4.

[23] Burrows, *Extremist for Love*, 52–53.

[24] Darryl M. Trimiew, "Political Pariahs, Political Messiahs: The Problem of Moral Leadership in America," *The Annual of the Society of Christians Ethics* 30 (2010): 63–78.

tinue the struggle for the Beloved Community with the clear knowledge of King's clay feet. He was a philanderer, a plagiarist, and a servant of God who died as a martyr serving God.[25] And he was sexist. He did not transcend the gender-role mores of his time, just as Rauschenbusch embraced the white supremacy of his time. Fifty years from now, if we are lucky, scholars will be analyzing our work, picking out the good and noting the bad and noting how we did not act properly because of our blind spots, our socialization into some sort of false consciousness that we currently regard as best practices. For those who want to both criticize the past and learn from it, the sins of ancestors must be understood even if not accepted. We must not throw out the baby with the bath water. In short, we cannot legitimately give King a pass on his shortcomings without, in some measure, also granting one to Rauschenbusch. And we should do so for the same reason King did. In order to effectuate change, in order to further the realization of the Beloved Community, we need to change the minds and hearts of as many people as possible. Those who because of racism will not listen to the claims for economic justice made by King, or Cone, or Cannon, might well convert and be transformed by the reintroduction of the White Social Gospel of Walter Rauschenbusch. It is a shame, in the twenty-first century, that justified claims for change can only be recognized by some whites if it is made by another white—but it is that way sometimes.

Yet Rauschenbusch may prove to be more influential today than he was in his own time. In Rauschenbusch's time, the movement for more social justice did not go forward in part because it was a freight train that would have had to carry black passengers. Because of Jim Crow, it could not do so. What was supplied instead was the stale hush puppy of white supremacy that Jim Crow provided to the whites of Rauschenbusch's era.

What do I mean by this? Let us hear the words of Martin Luther King Jr. at the conclusion of the Selma to Montgomery march on March 26, 1965. King spoke of this reality as follows:

> If it may be said of the slavery era that the white man took the world and gave the Negro Jesus, then it may be said of the Reconstruction era that the southern aristocracy took the world and gave the poor white man Jim Crow. (*Yes, sir*) He gave him Jim Crow. (***Uh huh***) And when his wrinkled stomach cried out for the food that his empty pockets could not provide, (*Yes, sir*) he ate Jim Crow, a psycho-

---

[25] Rufus Burrows, *God and Human Dignity*, 129–30.

> logical bird that told him that no matter how bad off he was, at least he was a white man, better than the black man. (***Right sir***) And he ate Jim Crow. (***Uh huh***) And when his undernourished children cried out for the necessities that his low wages could not provide, he showed them the Jim Crow signs on the buses and in the stores, on the streets and in the public buildings. (***Yes, sir***) And his children, too, learned to feed upon Jim Crow, (***Speak***) their last outpost of psychological oblivion. (***Yes, sir***)
>
> Thus, the threat of the free exercise of the ballot by the Negro and the white masses alike (***Uh huh***) resulted in the establishment of a segregated society. They segregated southern money from the poor whites; they segregated southern mores from the rich whites; (***Yes, sir***) they segregated southern churches from Christianity (***Yes, sir***); they segregated southern minds from honest thinking; (***Yes, sir***) and they segregated the Negro from everything. (***Yes, sir***) That's what happened when the Negro and white masses of the South threatened to unite and build a great society: a society of justice where none would prey upon the weakness of others; a society of plenty where greed and poverty would be done away; a society of brotherhood where every man would respect the dignity and worth of human personality. (***Yes, sir***)[26]

The "stale hush puppy" of Jim Crow cannot now be thrown to disaffected whites to satisfy them. Nor can the sad embrace of opioids. And so now the time is ripe for poor and working-class whites to join with blacks, Hispanics, and all others in the struggle for economic justice and human rights. Here is where Rauschenbusch may now be heard again. Over time, as people understand more fully how poorly the manure of wealth distribution has been made over the farm of America, hearts and ears may be open to hear King, Cannon, Cone, and others.

CONCLUSION

It is my hope that despite my finding that Walter Rauschenbusch did not significantly affect the black church of his era, he will not be forgotten. My additional finding that his work may be of great value in the twenty-first century should spur some reconsideration of his theology. This cannot be

---

[26] Martin Luther King Jr., "Our God Is Marching On," American Public Media https:Americanradioworks.publicradio.org/. Accessed 29 October 2017.

done by revisionism, but by accepting the sins and errors of Rauschenbusch's white supremacy, by eating the meat of his God of justice and spitting out the bones of racist contention. This can be done, this should be done, but it is not yet clear that it will be done. The election of President Donald Trump is a clear rejection of the struggle to build a Beloved Community. His atrocious performance might, however, be the best argument against rebuilding a "Rauschenbusch America." A gathering force seems to be arising. The Reverend William Barber III and the Kairos Coalition is renewing King's organization of the Poor Peoples March. This is more than just a push for more money for the poor. When the unjust tax cuts and the removal of Glass/Steagall protections generate a new collapse, working people of all colors will be open to working together in a new struggle. This struggle will be for a just, participatory, and sustainable community. This will be a struggle to establish a Beloved Community by moral change, spiritual renewal, and economic justice for all. We can join in that struggle, and as the struggle continues, sense the reign of God is in our midst.

Chapter 9

Walter Rauschenbusch's Theology of the Cross: A Postcolonial Reflection

Dominik Gautier

I hesitate to write about the cross, this central symbol of Christianity. In Germany, where I come from, Christianity is invoked by many as a cultural power against those who are deemed as "others." Christianity is invoked against migrants and refugees, who are simply addressed as Muslims (whether they are Muslims or not), and against those who advocate a more open society. Christianity, and with it its central symbol, seems to become entangled with the dominant discourse of national identity that has to be defended against those who are not "us." In German critical race theory, this is currently referred to as the "demonization of others." These "others" are imagined to be backward, criminal, and sexually dangerous. By this, the "demonization of others" draws—subtly or not—on images from the repertoire of racism to make plausible a policy of isolation and to facilitate violence against these "others"—always by referring to "our" Christian culture, which must be asserted.[1] That is why I hesitate to write about the cross.

In this text, however, I do not want to leave Christianity's discursive involvement with violence unchallenged. So, I want to approach the cross cautiously, from a perspective in which violence is not promoted but questioned. In part, Walter Rauschenbusch's theology of the cross, as I read it, helps me with this. When he talked about the cross, he was addressing the violence that structures our societies—and he was reflecting on whether a theology of the cross can help us to change society so that it corresponds more to what Rauschenbusch understood to be the reign of God. In the first part of this text, I will therefore trace Rauschenbusch's thoughts on the cross, based on the last chapter of his *Theology for the Social Gospel.* By tracing his ideas, I will suggest that even his theology is not free from thinking

---

[1] See *Die Dämonisierung der Anderen. Rassismuskritik der Gegenwart*, eds. Paul Mecheril and María do Mar Castro Varela (Bielefeld: transcript, 2016).

in the mode of "us" and "them" when he left the violence of race and racism widely unquestioned.

The second part of this text then deals with a postcolonial exploration of his theology of the cross, in which I delve a bit deeper into the relationship between his theology, modern religion, and race. This is not about reckoning with his work, but about what Hannah Arendt has called an "extended way of thinking": showing appreciation through analyzing complexities and contradictions as well as searching for ways of thinking differently about the issue that is at stake.[2] I therefore conclude with two postcolonial reflections, hoping to supplement Rauschenbusch's critique of violence in the interest of a more just society that is less obsessed with the often racially coded distinction between "us" and "them." To put it differently: is there a way out of this distinction toward more equality?

WALTER RAUSCHENBUSCH'S THEOLOGY OF THE CROSS

How can one make sense of the death of Jesus? With this question, I turn to Walter Rauschenbusch's theology of the cross as he developed it in his 1917 work *A Theology for the Social Gospel.* This work comes closest to a systematic theology of the Social Gospel movement.

As a theological liberal, Rauschenbusch struggled with this question. He could not accept the traditional theories of the atonement as eternally valid. To regard Jesus's death biblically as a sacrifice or traditionally as an act of satisfaction is not denied by Rauschenbusch, but he emphasized that all theories of the atonement are historically relative interpretations of the cross, and so, for him, it was necessary to reinterpret its meaning constantly. For him, it was the concept of solidarity that is key to gain an access to what the cross could mean. "Our dominant ideas are personality and social solidarity. The problems which burden us are the social problems. Has the death of Christ any relation to these?"[3] With the concept of solidarity that emerged with the social sciences and the labor union movement in the nineteenth century, Rauschenbusch acknowledged and analyzed social structures

---

[2] See Hannah Arendt, *Eichmann in Jerusalem. Ein Bericht von der Banalität des Bösen* (München/Zürich: Piper, 2011 [1965]).

[3] Walter Rauschenbusch, *A Theology for the Social Gospel* (New York: Macmillan Co., 1917), 244.

and called for a social commitment to change so that our living together looks more like a society of solidarity.[4]

In the light of this sociologically informed thinking, Rauschenbusch thought he could trace "Christ's own theology"[5] and said that "we are in a better situation to understand the atonement than any previous generation."[6] How so? Rauschenbusch argued that social thought enabled us to recognize Jesus first and foremost as a Hebrew prophet who fought dehumanizing social structures and calls for human solidarity. This culminates in Jesus's prophetic message that God's reign is present and evolving. When talking about the cross, we therefore have to keep an eye on Jesus's prophetic life. His death is then the consequence of this life—it is a prophetic death, which Jesus suffered in the struggle for God's reign. With this, Jesus has included himself in God's fight against social sin. "[Jesus] entered that attitude, made it his own, and thus revealed God at the point where the sin of the world and the mind of God were in sharpest antagonism."[7] The first function of Rauschenbusch's theology of the cross was thus the awareness of this antagonism: the cross aims at the critical exposure of socially mediated sin.

The second function of his theology of the cross is to empower people to become prophetic agents for solidarity—aiming at social salvation. This implies that the crucifixion should not be interpreted as displaying Jesus's passivity but as showing his prophetic energy that he wants to share with his followers: in death, Jesus defiantly clings to God's reign. Therefore, Rauschenbusch remarked, "Christian art has misreported [Jesus] when it makes him suffer with head down. His head was up and he was in command of the situation."[8]

All in all, Rauschenbusch said, the cross "furnishes a mystic basis for the social revolution. It would be a theological conception which the Social Gospel could use and enforce."[9] In this prophetic movement, God and hu-

---

[4] See Gary Dorrien, "Society as the Subject of Redemption. Washington Gladden, Walter Rauschenbusch, and the Social Gospel," in *Economy, Difference, Empire. Social Ethics for Social Justice* (New York: Columbia University Press, 2010), 3–28, 11–15.

[5] Ibid., 259.

[6] Ibid., 204.

[7] Ibid., 261–62.

[8] Ibid., 266.

[9] Ibid., 267.

manity—grown together at the cross—fight for social salvation that eventually culminates in God's reign. With this progressive angle, one can speak of a goal-oriented, teleological theology of the cross in Rauschenbusch's work.

I will now take a closer look at the two functions of Rauschenbusch's interpretation of the cross: How does the cross expose social sin? How does it provoke prophetic action?

THE CROSS AND THE CRITICAL EXPOSURE OF VIOLENCE

Rauschenbusch struggled to interpret the difficult notion that Jesus died for "our" sins. How can this sentence be understood in the perspective of the social? His answer to this was not that Jesus, who is seen as free from sin, somehow vicariously takes up "our" sin. For such a view Rauschenbusch was much too modern and regarded guilt as a personal issue for which no other person can take responsibility. Also, Jesus does not take up sin by merely sympathizing with his fellow human beings whose lives are shaped by sin. For Rauschenbusch, the most convincing interpretation was that Jesus *experiences* the consequences of sinful social structures on his very own body. Jesus experiences the sin, to which—across time—all human beings contribute and under which all human beings suffer.[10] "These public evils so pervade the social life of humanity in all times and all places that no one can share the common life of our race without coming under effect of these collective sins."[11] Jesus "did in a very real sense bear the weight of the public sins of organized society, and they in turn are causally connected with all private sins."[12] If we see Jesus as being in solidarity with his time, then he is completely affected by the sinful violence of his time that pervades society. In the tradition of liberal theologian Albrecht Ritschl, Rauschenbusch called these social evils somewhat dualistically the "Kingdom of Evil" in contrast to the "Kingdom of God": "[Jesus] lived in the midst of that Kingdom," said Rauschenbusch, "and it was this which killed him."[13]

Thus, the cross provokes a critical reflection of violence that is inherent in social structures and by which Jesus, as well as humanity, is affected. According to Rauschenbusch, there are six forms of sinful social corruptions

---

[10] Ibid., 245–47.

[11] Ibid., 247.

[12] Ibid.

[13] Ibid., 246.

that bring Jesus to the cross. He named them very precisely. They are religious power, political power, the legal system, mob violence, militarism, and classism. I now want to trace how he reflected on these social sins. By doing this, I think we can learn something about how Rauschenbusch perceived society in his time and what he wanted to address critically in the interest of the common good. Also, I will observe in what way he engaged (or did not engage) race in his argument.

The first sin that leads to the cross is the corruption of religious power. Rauschenbusch said, "Jesus was killed by anti-prophetic, ecclesiastical religion. It takes religion to put a steel edge on social intolerance. Just because it is so high and its command of social loyalty so great, it is pitiless when it goes wrong."[14] This argument runs the risk of becoming an anti-Semitic accusation, that Jews are Christ-killers. But at least here Rauschenbusch did not direct his criticism of religious bigotry primarily to Judaism; rather, he critiqued religious justifications of violence in general. With this, Rauschenbusch emphasized the ambivalence of religion, how it can be used for the good but is often used to enforce injustice, such as a crucifixion.

The second sin that the cross exposes is the corruption of political power. According to Rauschenbusch, political power, like religion, could be used for enhancing justice but is repeatedly deformed in the interest of the dominant class. Because Jesus, as a prophet of widows and orphans, as the prophet of the marginalized, stood up for God's politics, he was killed by the dominant powers: "We are on sure ground," wrote Rauschenbusch, "when we realize that the prophetic leadership of Jesus endangered the power of the ruling class."[15]

The third sin, leading to crucifixion, was embodied by a corrupted legal system: by connecting Jesus's life to the parable of the unjust judge and the persistent widow, Rauschenbusch placed Jesus in the prophetic tradition as the victim of the legal system—condemned as a heretic and a traitor: "So Jesus made experience of one of the permanent sins of organized society, bearing in his own body and soul what so many thousands of the poor and weak have borne before and after, the corruption of justice."[16] Rauschenbusch emphasized that the injustice was to be found in the structures of the legal system and not first and foremost in the misbehavior of individuals.

[14] Ibid., 249.
[15] Ibid., 251.
[16] Ibid., 254.

"Even if the judge is wholly free from bias," Rauschenbusch wrote, "the law itself in all countries, presumably is on the side of property."[17] "What nation can claim to be free from this?"[18] He also linked this structural injustice to the lack of representation of those who are most affected by it, "Our own legislatures rarely contain any spokesman [*sic*] of the class which needs a voice most of all."[19] While Rauschenbusch related his analysis specifically to Russian prisons and World War I, he did not mention the 1896 legal justification of racial segregation in the American South which was supported by the dominant religious and political discourse he tries critically to address. Here, one can see how his sense of injustice remained bound to a privileged worldview of whiteness.

However, through his elaboration of mob violence, a fourth sin makes the picture more complex. The cross, for Rauschenbusch, is a symbol of mob violence. It is the mob who also wants Jesus's death. Through the mob, the social, which he considered to be good as a matter of principle, is turned into its opposite. Rauschenbusch wrote: "The mob spirit is the social spirit gone mad."[20] In this case, unlike his reflection on the corruption of the legal system, he referred to the legacy of race and racism in society and to lynching. However, he did not refer to the Black Social Gospel tradition that would have broadened his view as a tradition of those who are the sinned against and not the sinners: "When a Southern city degrades the whole nation by turning the savage inhumanity of a mob into a public festivity, we are continuing to sin because our fathers created the conditions of sin by the African slave trade and by unearned wealth they gathered from slave labour for generations."[21]

In his fifth argument, he reflected on the sin of militarism. For Rauschenbusch, having in mind the crisis experience of World War I, it is the culture of the gun that leads to the cross. This means Jesus fell into the hands of the war system that, as he suggested, is characterized by masculine dominance. Rauschenbusch argued, "When the soldiers stripped him, beat his back...and when they blindfolded and struck him, asking him to prophesy who it was and spitting in his face,—this was the humour of the barrack

[17] Ibid., 253.
[18] Ibid., 252.
[19] Ibid., 253.
[20] Ibid., 254.
[21] Ibid., 79.

room. This was fun as the professional soldiers of the Roman Empire saw it."[22]

Finally, and this is the sixth sin, the cross exposes classism. Capitalism, for Rauschenbusch, produces a hierarchy of social classes that benefits the few and exploits the many. Therefore, classism not only dehumanizes the exploited but also robs the privileged of their humanity. It was Jesus who was crucified by an instrument intended exclusively for the lower classes. This specific social violence becomes condensed in the cross: "When Jesus was nailed to the tree, therefore, he bore not only the lightning shoots of physical pain imposed by the cruelties of criminal law, but also that contempt for the lower classes which has always dehumanized the upper classes, numbed and crippled the spiritual self-respect of the lower classes, and set up insuperable barriers to the Kingdom of God."[23] It is notable here that his focus lies on the deep analysis of class but that he does not also analyze the ways in which the constructions of race set up a barrier to God's reign.

From this consideration of how the cross in Rauschenbusch's theology can sharpen the awareness of social sin, I now turn to the question of how he interpreted the cross as a source of empowerment for engaging in the project of social salvation.

THE CROSS AND THE PROJECT OF SOCIAL SALVATION

While Jesus experienced these social sins—"our" sins—how does that relate to working for a more just society? There are three effects of the cross that he shows us that evoke a movement toward social salvation. They are the redemptive awareness of sin, the disclosure of love as the basis of the new social order, and prophetic agency.

Firstly, the cross—and this is its ethical power I wrote about above—points to the depths of sin in society and to the suffering from this sin: "The cross forever puts a question mark alongside of any easy treatment of sin."[24] The awareness of sin, for Rauschenbusch, is already a moment of salvation, because some of its power is broken through naming it. For him, the awareness of sin is bound to a somewhat natural sensitivity to the suffering of others, though almost always obscured by other interests. The cross,

---

[22] Ibid., 256.
[23] Ibid., 257.
[24] Ibid., 268.

however, when it is truly meditated, disrupts these other interests and urges us to work for a different style of living together.[25]

Secondly, the cross reveals love as the power of social redemption—and not just as common love but as sacrificial love. Jesus gives himself both for God and for God's reign. Hereby at the same time God gives Godself to humanity. This, for Rauschenbusch, initiates a response that takes form in advocacy for social change: "The atonement," wrote Rauschenbusch, "is the symbol and basis of a new social order."[26] For him, this new social order was radical democracy that the West had already realized to some extent. However, for those who were at the underside of this democracy at that time, this phrase must have sounded ironic. He said: "Suppose that instead of the Father of Jesus Christ we had a God who embodied the doctrine of the survival of the fit, the rule of the strong, and the suppressing of the weak, how would that have affected the spiritual character of Western civilization? How much chance would there have been for democracy?"[27]

Thirdly, the cross can have the function of motivating people to take a prophetic stand. This, now, makes clear that radical democracy is not at all achieved. "The prophet is always the predestined advance agent of the Kingdom of God. His religion flings him as a fighter and protester against the Kingdom of Evil."[28] The cross—and with this we catch the essence of Rauschenbusch's perspective of the cross—"has compelled reflection on the value of the prophets for the progress of humanity."[29] Against the Social Gospel cliché that God's commonwealth would simply evolve, Rauschenbusch's *A Theology for the Social Gospel* ended with the realistic idea that the cross finds an ongoing echo in the suffering of those constantly working for justice.

It would be important for further analysis to reflect on the problematic notion of sacrificial love and how it relates to the sacrifices especially the marginalized have to make.[30] However, I now want to look at Rauschenbusch's theology from a postcolonial perspective.

---

[25] Ibid., 269.

[26] Ibid., 274.

[27] Ibid., 271.

[28] Ibid., 277.

[29] Ibid., 278.

[30] Delores Williams, *Sisters in the Wilderness: The Challenge of Womanist God-Talk* (Maryknoll, NY: Orbis Books, 2013), 143–48.

A POSTCOLONIAL REFLECTION ON WALTER RAUSCHENBUSCH

Rauschenbusch's progressive interpretation of the cross has contributed theologically to backing up the commitment to a more just society. However, he shows an ambivalent perspective on race, as I have learned through reading Gary Dorrien's analyses. Rauschenbusch imagined a future in which racial injustice remained mostly unquestioned. On the one hand, he condemned lynching culture as a social sin. On the other hand, he spoke in a paternalistic way of the "belated races" and affirms racism; for example, he referred to African Americans as threatening—in opposition to the "qualities" of white Germans.[31] By leaving violence against those constructed as "other" largely unquestioned, Rauschenbusch supported the dominant discourse. This discourse, after all, and as unintended as it may be, requires relative ignorance about the suffering of others to uphold its "rightfulness."[32] Although Rauschenbusch understood the cross as heightening the sensitivity to violence, he did not come to see the lynching tree as the cross in America, as James H. Cone put it in accordance with Black Social Gospel proponents.[33]

This could also be due to the fact that Rauschenbusch's theology is discursively bound to the optimistic and teleological thinking of modernity that makes it very hard to reflect on its contradictions. To put it polemically, racism at the root of both the European and American project just cannot be true. Theodore Vial has argued that the teleology of modern religion, this "pressing forward," has brought many good outcomes, such as the recognition of individual rights and a powerful sense of solidarity, but at the same time it is mixed with racial thinking. This is articulated, for example, in the idea that some groups are already closer to salvation than others, that there are therefore more developed and less developed groups. Traditionally, Europeans are associated with being closer to the "goal" than Africans, and

---

[31] Gary Dorrien, "Social Ethics in the Making. History, Method, and White Supremacism," in *Economy, Difference, Empire*, 392–409; 404–405.

[32] Ben Sanders III, "Walter Rauschenbusch on Society," in *Beyond the Pale: Reading Ethics from the Margins*, eds. Stacey M. Floyd-Thomas and Miguel A. De La Torre (Louisville, KY: Westminster John Knox Press, 2011), 111–18.

[33] James H. Cone, *The Cross and the Lynching Tree* (Maryknoll, NY: Orbis Books, 2011).

European Americans are closer than African Americans.[34] Vial argues: "Religious studies, as the quintessential modern project in many ways is fully imbricated with race. This aspect of the modern project, intertwined with the parts we want to praise, we have [yet?] to come to terms with in any serious way."[35] Kelly Brown-Douglas, for example, explains how dominant Christianity needs blackness as "other" to assert white culture. She emphasizes that this culture is also supported by the discourse of being able to defend oneself—to defend oneself against those who are constructed as criminal and sexually dangerous in order to make violence plausible and legitimate.[36] This resonates in part with what I wrote about the "demonization of others" in German society.

When Rauschenbusch's theology is involved in this ambivalence of modern religion, how could we rethink his work? Supplementary to his focus on the coming of God's commonwealth, I want to emphasize the moment of crisis, disruption, and confusion that I think can open up possibilities of self-critical questioning of our visions for the future. I want to do this by referring to postcolonial criticism.

Postcolonial thinking, for me, is in its widest sense the critical treatment of the hierarchical distinction between "us" and "them" that has grown powerfully out of the colonial imagination. For me, this is not about designing counter-theories, but about constantly supplementing existing narratives, and thereby changing them—always with an interest in how to imagine a future where people can have a more livable life because they are less bound to restrictions made up by race, class, gender, or sexuality.[37] Therefore, I do not intend my following reflections on the cross to be counter ideas, but supplements, which I want to "insert" into Rauschenbusch's elaborations on the cross, and into his thoughts on both sin and prophetic action.

---

[34] Theodore Vial, *Modern Race, Modern Religion* (New York: Oxford University Press, 2016), 221–54.

[35] Ibid., 254.

[36] Kelly Brown-Douglas, *Stand Your Ground: Black Bodies and the Justice of God* (Maryknoll, NY: Orbis Books, 2015), 48–89.

[37] María do Mar Castro Varela and Nikita Dhawan, *Postkoloniale Theorie. Eine kritische Einführung* (Bielefeld: transcript, 2015), 339–40.

THE CROSS AND THE POWER OF CONFUSION

As a starting point for thinking about the productiveness of confusion, I am interested in Rauschenbusch's silence concerning racism. Rauschenbusch said, "For years the problem of the two races in the South has seemed so tragic, so insoluble, that I have never yet ventured to discuss it in public."[38] In this silence, there seems to be some potential to reflect on how critique of race and racism is never easy and simple, but that there is a need for deep criticism. I would like to develop this by referring to postcolonial critic Gayatri Chakravorty Spivak. Spivak has urged Western intellectuals who advocate social change to a profound self-criticism, to questioning their own social position and privilege, so that they ultimately end up in a state of confusion. This is necessary because Western intellectuals are discursively involved in a worldview that silences others, those "others" who are constructed as backward, unemancipated, or dangerous. Only when modern thought and its thinkers bring themselves in this state of confusion, when they become somewhat speechless, can change take place—as slow and difficult as it may be. Change happens when space is opened up for articulation of those whose voices were silenced as well as when those who are in hegemonic positions learn to speak differently—aimed at a society that does not rob others of their dignity.[39]

Can the cross, this shocking symbol of violence, be seen as invoking this confusion? Can it interrupt our plans for imagining the world productively? I think Rauschenbusch has offered us helpful insights when he understood the cross as a disclosure of violence, and when he has emphasized that Jesus became the victim of the mob and suffered a death reserved for the lowest classes of society. The cross, seriously approached, should do nothing but induce speechlessness. Theological interpretations should be secondary. They even run the risk of relativizing violence and silencing, so to speak, the voice of Jesus, who also stands in for those who experience violence. However, Rauschenbusch, though not too far from it theologically, did not relate this to racism. He inserted his theology of the cross into his teleological worldview, and thus was not able to see the cross's disrupt-

---

[38] Gary Dorrien, "Social Ethics in the Making. History, Method, and White Supremacism," in *Economy, Difference, Empire*, 404.

[39] Gayatri Chakravorty Spivak, "Can the Subaltern Speak?," in *Marxism and the Interpretation of Culture*, eds. Cary Nelson/Lawrence Grossberg (Chicago, IL: University of Illinois Press, 1988), 271–313, esp. 308.

ing potential. He did not understand the cross to be so profound in its effect that it also exposes the violence that might be inherent in his *own* imagination. So, I would like to suggest that the cross puts us into the profound state of confusion that Spivak is looking for. It confronts us with violence and urges us to question the violence of exclusion that creeps into our very own thinking. A constant reflection of one's own visions could maybe create spaces for alternative and even conflicting approaches that are necessary to imagine a more just society.

THE CROSS, GRIEF, AND SOLIDARITY

The question of advocating for a more just society is closely linked to the question of solidarity, which is used by Rauschenbusch as a key perspective for interpreting the cross and which is central to the prophetic struggle for God's reign. For supplementing his thoughts, I want to refer to Judith Butler's work on the politics of grief. Butler's perspective is based on the analysis that the hierarchical structure of society shapes even our emotions, our affects, so that we are made to see every life as not equally grievable. From this feeling of grief, we get a sense of who we think belongs to the "we" and who does not. Let me mention, for example, the past and present socially produced ungrievability of those who died and die of AIDS. At the same time, for Butler, the feeling of grief holds the potential to confuse this hierarchy of emotions. In which way? To put it more personally, the grief I feel for a lost life of a person close to me makes it clear to me that I am more than myself. Grief is the feeling that I not only lose a person, but that I lose myself. More socially speaking: in grief we could feel that all life is implicated in the lives of others; we feel our interdependence. Grief thus exposes the constructed distinction between "us" and "them" and questions it: Whose life do we regard as grievable?[40] With whom do we want to be allied? Here opens up the small chance for experimenting with a different kind of solidarity, that is, the solidarity with those who are deemed as "other." The political protest of the die-in, for example, the performance of one's own death, used by #BlackLivesMatter activists in the US as well as in Germany, provokes exactly this question: do you think black lives are grievable?

---

[40] Judith Butler, "Violence, Mourning, Politics," in Judith Butler, *Precarious Life. The Power of Mourning and Politics* (New York: Verso, 2004), 19–49, esp. 44–49.

What would it look like to interpret the cross against this background?[41] The cross can be seen as a symbol of sorrow. The story of the cross provokes grief for the lost life of the executed other who stands in for the many others executed. The body of Jesus that is mourned by Christianity is a body that points to the unmourned others who count as the "not us." The story of the cross could be a story that disrupts our imagination and questions what we mean by solidarity. Thinking of a theology of the cross, solidarity would then not be understood first as a solidarity among those who are the same, but as solidarity among those who are different. I think the cross urges us, as complicated as it is, to become less dependent on our groups and toward alliances with people who do not belong to our group. This would be an understanding of solidarity that could enable us to imagine a future that is more pluralistic, a future in which we are not so much bound to our identities and in which we enter into a movement of equality, in which fewer and fewer lives will be considered ungrievable—and that could be called God's equality.

---

[41] See also Wonhee Ann Joh, "A Postcolonial Spectrality of the Cross," *Concilium*, 2 (2013): 41–50.

Chapter 10

Sowing Seeds: How *For the Right* Germinated Rauschenbusch's Later Muckraking

Christina Littlefield

Social Gospel leader Walter Rauschenbusch is famous for waking up churches to America's social ills with his 1907 *Christianity and the Social Crisis.*[1] Throughout his works, Rauschenbusch mimicked the techniques of the secular muckrakers—the turn-of-the-century investigative journalists who helped give birth to the Progressive Era in American politics.[2] Rauschenbusch's books often used data and anecdotes to document the social ills created by rapid industrialization and urbanization and show how Christians should address those problems. But his first foray into muckraking dates far earlier, to a little-known and little-read journalistic venture with fellow New York Baptist clergyman Leighton Williams. Together, they produced a paper for working people titled *For the Right,* from October 1889 through March 1891.Though the newspaper ultimately failed, it was the testing ground for Rauschenbusch's later ideas, both his Christian Socialism, with its modified yes/no critique against other forms of Socialism, and his vision of the kingdom, which fueled his reform efforts. It was also the beginning of the Brotherhood of the Kingdom reform efforts. Rauschenbusch hoped *For the Right* would better the lives of working people like those whom he served as pastor at Second German Baptist Church in Hell's Kitchen, New York City. The front-page mission statement affirmed that

---

[1] Walter Rauschenbusch, *Christianity and the Social Crisis in the 21st Century: The Classic That Woke Up the Church,* ed. Paul B. Raushenbush (New York: HarperOne, 2007). First published 1907. See also *Walter Rauschenbusch: Published Works and Selected Writings, Vol. I,* ed. William H. Brackney (Macon, GA: Mercer University Press, 2018), ixxv–293.

[2] Judith Serrin and William Serrin, *Muckraking! The Journalism That Changed America* (New York: New Press, 2002); Arthur and Lila Weinberg, *Muckrakers: The Era in Journalism That Moved America to Reform* (New York: Simon & Schuster, 1961).

For the Right aimed to "reflect in its pages the needs, the aspirations, the longings of the tens of thousands of wage-earners who are sighing for better things; and to point out, if possible, not only the wrongs that men suffer, but the methods by which these wrongs may be removed."[3]

Coming from what the editors of *For the Right* called a "New Testament Christian" standpoint, they promoted a form of Christian Socialism. The editors focused on labor rights and living conditions for the working poor and promoted equal rights for women, American Indians, and blacks. They believed every individual should have basic comforts and the opportunity to pursue success. The paper was politically conservative in that it focused on how workers could help themselves through personal regeneration. The paper rarely called for legislative change, save for the public ownership of utilities and transportation services.

The paper's target audience was working people, though its readership was more likely middle-class churchgoers and like-minded pastors. However, the editors were forerunners in promoting the Social Gospel and earned praise from the religious press and *The New York Times*, which described the paper as "radical yet Christian, [saying] boldly what in their opinion every pulpit in New York ought to be saying."[4] *For the Right* was one of many Social Gospel newspapers hoping to usher in the kingdom of God, and this essay showcases how Rauschenbusch, like others of his ilk, "muckraked" alongside his more secular peers to promote a reform agenda that was intent on working toward the kingdom of God.

LITERATURE REVIEW

The Social Gospel was a late nineteenth-century movement in England, Germany, and the United States to apply the teachings of Jesus to every aspect of life: individually, socially, politically, and economically. As Charles Howard Hopkins wrote, "Social Christianity involved a criticism of conventional Protestantism, a progressive theology and social philosophy, and an

---

[3] Walter Rauschenbusch and Leighton Williams, *For the Right* (November 1889–March 1891), Microfiche, American Baptist Historical Society, Atlanta, Georgia: hereinafter ABHS, November 1889.

[4] "Clergyman Who Are Socialist" TimesMachine: 8 November 1890, 2, https://timesmachine.nytimes.com/timesmachine/1890/11/08/103277437.html?pageNumber=2. Accessed 28 May 2018. For The Right editors cite this in November 1890, 2.

active program of propagandism and reform."[5] Many Social Gospel thinkers edited their own periodicals, covering social issues in the decades before the more well-known muckrakers and during the muckrakers' heyday of the early 1900s.[6] Scholars have done little detailed work on the journalistic efforts of the Social Gospelers, as journalism historians focus on the mainstream muckrakers, and church historians only mention the newspaper work of theologians in passing.[7] The Social Gospel leaders developed their own reform periodicals because they believed the Gospel was the best hope for addressing the ills of rapid industrialization, urbanization, and immigration. Newspapers were one way to shape the public mind toward individual and societal regeneration.

Here I define muckraking, or exposure literature, as a form of advocacy journalism that uses detailed investigations, individualized anecdotes, and sociological data to concentrate public attention on social ills in hopes of ushering in reform.[8] As journalism historian Doug Underwood has argued,

---

[5] Charles Howard Hopkins, *The Rise of the Social Gospel in American Protestantism* (New Haven, CT: Yale University Press, 1940), 1. Critical works on the Social Gospel include Christopher H. Evans, *The Social Gospel in American Religion: A History* (New York: New York University Press, 2017); Robert T. Handy, *A Christian America: Protestant Hopes and Historical Realities*, 2nd ed. (New York: Oxford University Press, 1984); Ralph Luker, *The Social Gospel in Black and White: American Racial Reform, 1885–1912* (Chapel Hill: University of North Carolina Press, 1991); Martin Marty, *Righteous Empire: The Protestant Experience in America* (New York: Dial Press, 1970).

[6] Much of this brief overview of the religious roots of the muckrakers is part of a larger book project and first appeared in Christina Littlefield and Falon Opsahl, "Promulgating the Kingdom: Social Gospel Muckraker Josiah Strong," *American Journalism* 34/4 (2017): 289–312.

[7] Rauschenbusch's contemporary biographers, Paul Minus and Christopher Evans, spend a few pages on *For the Right* but don't dig into primary sources; see Paul M. Minus, *Walter Rauschenbusch* (New York: MacMillan Publishing Company, 1988), 65–67; Christopher H. Evans, *The Kingdom Is Always but Coming* (Grand Rapids, MI: Eerdmans, 2004), 83–89.

[8] Scholars debate whether the muckrakers were liberal reformers, crusading for the people against big business and corrupt politicians, or upholders of middle-class sensibilities, friendly toward business and conservatively addressing only the most pressing issues of the Gilded Age. See Harry H. Stein, "American Muckrakers and Muckraking: The 50-Year Scholarship," *Journalism Quarterly* 56/1 (Spring 1979): 9–17; David Mark Chalmers, *The Social and Political Ideas of the Muckrakers* (New

muckrakers often used proselytizing or prophetic language to push for a more humane and sometimes radically Christian social order.[9]

Scholars most often credit Theodore Roosevelt, a friend of the Social Gospel leaders, for coining the term "muckraking" when he compared the investigative journalism of the Progressive Era to the "muck-raker" in *Pilgrim's Progress,* who was so focused on "raking the muck" that he failed to see the crown he was being offered.[10] Traditionally, scholars have limited the muckraking period to the early 1900s and focused on the work produced by the *McClure's Magazine* team of Ida Tarbell, Lincoln Steffens, and Ray Stannard Baker. However, a growing number of scholars have pushed back on this narrow definition, noting that investigative work started as early as the 1840s, developed during the New Journalism of the 1880s and 1890s, and continues on through today.[11]

Exposure literature flourished over the turn of the nineteenth and twentieth centuries, as a steady stream of reform literature, magazine articles, and newspaper reports identified various social ills, such as overcrowded tenements, dangerous factory conditions, the underhanded business practices of trusts, child labor problems, and tainted food. The *McClure's* team, particularly Tarbell and Baker, were known for meticulously report-

---

York: Citadel Press, 1964); Louis Filler, *Crusaders for American Liberalism* (New York: Collier Books, 1961); Richard Hofstadter, *The Age of Reform: From Bryan to F.D.R.* (New York: Vintage Books, 1955), 186–210. The same debate exists about Progressive reforms et large, see Sean Dennis Cashman, *America in the Age of the Titans: The Progressive Era and World War I* (New York: New York University Press, 1988); John Whiteclay Chambers, *The Tyranny of Change: America in the Progressive Era, 1890–1920* (New Brunswick, NJ: Rutgers University Press, 1992); Lewis Gould, *America in the Progressive Era, 1890–1914* (Harlow, UK: Pearson Education Limited, 2001); Janette Thomas Greenwood, *The Gilded Age: A History in Documents* (New York: Oxford University Press, 2003).

[9] Underwood, *From Yahweh to Yahoo!: The Religious Roots of the Secular Press* (Urbana: University of Illinois Press, 2002), 76–87; Chalmers illustrates this point across *Social and Political Ideas of the Muckrakers.*

[10] Donald K. Gorrell, *The Age of Social Responsibility: The Social Gospel in the Progressive Era 1900–1920* (Macon, GA: Mercer University Press, 1988), 36.

[11] See Stein, "American Muckrakers"; Roy J. Harris Jr., *Pulitzer's Gold: Behind the Prize for Public Service Journalism,* revised edition (Columbia, MO: University of Missouri Press, 2010); Jon Marshall, *Watergate's Legacy and the Press: The Investigative Impulse* (Evanston, IL: Northwestern University Press, 2011).

ing their stories. Other muckrakers focused on the more salacious details and were sometimes loose with facts. Outrage drove the muckrakers. Like contemporary reporters, they believed that if they exposed the depth of the problem, the public would demand change. Whereas some muckrakers tried to restrain their activism to focus on the facts, others turned their exposés into crusades.[12] Social reformers and politicians, including Roosevelt, used the journalistic findings in their campaigns for industrial regulation, social legislation, and housing projects.[13]

A few historians, principally Bruce J. Evensen, Ronald R. Rodgers, and Underwood, have acknowledged how Social Gospel leaders influenced key muckrakers and helped fuel Progressive reforms.[14] Historian Donald Gorrell has described muckrakers and Social Gospelers as kindred spirits:

> Muckrakers worked with a sensitive social conscience that was essentially Protestant as well as middle class in its morality. Using such words as sin, greed, guilt, salvation, righteousness, and soul in their descriptions of the flaws they discerned in society, these writers expressed an evangelical understanding of human nature.... The muck-

---

[12] Robert Miraldi, *Muckraking and Objectivity: Journalism's Colliding Traditions* (New York: Praeger, 1990); Miraldi, *The Pen Is Mightier: The Muckraking Life of Charles Edward Russell* (New York: Palgrave Macmillan, 2003).

[13] Chalmers, *Social and Political Ideas of the Muckrakers*; Christopher B. Daly, *Covering America: A Narrative History of a Nation's Journalism* (Amherst: University of Massachusetts Press, 2013), 143–48; Hofstadter, *Age of Reform*, 186–210; Frank Luther Mott, *American Journalism: A History, 1690–1960* (Macmillan, 1962), 575–76; Rodger Streitmatter, *Mightier than the Sword: How the News Media Have Shaped American History* (Boulder, CO: Westview Press, 2012), 83–92.

[14] Bruce J. Evensen, "The Evangelical Origins of Muckracking" in W. David Sloan, *The Media and Religion in American History* (Northport, AL: Vision Press, 2000), 186–205; Ronald R. Rodgers, "The Social Gospel and the News," *Journalism & Communication Monographs* 13/ 2 (20 June 2011): 69–134; Ronald R. Rodgers "The Press, Pulpit and Public Opinion: The Clergy's Conferral of Power and the Concomitant Call for a Journalism of Advocacy in an Age of Reform," *Journal of Media and Religion* 9/ 1 (2010): 1–18; Doug Underwood, "Transcending the News: Religious Ambivalence among the Famous Journalist-Literary Figures and Literature as the Uncertain Path to Immortality," *Journal of Media and Religion* 6/4 (2007): 249–50; Doug Underwood, "Religion in Print Media" in *The Oxford Handbook of Religion and the American News Media*, ed. Diane Winston (New York: Oxford University Press: 2012), 122–23.

> rakers sought to stimulate public conscience by appealing to personal morality, with the expectation that citizens would act morally when informed of the evil conditions in their environment. Leaders of the Social Gospel movement recognized their kinship with those ideas and drew heavily on the data uncovered by the muckrakers.... In turn, muckrakers evidenced the influence of social-gospel advocates in developing their own values, even though a number abandoned the organized church.[15]

Underwood documents the evangelical roots of key muckrakers, such as Tarbell's girlhood conversion on a Methodist mourners' bench, Steffens's Methodist upbringing, and Baker's Presbyterian roots.[16] Underwood also notes that the social-political world of the muckrakers was steeped in an evangelical mindset. Decades of nonstop revivals developed alongside and intermingled with Populist and Progressive reform movements to address the issues caused by rapid industrialization, urbanization, and immigration in the late nineteenth century. Underwood writes:

> In claiming Jesus as their greatest antecedent, the muckrakers preached a fiery brand of reform politics that was known then as the social gospel. Drawing largely from the Sermon on the Mount (Matthew 5–7) and the radical social elements in Jesus' teachings, the muckrakers distilled the Christian message into a reform agenda that denounced moral corruption, worldly excess, social inequality, exploitation of the poor, and inhuman treatment of any kind. Inspired by the Hebrew prophets, the muckrakers held up the prophetic strain in Christianity as the proper model for dealing with the failings of the social order.[17]

Following the lead of earlier abolitionists, most evangelical Social Gospel leaders in the United States and Great Britain edited or contributed to religious and secular newspapers as part of their reform efforts, starting with Frederick Denison Maurice's Christian Socialist newspaper *Politics for the People* for English dockworkers in the 1840s and continuing through Lyman Abbott's *The Outlook* in the US in the early 1920s. Rauschenbusch's paper was inspired by Maurice's publications and by the work of William

---

[15] Gorrell, *Age of Social Responsibility*, 37.
[16] Underwood, *From Yahweh to Yahoo*, 76–77.
[17] Ibid.

Dwight Porter Bliss, who published the Christian Socialist paper *The Dawn* in the 1890s and later contributed to Josiah Strong's *The Gospel of the Kingdom.* Strong edited three periodicals over the last seventeen years of his life, all dedicated to social reform. Congregationalists Washington Gladden and Lyman Abbott balanced their ministerial work with regular journalism work, primarily in *The Outlook.*

In Britain, where reform movements, exposure literature, and Social Christianity developed earlier, Congregationalist W. T. Stead, author of the Social Gospel book *If Christ Came to Chicago*, went to jail while he was editor of the *Pall Mall Gazette* for his series exposing child prostitution. Hugh Price Hughes tirelessly produced the weekly newspaper *The Methodist Times: A Journal of Religious and Social Movement* from 1885 until his sudden death in 1902. Robert William Dale, known for promoting the Civic Gospel in Birmingham, used the pages of *The Congregationalist* to fight for universal education and the religious liberty of nonconformists. Anglicans Henry Scott Holland, founder of the Christian Social Union, and Stewart Headlam, founder of the more liberally Socialist Guild of St. Matthew, also wrote for and edited newspapers to promote social reform.

Save for a few like Stead, Social Gospelers rarely did the kind of hands-on investigative work as Tarbell or Baker, and none pretended to be objective or unbiased in their arguments. However, Social Gospelers did significant research on social issues and their causes and brought these issues to their religious readers to take action.[18] Furthermore, they promoted solutions using pragmatic arguments, theological reasoning, and a prophetic vision of the kingdom of God, which gave a spiritual impulse to their calls for reform that helped undergird secular reform efforts. If the muckrakers were the "press agents for the Progressive era" as Andrew and Lila Weinberg argue, the Social Gospelers were the spiritual foundation that made muckraking and the Progressive movement possible.[19] This essay is part of an ongoing study looking at Social Gospel journalism work in the United States and Great Britain, and includes both quantitative and qualitative analysis of *For the Right.* The qualitative analysis is my own, but the quantitative coding is thanks to my graduate assistant Falon Opsahl.

---

[18] Rodgers, "The Social Gospel and the News," 91; Rodgers, "The Press, Pulpit and Public Opinion," 5.

[19] Weinberg, *Muckrakers*, xviii.

WALTER RAUSCHENBUSCH

Beyond *Christianity and the Social Crisis*, Walter Rauschenbusch was a player in the creation of the Federal Council of Churches of Christ's Social Creed in 1908, wrote *Christianizing the Social Order* in 1912, and gave theological weight to the movement with his 1917 *Theology for the Social Gospel.*[20] Rauschenbusch grew up in a family embedded in the quiet piety of their German fatherland, the democratic values of their adopted homeland, and the conservative, traditional, individualistic theology of the Baptists of the Northern states. Rauschenbusch became pastor at the Second German Baptist Church in one of the most impoverished areas of New York. It was working and living at West 45th Street and Tenth Avenue that opened Rauschenbusch's heart to social ills. Rauschenbusch's German Baptist church was almost solely made up of working-class immigrants, as seen in the marriage rosters he kept.[21] Surrounded by crowded tenements and factories and ministering to German immigrants in the city that had been the first home of his own father, personal contact with the worst social ills of urbanization and immigration transformed him: "When I saw how men toiled all their life long, hard, toilsome lives, and at the end had almost nothing to show for it; how strong men begged for work and could not get it in the hard times; how little children died—oh, the children's funerals! they gripped my heart—that was one of the things I always went away thinking about—why did the children have to die?"[22]

Speaking to a crowd in Cleveland, Rauschenbusch shared his struggle with how to unite his personal religion with his new social outlook. Baptist teaching seemed to focus on the individual sinner, the soul and not the man. He desired a faith that united the two, "a holistic Christianity that served the spiritual, physical, emotional and intellectual needs of man."[23]

---

[20] Biography consolidated from Minus, *American Reformer*; Evans, *The Kingdom Is Always but Coming*, American National Biography, archival research. Some of this basic biographical material appears in Christina Littlefield, *Chosen Nations: Pursuit of the Kingdom of God and Its Influence on Late Nineteenth Century Britain and the United States* (Minneapolis, MN: Fortress Press, 2013).

[21] Rauschenbusch marriage rosters (Box 97, Rauschenbusch Family Collections, ABHS).

[22] Rauschenbusch, "Cleveland Kingdom of God Reminiscence," 2 January 1913 (Box 39, Rauschenbusch Family Collections, ABHS).

[23] Ibid.

He found that in the concept of the kingdom of God, an idea he had been contemplating since his days at the German gymnasium before seminary.[24] This concept made God the center and inspiration for all social reform and helped people to live in righteousness and bring their society into righteous living.[25] While he did not publish his views widely until 1907, they were developed in the 1880s and 1890s in articles and can be seen in his *For the Right* newspaper.

FOR THE RIGHT

Convicted by the ills he saw in the city, and convinced Christianity could provide the moral vision needed to correct the course, Walter Rauschenbusch first wrote on the "social question," as it was then called, in a paper on Henry George read privately to friends in 1887. Biographer Paul Minus has noted that Rauschenbusch's "gentle muckraking" continued with a sorrowful tale of an employer denying a tailor the time off to visit his dying daughter, asking middle-class readers to see the misery beneath the surface.[26] This was the only time Rauschenbusch failed to put his name on his work, publishing it only as a "New York Pastor."

Such gentle muckraking would be the norm when Rauschenbusch gained the courage to launch *For the Right* with his close friend Leighton Williams in October 1889. Williams was a minister at Amity Baptist Church and a steady student of social issues who attended Columbia University with classmate Richard Ely, according to the *New York Times* write up of their newspaper.[27] Their inspiration came from Frederick Denison Maurice, a British Christian Socialist Rauschenbusch and Williams were reading, and a meeting with William Bliss at a conference in Boston in May.[28]

Like most of the British and American Social Gospel thinkers, Maurice's work deeply influenced Bliss and Rauschenbusch. In Maurice's *King-*

---

[24] Minus, *American Reformer*, 51.

[25] For more on Social Gospel theology, see Littlefield, "Chosen Nations," chapter 3, and William H. Brackney, "Theological Introduction" to volume III, *Walter Rauschenbusch: Published Works and Selected Writings.*

[26] Minus, *American Reformer*, 65.

[27] "Clergymen Who Are Socialist."

[28] Evans, *Kingdom Is Always but Coming*, 83–84, Minus, *American Reformer*, 66–67.

dom of Christ and his *Social Morality*, one finds the roots of Social Gospel theology, with its emphasis on the incarnation, the fatherhood of God and the brotherhood of all men, and the Kingdom of God. [29] Maurice's work on a short-lived paper for London dockworkers likely inspired Bliss and Rauschenbusch's newspaper work. *Politics for the People* ran weekly for seventeen issues from March 5 through July 29, 1848, responding to the Chartist crisis in Great Britain.[30] When Bliss and Rauschenbusch met, Bliss had just launched his own periodical, *The Dawn*, which ran from May 1889 to March 1896.[31] In addition to leading the American branch of the Society of Christian Socialists, Bliss had also been a major advocate in the Episcopal Church's development of the Church Association for the Advancement of the Interests of Labor (CAIL) in 1887, which promoted church interest in the issues facing working men and in advocating for arbitration in labor disputes.[32]

Their main benefactress was New York philanthropist and social reformer Grace Hoadley Dodge. Winthrop Hudson has noted that Dodge's family of merchants regularly funded evangelical causes and that most of their money came from the mining firm of Phelps, Dodge and Co., Dodge went on to become president of the national board of the YWCA and founded working girls' clubs and Columbia University's Teacher's College. [33] Rauschenbusch and Williams recruited fellow Baptist pastor J. E. Raymond, of Fordham, New York, who the *New York Times* described as near-

---

[29] Maurice, *The Kingdom of Christ: Or, Hints on the Principles, Ordinances, and Constitution of the Catholic Church in Letters to a Member of the Society of Friends* (London: Darton and Clark, 1838), I: 41, 55, 56; Vol. 2, 295; Maurice, *Social Morality: Twenty-One Lectures Delivered in the University of Cambridge* (London: Macmillan, 1869).

[30] *Politics for the People* (London: John S. Parker, West Strand).

[31] William Dwight Porter Bliss, *The Dawn: A Journal of Christian Socialism* (Boston, MA: Society of Christian Socialists, 1889–1896).

[32] Evans, *The Kingdom Is Always but Coming*, 83–84.

[33] See Winthrop S. Hudson, *Walter Rauschenbusch: Selected Writings* (New York: Paulist Press, 1984), 19; "Laud Miss Dodge as Girls Friend, "TimesMachine: February 10, 1915 - NYTimes.com," accessed 27 May 2018, https://timesmachine.nytimes.com/timesmachine/1915/02/10/100138361.html?pageNumber=5 and "Grace Hodge Dead; Noted for Charities," "TimesMachine: 28 December 1914 - NYTimes.com," accessed 27 May 2018, https://timesmachine.nytimes.com/timesmachine/1914/12/28/100129483.html?pageNumber=9.

er "the heart and purpose of the wage earner than any other clergyman in the city." Raymond served as business manager and coeditor with Rauschenbusch, Williams, and Elizabeth Post. Little is known about Post, who served as managing editor. Hudson noted that she may have been related to reformer and journalist Louis Freeland Post.[34] She would have been an older contemporary of the famous etiquette maven Emily Post, but there is no relation.

For the Right's November 1889 issue opens with a notice from Raymond that declared their Christian Socialist viewpoint, their desire to serve workers, and explained the choice of title:

> This paper is published in the interests of the working people of New York City. It proposes to discuss, from the standpoint of Christian-socialism, such questions as engage their attention and affect their life. The paper is not the organ of any party or association whatever. Nor has it any new theories to propound. Its aim is to reflect in its pages the needs, the aspirations, the longings of the tens of thousands of wage-earners who are sighing for better things; and to point out, if possible, not only the wrongs that men suffer, but the methods by which these wrongs may be removed. The editors freely give their time and labor to this undertaking, animated solely by the hope that their efforts may aid the advancement of that kingdom in which wrong shall have no place, but Right shall reign for ever more.[35]

Raymond also immediately invited submissions from "friends of social reform" and "wage earners" and offered commissions for those who brought in subscribers. The January 1890 edition advertised a 10-cent commission on every 50-cent annual subscription. When a mocker, early on, questioned whether the editors thought they could reform society with their little paper, they replied that

> far be it from us to attempt what greater men have failed to do. But we do aim to point out the wrongs that men suffer, and the methods by which these wrongs may be righted: to say a word now and then to the toiler along the high-way of life that will make life seem

---

[34] See Hudson, *Walter Rauschenbusch*, 19.

[35] J. E. Raymond, *For the Right*, November 1899. The American Baptist Historical Society collection starts with issue number 2.

> brighter, and the world better: to put our hands under the burdens that men bear, and let the love of our hearts go out towards them, and prove to them there is a spirit in the world which is not of the devil.[36]

Though *For the Right* claimed to come from a viewpoint of Christian Socialism, it was of the modified yes/no variety of Socialism Rauschenbusch promoted in a later journal article entitled "The Ideals of Social Reformers." Rauschenbusch's Socialism was of the gas and water variety, he wanted to see all natural resources, public utilities, and transportation in the hands of the public. But he was also deeply critical of Socialism's denunciation of Christianity, its denigration of democratic values and erosion of the family.[37] Both Rauschenbusch and Williams joined the Society of Christian Socialists in February 1890, and Williams became vice president. The editors believed Christian Socialism entailed cooperative businesses and trade unions, insurance societies and fraternal brotherhood in all relations, but also government ownership of utilities and transportation companies, and the building of city facilities such as roads, bridges, parks, libraries, galleries, prisons, courts, and legislatures. They did not support the full government takeover of all private industry.[38] They regular supported cooperative efforts, including homemakers rallying together to buy needed food. The writings of economist Henry George and Italian activist Giuseppe Mazzini were often reprinted in the paper, both heroes to Rauschenbusch.

Rauschenbusch also glorified the utopian vision of Edward Bellamy's book *Looking Backward*, which described an ideal Socialist society 100 years in the future, where all people have their needs met and equal opportunities. In the clip reprinted in *For the Right*, Bellamy compared nineteenth-century individualism as being individual umbrellas over people's heads, while in the twentieth-century there are sidewalk awnings that protect everyone's head.[39] In March 1890, Rauschenbusch advised readers to read Bellamy and the Gospel of Luke and judge for themselves "what our master

---

[36] *For the Right*, December 1889, 1.

[37] Rauschenbusch, "The Ideals of Social Reformers," *American Journal of Sociology* 2 (July 1896): 217–18; (Kingdom of God pamphlets, ABHS, Atlanta, Georgia).

[38] Williams, *For the Right*, March 1890, 2.

[39] Edward Bellamy, *For the Right*, January 1890, 8

had to say about these things."[40] In May 1890, Rauschenbusch wrote about the suffering in Russia and prayed for Czar Alexander's abdication to end the suffering of his people, noting that the American Revolution would have been crushed without the rights of a free press and the rights to assemble.[41]

In June 1890, responding to a reader question about the paper's intent, the editors responded theologically that they were New Testament Christians. They boiled their answer down in July 1890 to three "simple articles of faith": "The existence of God, the atonement of Jesus Christ, and the unity of the human race. Upon the first we base our hope of the world's future happiness; upon the second we rest our assurance of the ultimate victory over sin, and the third is the ground of our expectation that a day is coming when the brotherhood of man will no longer be a mere term on the lips of social reformers."[42]

As social reformers, they looked for "the improvement of society and the readjustment of human relations in conformity to the teachings of Jesus."[43]

Rauschenbusch argued the paper was distinct in its attempt to try to balance both personal regeneration and societal regeneration. He and his fellow editors differed from secular Socialists because they believed greater material equality mattered little if people didn't also have personal morality and a spiritual foundation in God. "Only if the number of such God-conquered souls is great and increasing in any nation, will the progress of that nation in material wealth be of a real benefit to the people!," Rauschenbusch wrote in August 1890.[44] But they differed from Christians who focused solely on individual morality because they believed social wrongs had to be righted alongside evangelical efforts, that good institutions bred good men. "This is essentially a function of those who profess to know and love God's will, and we raise the charge of negligence and sloth against the church of God in suffering injustice to be incorporated in the very construction of society."[45] The December 1890 front-page editorials affirmed that

---

[40] Rauschenbusch, *For the Right,* April 1890, 3.
[41] Ibid., May 1890, 2.
[42] *For the Right,* July 1890, 1.
[43] *For the Right,* June 1890, 1.
[44] *For the Right,* August 1890, 2
[45] Ibid.

personal regeneration was first and foremost for the paper's editors, but that Christianity was the only effective remedy for modern ills. The January 1891 front page affirmed that one had to work at both personal and societal regeneration simultaneously because "neither is possible without the other."[46]

The paper promoted many of the same concepts, though in simpler form, that Rauschenbusch elaborated on nearly two decades later in *Christianity and the Social Crisis.* The paper was the first laboratory for his ideas and helped shape his thought on many of the social issues he addressed later in his books. Throughout the paper, the editors established their base for reform in the teachings of Jesus, who they believed taught that the social system was out of order.[47] They covered labor rights, natural and unnatural monopolies, trade tariffs, unearned income, property tax, workplace injuries, sweatshops, domestic servants, and public ownership of utilities and transit. They also addressed the problem of adulterated food, poor nutrition, and the saloon problem. The editors promoted the rights of women to vote, because they knew that women would do far more to help defeat the evils facing their homes than men.[48] They believed wholeheartedly in democracy and believed that every individual should have the basic comforts and the opportunity to pursue success in life.

Rauschenbusch wrote twenty-seven articles over the seventeen issues of *For the Right.* Like many of his fellow Social Gospelers, Rauschenbusch's editorials were twice as likely to be pragmatic in tone than theological. Only five interweaved both pragmatic and theological arguments. The paper intermixed editorials and letters with stories and poems that attempted to make a point on social reform, such as Rauschenbusch's story of the three miners trying to fix a smoking stove. The successful miner got at the root of the problem, rather than trying to treat the symptoms. Similarly, Christians needed to get at the root of the social problems.[49] In the following issues, he attacked possible crow's nests that were stopping up the stove on social problems, such as the unjust distribution of money, and looked for solutions, such as Henry George's proposed single tax.[50] Several readers wrote in

[46] *For the Right*, January 1891, 1.

[47] *For the Right*, November 1889; 1–2, August 1890, 1.

[48] *For the Right*, December 1889, 2.

[49] *For the Right*, November 1889, 2–3.

[50] Rauschenbusch, *For the Right*, February 1890, 2–3.

over multiple issues to give their own takes on what the crow's nest was and offer possible solutions, which led to a back-and-forth between Rauschenbusch and readers.

Comparing *For the Right* to its inspirations, quantitative coding showed that *Politics for the People*, responding as it was to the Chartist movement, emphasized voting rights and issues surrounding poverty almost equally, as well as class stratification, the need for fair wages, government corruption, and general morality. The paper addressed Socialism but not as its dominant theme. Defending Christian Socialism dominated every issue of Bliss's *The Dawn*, with fair wages coming second, followed by equal attention to church responsibility for social issues, working hours, housing, and morality questions. *For the Right* addressed fair wages the most, followed by almost equal time spent on morality questions, access to food, and women's labor. Coming third in importance were equality issues, Christian Socialism, church responsibility, the family, and the cost of rent.

In *For the Right*, Rauschenbusch focused on the need for democratic values and greater equality in American society. In September 1890, he argued that God's full vision for equality had not been reached in America, that Americans needed political and social equality, and that political freedom was the means to end class privileges. "Wherever selfishness has been incorporated in laws and customs; wherever the property of all is being appropriated by the few; there the ballot, the political power of the people, should be applied in the cause of justice."[51] In December 1890, Rauschenbusch argued that churches had lost sight of the fact that Jesus was a working man who lived amongst the common people. He called working people back to the true faith of Christ and challenged churches to drop their worldly airs: "It is possible for any workingman to begin right now the life of a true disciple of Jesus Christ, and to get others to join him in it. Christ is still the Christ of the common people, and if some have made Christianity an aristocratic religion, let us go back to Christ himself and make it once more a democratic religion."[52]

In speaking up for an eight-hour workday, Rauschenbusch sounded middle-class alarm bells that such moderate reforms were needed to stave off revolution:

---

[51] Rauschenbusch, *For the Right*, September 1890, 2.
[52] Rauschenbusch, *For the Right*, December 1890, 4.

> The great and powerful are probably rejoicing because they once more succeed in stifling the voice of the poor. But they are only sealing their own doom. The only safety lies in justice and mercy. If they would hear the voice of God in the voice of the people and surrender to the labourer the hire which is by fraud kept back, there need be no fear of violence or revolution. But if they refuse to harken, and the evil becomes intolerable, then it is they who have brought disaster on their country and destruction upon themselves.[53]

Earlier, in answer to a critic who said the paper was stirring up discontent, the editors insisted they were exposing the social agitation going on all around.[54]

Most editorials, by Rauschenbusch or the other writers, included some kind of call to action for Christians to follow. Rarely, however, did this include legislation. Rauschenbusch directly called for ballot reform in March 1890, for a change to the parcel post in May 1890, and for eight-hour workdays in June 1890. He called for public rapid transit in New York in February 1890 and for railroads to be become publicly owned. Williams called for public ownership of certain lands and natural resources in July 1890 and more direct representation of citizens on the city legislature in November 1890.

More often, the paper included personal calls to action. Beyond telling people to get to the root of social problems, Rauschenbusch invited readers to investigate Christian Socialism in April 1890, entreated readers to make Christianity a religion of the common people in December 1890, and argued for churches to avoid government funding in January 1891. John Raymond promoted training schools for domestic servants in December 1889, attacked industrial slavery in March 1890, urged readers to focus on Jesus and reform would follow in May 1890, argued for abolishing saloons to abolish poverty in June 1890, and critiqued selfishness and urged following Christ's sacrificial example in March 1891. Grace Dodge and Elizabeth Post mostly promoted personal morality among individuals and in the home. The September 1890 edition urged people to action by helping support the paper, among other steps: "How many readers of For the Right are doing any work in the good cause? Have you tried to make any converts? Have you given your papers to others? Have you asked any one to sub-

---

[53] Rauschenbusch, *For the Right*, June 1890, 3.
[54] *For the Right*, March 1890, 1.

scribe? Have you ever prayed to God to let His Kingdom come on earth and to make use of you in making it come?"[55]

The editors helped launch an investigation into problems with women's and children's work in retail stores, bringing pressure to bear on the store owners and supporting a boycott of stores that persisted in the ill treatment of employees. Problems included excessive, unpaid hours, inadequate wages, unsanitary and unwholesome conditions, and excessive fines for mistakes or tardiness, Williams wrote, demanding immediate change: "A temperate, industrious, God-fearing people cannot be enslaved or kept down."[56] The work helped launch the Consumer's League and public lobbying of the New York State Legislature to place retail establishments under surveillance via the factory law.[57]

Almost a year into the paper, editors explained in an unsigned editorial in September 1890 why there weren't many calls for legislation:

> If it were possible to get men to vote for right things, we would believe in the ballot as a means of social reform. But at present the most that can be expected from a political movement is a temporary purification of the local government. So soon as the wave of reformation has passed over, the old order will establish itself again. Our hope, our only hope, is in the education, in the enlightenment of the public conscience by a patient, persistent promulgation of the moral law, and the application of that law to the life of the individual, the home, the community and the State.[58]

This lack of political advocacy isn't surprising given that Social Gospel calls for legislation grew exponentially with the advent of the Federal Council of Churches of Christ's Social Creed in 1908 and peaked with the revised version of 1912, when President Woodrow Wilson signed some of their goals into law.[59]

The paper has been called paternalistic and patronizing, and there is certainly evidence to justify that consensus, such as the regular use of stories

---

[55] *For the Right*, September 1890, 1

[56] Williams, *For the Right*, March 1890, 4–5. See also Grace H. Dodge, February 1890, 5–6, Williams, May 1890, Lizzie C. Fennimore, May 1890, 4.

[57] Williams, *For the Right*, February 1891, 3.

[58] *For the Right*, September 1890, 1.

[59] Gorrell, *Age of Social Responsibility*, 257, Cashman, *American in the Age of the Titans*, 125–31; Chambers, *Tyranny of Change*, 197, Gould, *Progressive Era*, 77.

that knock one over the head with their unhidden meaning or the clearly Socialistic serial Jericho Road.[60] A November 1889 front-page editorial eagerly sought out the views of working people, noting that the paper's intention was not to serve as preachers or teachers but to explore social questions in "hearty sympathy" with all who toil.[61] However, in October 1890, a front-page editorial explained that *For the Right* was here to stay, but was moving slowly because they were trying to "teach men." It is unclear which men they meant—the working men initially targeted or the clergymen or middle-class Christians more likely reading the paper. Whichever audience, they did not think their readers were ready for the whole truth. The majority of the people were "just beginning to think" about social problems, so they must state their "principles carefully and gradually."[62] Moreover, they did not have answers to all of the social evils "under the sun."[63]

Rauschenbusch biographer Christopher Evans has argued that *For the Right* was likely undercut by a growing American labor movement that increasingly felt alienated by pastors who meant well but knew little about the day-to-day realities laboring people faced.[64] The editors did criticize the labor movements for squabbling over small matters, particularly an August 1890 meeting of forty labor organizations that could not agree on anything.[65] Rauschenbusch and Williams declared that the only hope was propaganda, that is, moral education and the uplifting of society to live by new Christian principles of love and brotherhood and service.[66] Some of the articles, more by Raymond, Dodge, or Post, promote the mythos of the Protestant work ethic in ways that can be seen as diminishing the hardship many suffered in factories and mining jobs.[67] The editors were combating what they saw as a growing belittlement of work that fueled discontent. Given the wealth they could see in New York, the working class often dreamed of riches and luxury and diminished the value of their own jobs. In

---

[60] Evans, *The Kingdom Is Always but Coming*, 87–88.

[61] *For the Right*, November 1889, 1.

[62] *For the Right*, October 1890, 1.

[63] Ibid., 1.

[64] Evans, Kingdom Is Always but Coming, 88.

[65] *For the Right*, August 1890, 1.

[66] *For the Right*, September 1890, 1–2;

[67] Raymond, *For the Right*, November 1899, 3–4; Dodge, *For the Right*, February 1890, 4.

promoting the dignity of labor, the editors saw themselves as protecting workers from themselves as much as the elite.

There's no doubt that the paper was maternalistic. The most condescending articles were Post's "Charming Home" series, which addressed the need to improve the home life of workers in New York City but failed to understand the conditions of tenement life. She wrote about the importance of making the home cheerful, bright, and clean, to make one's kitchen "the sweetest place on earth."[68] For families whose kitchen was but a four-by-four-foot room that doubled as dining room, laundry room, bathing facility, and often workplace for home clothing sweatshops, the idea of ever being able to make it cheerful and bright could appear to be a cruel joke. Likely, it was also never read by those homemakers most in need—and in want—of advice. Post left the paper in January 1891, allegedly because she felt it was becoming too radical.[69]

Williams and Rauschenbusch worked and lived among working people in their respective churches, and one can see their sincerity in wanting to make the paper a "people's paper: one that shall express their best sentiments, their highest thoughts, their truest aspirations, and their sincerest opinions on all matters of a practical, social, literary, or religious significance."[70] They deserve credit for trying and being among the few in those early days trying to bring attention to the needs of the working people. It's an anthropological question of whether people raised outside of a culture can ever truly write as an insider—having had middle-class childhoods and benefited from higher education, could Williams and Rauschenbusch ever have come across as anything other than outsiders. They believed however, that they could stimulate workers to help themselves, as seen in the January 1890 edition: "We can help you, but we cannot do it for you. Read For the Right. It will help you to understand one thing after the other."[71]

They also believed that by promoting the ideas of Christian Socialism, they were paving the way for reform work. For instance, they believed a successful carpenter's strike that secured an eight-hour day was aided by a worldwide movement spreading the need for labor rights and the sense that

---

[68] Post, *For the Right*, November 1889, 4.

[69] Evans, *The Kingdom Is Always but Coming*, 85.

[70] *For the Right*, November 1889, 1.

[71] Rauschenbusch, *For the Right*, January 1890, 4

workers weren't getting their fair share. People laugh at *Looking Back*, *Progress and Poverty*, *For the Right*, and "call it all talk," Rauschenbusch wrote:

> But this talk and this dreaming is working in the hearts of men as the yeast works in the baker's dough. Little by little men learn and understand. They begin to hope and expect and work. And when the time comes to take a step forward, men are ready for it, and those who would like to hinder, dare not. Take courage. If you can do nothing now but talking and spreading ideas, do that. Ideas are more powerful than dynamite, and a thousand times more helpful. They not only destroy, but build up.[72]

The paper lasted eighteen months. The publishers commenced on an optimistic tone, telling readers in page-one editorial notes in February 1890 that they aimed to gain 5,000 readers throughout New York. By July 1890, they were dreaming of raising $5,000 for a model club house. They announced in August 1890 that they would soon be able to enlarge the paper and were planning a special edition for October 1890. The August 1890 and September 1890 editions called for contributions to send out 2,000 free copies of the October issue to clergymen, which the October issue indicated happened. But the paper hit bumps early on. They went through three printers, changing in February 1890 because the printer kept delaying their delivery, and in May 1890 because the printer messed up several pages, including printing an early draft of the principles for the Society of Christian Socialists. It managed to sell a few pages of advertising each month.

Christopher Evans has reported that *For the Right* never enlisted more than 200 subscribers.[73] Gary Dorrien, in the second of his three-volume *The Making of American Liberal Theology*, argued that it was "too radical for most of its desired audience and too Christian for disaffected workers who were already radicalized."[74] It is unclear how many readers were from its target audience.[75] The paper did receive several letters over the first year in

[72] Rauschenbusch, *For the Right*, June 1890, 3.

[73] Evans, *The Kingdom Is Always but Coming*, 88. His source is unclear. The paper does not list the circulation anywhere.

[74] Gary Dorrien, *The Making of American Liberal Theology: Idealism, Realism and Modernity, 1900–1950* (Louisville, KY: Westminster John Knox Press, 2003), 87.

[75] January 1890 issue notes thirty-four subscribers from one factory.

response to Rauschenbusch's "Crow's Nest" series, and a few came from working men and women.

For the Right ended abruptly in March 1891, right in the middle of Henry Holman's Jericho Road serial about the downfall of one middle-class family due to illness. Trouble had been brewing—the January issue was smaller and didn't include Post's "Charming Home" column. Suddenly, whereas Post, Raymond, Rauschenbusch, and Williams had all been listed as editors, the February issue listed only Raymond as editor and Williams as business manager. February's front-page notes indicated that the personnel changes occurred in January and were responsible for the shortened paper. The editors also offered a special deal that month to get the rest of the year's subscription for only 25 cents—half the usual rate. In the last edition, editors requested $200 in donations to help expand the paper's circulation and indicated that the Jericho Road serial would continue for three to four more issues. Rauschenbusch's editorials appeared through the final issue, which announced he was *en route* to a sabbatical in Germany and that he would publish articles from abroad. He was seeking a cure for a roaring in his ears after a flu virus left him mostly deaf.[76]

One of Rauschenbusch's last contributions is titled "The Railroads and the Press," where he critiqued the New York *Daily Recorder* for possibly being a railroad organ. For him, this is another example of big corporate money foiling the will of the people by using the press to mislead people. But he also notes in the piece the power of the press to influence public opinion and the "tremendous power" of public opinion itself. He affirmed both the need to nationalize the railroads and that *For the Right* was on the winning side:

> Men say to us: You do nothing but talk. It is true; but when we talk, we do something. The people who back the *Recorder* know what talk is worth. Will not the people for whom *For the Right* works comprehend it also? *The Recorder* has money to back it. We have only our brains and the love of our friends. *The Recorder* blows a big steam whistle. We have only our fingers to whistle on. But we are on the winning side, for we are on the side of God and the people. Let who will be on the side of Mammon and the classes.[77]

---

[76] Minus, *American Reformer*, 76.

[77] Rauschenbusch, *For the Right*, March 1891, 4.

A final editorial from Rauschenbusch that month promised readers that the kingdom of God "shall be," "with or without your help."[78] In Germany he developed the seeds of his prophetic vision of the kingdom of God.

It is unknowable how much, if at all, the failed *For the Right* helped anyone's thinking, but Rauschenbusch and Williams did add to the social-mindedness that was building in New York City and the broader Northeast. Rauschenbusch could point to reform success with *For the Right*, given the paper's success in launching a boycott of retail stores that maintained oppressive working conditions for women and children. Rauschenbusch and Williams also started the Brotherhood of the Kingdom, which was mostly an intellectual discussion group on social ills and proposed solutions. However, it morphed into local chapters that were involved in their communities' needs, such as an early campaign for children's playgrounds in New York City that used newspaper editorials to promote the cause.[79] After *For the Right* ceased publication, Rauschenbusch continued his muckraking work piecemeal, writing articles for the *Examiner* or for more intellectual journals, such as the *American Journal of Sociology*, and giving numerous papers and lectures in the year preceding his breakout book. While some of the *Examiner* pieces followed the ham-fisted sentimentality of the coalminer's stove story, such as the 1892 "Pilate's Wash Bowl," others are more powerful analyses, such as the 1894 "How Rich Do I have a Right to Be?"[80] Rauschenbusch also wrote articles in favor of the 1895 Brooklyn Street Car strikers and to attack the dangers of premillennial thinking in 1896.[81]

Rauschenbusch's deafness made serving as a pastor gradually impossible. He took over the Rochester Theological Seminary German Department

---

[78] Ibid., 6.

[79] See Brotherhood of the Kingdom Pamphlets (Rauschenbusch Family Collection, ABHS); specifically, Williams, No. 11, "Municipal Reform: The Need of a Positive Program." The Brotherhood successfully petitioned the New York's Park Commissioners to set aside several sand piles for children to play in, "Sand Piles for the Children," *New York Herald*, January 1896); Rauschenbusch, "Playgrounds for the Children," *Examiner*, 18 August 1892 (Minus, Paul RG-1478. Boxes 1–12, Rauschenbusch Family Collection, ABHS).

[80] Dores Robinson Sharpe, *Walter Rauschenbusch* (New York: Macmillan Company, 1942), 98–102.

[81] Ibid., 111–15.

once administered by his father in 1897, moving to the church history department of the English Department in 1902 to focus on his "kingdom theology." He worked for local social reform in Rochester, including advocating for public takeover of utilities and doing a comprehensive survey of social needs for the YMCA. Publication of *Christianity and the Social Crisis* launched Rauschenbusch into advocacy for national reform work, helping to inspire the progress of the Federal Council of Churches of Christ's Social Creed and working on various commissions and leagues to promote the work.[82] Baker called him the "prophet of the new times" in "Do It for Rochester," a 1910 *American Magazine* article highlighting religiously minded local civic reform work.[83]

Rauschenbusch continued his muckraking mission in *Christianity and the Social Crisis*, where he detailed the social problems and illustrated how they violated Christian concepts of the worth of the individual soul and of man's fellowship with his or her fellow human beings. He believed the affluent "must be made to see the human costs of the economic system that gave them their wealth."[84] In *Christianity and the Social Crisis*, Rauschenbusch described in detail how machine production revolutionized the world, creating new class divisions, killing independence and equality, dragging women and children to work, crafting modern cities around the factories, and intensifying poverty even as it created wealth. His descriptions are often littered with statistics to back up his argument, followed by emotional appeals:

> From 1760 to 1818 the population of England increased 70 percent; the poor relief increased 530 percent. Here, then, we have the incredible paradox of modern life. The instrument by which all hu-

---

[82] Rauschenbusch served as a "Social Evangelism" worker for the Federal Council of Churches of Christ Commission on the Church and Social Service, helping to lead the initial rally meetings and Bible studies to foster community action in different cities. He later served on the Social Service Commission of the Baptist World Alliance and the Northern Baptist Convention, the League for Social Service, the Men and Religion Forward Movement, and the Religious Citizenship League.

[83] Ray Stannard Baker, "Do It for Rochester," *American Magazine*, September 1910, 685.

[84] Minus, *American Reformer*, 65.

> manity could rise from want and the fear of want actually submerged a large part of the people in perpetual want and fear....[85]
>
> That such an evil turn could be given to an event that held such a power for good is a crushing demonstration that the moral forces in humanity failed to keep pace with its intellectual and economic development. Men learned to make wealth much faster than they learned to distribute it justly. Their eye for profit was keener than their ear for the voice of God and humanity. That is the great sin of modern humanity, and unless we repent, we shall perish by that sin.[86]

Walter Rauschenbusch's books document how the American pursuit of profit was disintegrating human life, and it was in large part the muckraking of *Christianity and the Social Crisis*—where he documented the ills he saw—that woke up the churches, as much as his vision for what the kingdom should look like. The Progressive Era saw a series of reforms to correct the worst excesses, protect laborers, rein in alcoholism, and extend women's rights. As Rauschenbusch later wrote, it began with only a few prophetic voices shouting in the wilderness.[87] *For the Right* helped them shout.

---

[85] Rauschenbusch, *Christianity and the Social Crisis*, 181.

[86] Ibid., 182.

[87] Rauschenbusch, *Christianizing the Social Order* (New York: The Macmillan Co., 1912), 9.

Part IV

The Largeness of the Rauschenbusch Legacy

Chapter 11

"Social Christianity's Greatest Prophet"?

Walter Rauschenbusch's Place in History

Heath W. Carter

A century after Walter Rauschenbusch's death, his name remains a kind of metonym for Social Christianity in the United States. And little wonder, given the terms in which first his contemporaries and then later interpreters framed his significance. When in 1918 Rauschenbusch died at just fifty-six years of age, Harry Ward, himself a leading Social Gospeler, declared, "When the record of these times is measured it will be found that none exercised a greater influence than he upon the development of Christian thought and action."[1] Nearly two decades later, Reinhold Niebuhr identified Rauschenbusch as "not only the real founder of social Christianity in this country but also its most brilliant and generally satisfying exponent."[2] Dores Sharpe argued in his 1942 biography that Rauschenbusch not only "changed both the emphases and the direction of American Protestantism" but also "influenced the whole Christian movement."[3]

Historians of American Christianity have largely echoed such bold characterizations. Charles Howard Hopkins identified Rauschenbusch as "Social Christianity's greatest prophet" in 1940 and succeeding decades witnessed only the slightest of variations on the theme.[4] Robert Handy called him "the leading prophet of the Social Gospel in American Protes-

---

[1] "Walter Rauschenbusch," The Social Service Bulletin in the Rauschenbusch Family Collections, Box 138, Folder 1 (American Baptist Historical Society, Atlanta, Georgia.)

[2] Quoted in Robert T. Handy, "Walter Rauschenbusch in Historical Perspective," *Baptist Quarterly* 20/7 (1964): 313.

[3] Dores Robinson Sharpe, *Walter Rauschenbusch* (New York: Macmillan Co., 1942), 402.

[4] C. Howard Hopkins, *The Rise of the Social Gospel in American Protestantism, 1865–1915* (New Haven, CT: Yale University Press, 1940), 27.

tantism," while Winthrop Hudson cast him as "the outstanding prophet of the Social Gospel."[5] Sydney Ahlstrom began the chapter on the Social Gospel in his magisterial 1972 book, *A Religious History of the American People*, with these two sentences: "When the Social Gospel movement began and when it came to a close are much disputed questions. But nearly everyone agrees that it was more fully represented by Walter Rauschenbusch than by anyone else, and that it gained classic utterance in 1907 with the publication of his *Christianity and the Social Crisis*."[6] That consensus has proven remarkably durable even in the decades since Ahlstrom's magnum opus. Martin Marty has called Rauschenbusch Social Christianity's "greatest representative," while Mark Noll has identified him as "the most important exponent of the Social Gospel."[7] Gary Dorrien argued in 2003 that "Rauschenbusch deserves his standing as the symbol and champion of American social Christianity," while just last year Christopher Evans contended, "Between 1907 and his death in 1918, Walter Rauschenbusch was the most influential prophet of the Social Gospel movement in America."[8]

I want to revisit this consensus. To be clear, I share in common with my aforementioned colleagues a sense of deep appreciation for Rauschenbusch's many sterling and far-reaching contributions. My questions have less to do with the significance of his work and more to do with the depth and breadth of American Social Christianity. So far as I can tell, this view of Rauschenbusch as not just a great but *the greatest* prophet speaks to the endurance of a venerable story, first told by the likes of Hopkins and Henry

---

[5] Robert Handy, "Walter Rauschenbusch in Historical Perspective," 1964; and Winthrop S. Hudson, *Religion in America* (New York: Charles Scribner's Sons, 1965), 313.

[6] Sydney E. Ahlstrom, *A Religious History of the American People*, 2nd edition (New Haven, CT: Yale University Press, 2004), 785.

[7] Martin E. Marty, *Pilgrims in Their Own Land: 500 Years of Religion in America* (Boston, MA: Little, Brown, and Company, 1984): 347; and Mark A. Noll, *A History of Christianity in the United States and Canada* (Grand Rapids, MI: Eerdmans, 1992), 306.

[8] Gary Dorrien, *The Making of American Liberal Theology: Idealism, Realism, & Modernity, 1900–1950* (Louisville, KY: Westminster John Knox Press, 2003), 6; Christopher H. Evans, *The Social Gospel in American Religion: A History* (New York: New York University Press, 2017), 78.

May all the way back in the 1940s and 1950s.[9] Their pioneering books gave shape to an emerging field of Social Gospel studies. That first generation conceived of Social Christianity as a heady, theological movement, a reform-minded tributary of the Protestant liberalism that came of age in the late nineteenth and early twentieth centuries. It thrived in the Progressive Era but was dealt a heavy blow by the First World War, which exposed the naiveté of its optimism; Reinhold Niebuhr and the neoorthodox theologians then went on to finish the job. Niebuhr and company could do so because, in this classic version of the story, Social Christianity was not just highly intellectual, but also unmistakably elite. Writing before the social history turn, Hopkins, May, and the rest emphasized almost exclusively the contributions of elite, white, male Protestant pastors, professors, Socialists, and social reformers. Their understanding of Social Christianity was, in fact, remarkably similar to that of the historical actors at center stage in their narratives—indeed, as I will argue, similar to the way that people like Walter Rauschenbusch conceived of it.

But as large as Rauschenbusch looms in this story, it has not, in the long run, served his legacy very well. While fifty years ago many historians of American religion located the Social Gospel near the heart of their stories, today it is relegated to the margins—and if that is the case in American religious history circles, it is all the more so in the broader American historical guild. Textbooks and survey classes mention Social Christianity only briefly, if at all. Beyond the academy, few these days have any sense of what we even mean by the phrase.

Building on a more recent generation of scholarship, including studies by many fellow scholars whose essays are in this volume, I want to suggest today that it is time for a new story, one which features a fundamentally different conceptualization. We need to start distinguishing between the early twentieth-century Social Gospel *movement*—a self-consciously Protestant and almost exclusively white male phenomenon, which prioritized formal theology and imagined churchly institutions as the leading agents of change—and a wider Social Christian *tradition*, which sprung from the grassroots in the nineteenth century and which only reached the apex of its mighty influence in the post-World War II era, with its massive, faith-infused labor and civil rights movements. This heterogeneous tradi-

[9] See Hopkins, *The Rise of the Social Gospel* and Henry F. May, *Protestant Churches and Industrial America* (New York: Harper & Brothers Publishers, 1949).

tion, which profoundly shaped not only the Progressive Era, but, in fact, much broader currents of life in the modern United States, has at its core several distinctive intuitions: first, that inequality is sinful; second, that the source of inequality is, first and foremost, outside of the individual in systems and structures; and therefore, third, that Christian faith requires participation in fights for the reform and reconstruction of unjust systems. White middle-class clergy such as Rauschenbusch have played key roles in the development of Social Christianity, but so have factory workers and settlement-house volunteers, women's suffragists and tenant farmers, civil rights activists and grape pickers, folk musicians and more. While some Social Christians have poured their energies into constructing systematic theologies, many more have prioritized action over contemplation. In the moment, they did not always recognize their similarities for their differences. More than that, they sometimes fought at cross-purposes, their universalizing rhetoric belied by deep and enduring cleavages down lines of race, class, ethnicity, and gender. The question of "whose equality" was almost always germane. But there are nevertheless so many reciprocal influences, overlapping networks, and common threads running through their stories that, in retrospect, we can see them as cultivators of a vital, if fractious, tradition of Christian thought and practice—one that grew up in and around not just mainline Protestant churches but also evangelical, Pentecostal, and Catholic ones. This tradition evolved somewhat differently in these various ecclesial contexts, but in nearly every case, churchly institutions were slow to embrace a Social Christian vision and halting in their efforts to make good on it. The energy and insistent pressure came first and finally from the grassroots.

I want to situate Rauschenbusch in the context of a wider tradition. I hope to show that even if he is not quite as *sui generis* as we've sometimes thought, his place in history is, in this way of thinking about American Social Christianity, all the more secure.

DISCHARGING A DEBT

"I have written this book to discharge a debt," Rauschenbusch declared in the poignant final paragraph of the introduction to *Christianity and the Social Crisis*, the 1907 title that launched him into the public eye. He went on to elaborate:

> For eleven years I was pastor among the working people on the West Side of New York City. I shared their life as well as I then knew, and

> used up the early strength of my life in their service. In recent years my work has been turned into other channels, but I have never ceased to feel that I owe help to the plain people who were my friends. If this book in some far-off way helps to ease the pressure that bears them down and increases the forces that bear them up, I shall meet the Master of my life with better confidence.[10]

Rauschenbusch's sense of a debt likely sprung in part from the fact that it was his immersion in Hell's Kitchen that had sparked his own social awakening. He was part of a generation of late nineteenth-century Protestant ministers whose eyes were opened in the course of their first pastoral call, often to a small church in a struggling urban neighborhood, where the full brunt of the industrial crisis was on vivid display. Such experiences converted many, including Rauschenbusch, to a Social Christian faith.

But his debt to "plain people" was even greater than he let on. The larger framework for the book—the context within which his historical and theological work gained urgent relevance—was, of course, "the social crisis." At times, he wrote almost as though this crisis, which seemed to him "inevitable" and "irrepressible," had a life and agency of its own. But the reality was that the popular sense of crisis had grown in direct proportion to the might of the Gilded Age's grassroots movements, galvanized by farmers, freedwomen and men, and industrial workers. These movements were anything but inchoate. Both their leaders—including the likes of Henry McNeal Turner, Ida B. Wells, William Jennings Bryan, and Terence V. Powderly—and their rank and file cultivated Social Christian ideas and practices long before such gained currency among white, middle-class churchgoers. Given Rauschenbusch's location in Rochester, a Northern industrial city, it was hardly surprising that the labor movement was closest to the top of his mind. At one point, he alluded to the ongoing clash between "the vastness and the free sweep of our concentrated wealth on the one side" and "the independence, intelligence, moral vigor and political power of the common people on the other side."[11] Elsewhere in the book he urged his readers to support trade unions, casting their aims as fundamentally Chris-

---

[10] Walter Rauschenbusch, *Christianity and the Social Crisis in the 21st Century: The Classic that Woke Up the Church* (New York: Harper One, 2007), xxii.

[11] Ibid., xix.

tian. What he failed to mention was that working people had been making that argument for more than a generation.[12]

Consider the case of Andrew Cameron, a Scottish immigrant and printer, who in the wake of the Civil War founded the *Workingman's Advocate*, a newspaper that soon gained a national audience and vaulted him to the fore of the early American labor movement. For Cameron, questions about wages and the length of the workday were directly tied to others about the meaning of the Gospel for industrializing society. This became evident starting in the spring of 1867, when not a single Chicago minister came to the aid of what would ultimately prove a failed general strike for the eight-hour day. Immediately on the heels of this betrayal, Cameron lashed out, declaring, "In all reforms, in which labor and capital have been interested, the Church has thrown its influence in behalf of the money changers."[13] That was what he had to say *before* William W. Patton, one of Chicago's leading Congregationalist divines, poured salt in the wound, delivering a scathing critique of trade unionism in one of his denomination's leading newspapers. "For several years past preconcerted and systematic effort have been made by demagogues and so-called friends of American mechanics and labor men, to cause them to be dissatisfied and discontented with the position to which the Supreme Ruler of all has assigned them in this world," Patton sneered.[14] Incensed, Cameron issued a series of withering retorts. In one he argued that the clergyman had "prostitute[d] the function of a minister of the gospel to...sustain a villainy against which the vengeance of heaven is assured." As if that was not clear enough, he went on, "[Patton's] sentiments, sentiments too which are promulgated in nine-tenths of our sanctuaries, are repugnant alike to the teachings of Christ and the enlightened spirit of the age."[15] The framing of Cameron's critique was

[12] The omission is particularly striking given that in a letter to Frank Mason North the following year he argued "that the Christian religion began amid the laboring class and...that its noblest movements have always sprung from the plain people." Walter Rauschenbusch to the Reverend Frank Mason North, 28 August 1908 (Box 28, Folder 2, in the Rauschenbusch Family Collections, American Baptist Historical Society, Atlanta, Georgia).

[13] "A Small Stream from a Large Fountain," *Workingman's Advocate* 4/9 (21 September 1867).

[14] "The Working Men of the Present Day," *Advance* 1/4 (26 September 1867): 1.

[15] "Autor Ultra Crepidam!" *Workingman's Advocate*, 28 September 1867.

telling. He was convinced that the labor movement was not just fully compatible with but was, in fact, a tangible manifestation of "the gospel" and "the teachings of Christ." It was Patton who had gone astray. As Cameron went on to write, "Our fight is not against Christianity, but against those who use it as a cloak to secure their selfish purposes."[16]

Had Cameron been a lone voice crying out into the wilderness, church leaders might have ignored him, but he was far from it. Terence V. Powderly, the longtime grand master workman of the insurgent Knights of Labor, devoted nearly seventy pages of his autobiography to an account of "ecclesiastical opposition" to the labor movement. At one point in that chapter, Powderly, a lifelong Catholic, paused to reflect, "I need hardly tell you that I was taught to believe that the Catholic Church was of divine origin and the events I have related caused me to question that teaching. I have come to the conclusion that while the Catholic Church is a marvelous and wonderful institution, the practices of many of its spokesmen are neither godlike nor divine."[17]

Even as churchly institutions failed to inspire, late nineteenth-century union halls and labor newspapers crackled with theological energy and intuitions. In 1886, when one of the nation's leading Christian businessmen, John V. Farwell, insinuated that the Knights of Labor were not true believers, he found himself at the center of a firestorm. One Knight responded,

> As a "student of the four gospels" I have learned that there is a fair prospect for the Knights of Labor to reach the kingdom of heaven, but I can hardly see any chance at all for Mr. Farwell. It would be easier for a camel to go through the eye of a needle than for him to get there. That is the decision of the "New Testament." Mr. Farwell, of course, does not believe the New Testament, and the evidence of his infidelity is this, that although he is a richer man than any man that lived in Judea at the time of Christ, yet he is trying to be richer still. He is working very hard and very successfully to make him ineligible for a place in the kingdom.[18]

---

[16] "Christianity a Failure," *Workingman's Advocate* 4/42 (9 May 1868): 2.

[17] *The Path I Trod: The Autobiography of Terence V. Powderly*, eds. Harry J. Carman, Henry David, and Paul N. Guthrie. (New York: Columbia University Press, 1940), 371.

[18] Wheelbarrow, "A Reply to Mr. Farwell," *Knights of Labor* 1/18 (7 August 1886): 2.

It was one thing when these confrontations unfolded in print. It was quite another when they spilled over into—or better, out of—the pews. Throughout the Gilded Age, working-class Christians often warned that they would abandon the institutional church altogether if it continued to oppose organized labor. More than that, they insisted that Jesus, a workingman, would go with them. As the century wound toward a close and a growing number of wage earners made good on the threat—defying "scab ministers," walking out of "company churches," and in some cases even founding labor churches of their own—denominational leaders grew increasingly panicked about "The Workingman's Alienation from the Church," a phenomenon they feared would permanently erode their cultural authority.[19]

In this sense, even if Rauschenbusch's direct intellectual debts lay elsewhere, there was no question that grassroots activism laid fallow the ground for *Christianity and the Social Crisis*. Published in 1907, the book proved nothing short of a sensation. The religious press reveled in Rauschenbusch's brilliant provocation. *The Standard* gushed, "The publication of this book by a professor in a theological school is an event of extraordinary significance. The sweep of ideas is wide, the learning implied is impressive, the epigrams are numerous enough to enrich scores of sermons, and the conclusions maintained are simply revolutionary."[20] Meanwhile, the reviewer for *Unity* declared it "revolutionary," adding, "I know of no book that shakes a man up better, and leaves him uninspired of his old notions and satisfactions."[21] Unitarian minister John Haynes Holmes went so far as to call it "the first gospel of the new dispensation."[22] The book went through thirteen printings in its first five years, and, before all was said and done, more than

---

[19] H. Francis Perry, "The Workingman's Alienation from the Church," *American Journal of Sociology* 4/5 (March 1899): 621–29. For more on these currents see Heath W. Carter, *Union Made: Working People and the Rise of Social Christianity in Chicago* (New York: Oxford University Press, 2015).

[20] "The Church and Society," *The Standard* (Box 25, Folder 2, Rauschenbusch Family Collections, American Baptist Historical Society, Atlanta, Georgia).

[21] Review Clipping, Unity, 1 August 1907 (Box 25, Folder 2, Rauschenbusch Family Collections, American Baptist Historical Society, Atlanta, Georgia).

[22] Quoted in Rauschenbusch obituary (Box 35, Folder 1, Rauschenbusch Family Collections, American Baptist Historical Society, Atlanta, Georgia).

50,000 copies of it would fly off the shelves.[23] It was, as Christopher Evans has so aptly put it, "a manifesto for the white Protestant middle class."[24]

The book resonated with white, middle-class, Protestant audiences precisely because it seemed to illumine a way forward through the crises which Gilded Age activists—including many an everyday Social Christian—had intentionally brought to a head. It proved a source of particular encouragement to the many who were distressed about workingmen's apparent disaffection from the churches. Consider a few brief excerpts from the letters that Rauschenbusch received. A Congregationalist layman from Chicago wrote to Rauschenbusch, "I cannot refrain from writing to thank you for your book Christianity and the Social Crisis." He shared that he was preparing to send his copy "out among the working men" and went on to say, "I have for many years felt and said that working men will not come to the churches...because the church does not stand for their interests."[25] A Baptist minister in Concord, New Hampshire, penned a letter in the winter of 1908 relaying that he had read the book the year before "and ever since it has been working in my mind." He had spent the months immediately prior "trying to do something to arouse my church to the situation and to get into touch with the labor union men in Concord." His sermon on "The Church and the Labor Question" had, in fact, produced a relational breakthrough with the workers organized through that city's Central Labor Union, giving him hope for the future of the American churches: "If they are ready in conservative, aristocratic old Concord, they are almost anywhere," he reflected.[26] A Presbyterian pastor in Atlanta related that the book "has not only opened before me with fascinating power many new themes. It has given me a higher conception of the Kingdom of God and its blessed final coming here." Elaborating, he declared, "We of the South have not felt the cleavage between the church and the laboring classes as you have but it is

---

[23] Gary Dorrien, *Social Ethics in the Making: Interpreting an American Tradition* (Oxford: Wiley-Blackwell, 2011), 97.

[24] Evans, *The Kingdom Is Always but Coming*, 185.

[25] John Woollett to Walter Rauschenbusch, 27 September 1907 (Box 25, Folder 2, Rauschenbusch Family Collections, American Baptist Historical Society, Atlanta, Georgia).

[26] Virgil V. Johnson to Walter Rauschenbusch, 11 December 1908 (Box 25, Folder 3, Rauschenbusch Family Collections, American Baptist Historical Society, Atlanta, Georgia).

coming—I have been helped by this book and thus am enabled to help others."[27]

In provoking such anxieties, the activism of poor and working-class Gilded Age Americans had created an opening for the middle-class reformers of the Progressive Era. Few made more of it than Rauschenbusch. *Christianity and the Social Crisis*'s spectacular success was an important indicator that a new season in the life of American Social Christianity was underway. A tradition which had grown up outside of churchly institutions—in union halls and union leagues, among sharecroppers and tenement dwellers—was now taking root within. Ministers such as Rauschenbusch played an essential role in this process, persuading thousands of other white, middle-class believers to embrace Social Christianity. While it remained far from mainstream, the scope and pace of its advance was nonetheless breathtaking. Shortly after the book was published, Rauschenbusch headed to Europe for a year of study. He would later recall, "Meanwhile the social awakening of our nation had set in like an equinoctial gale in March, and when I came home, I found myself caught in the tail of the storm."[28]

THE TAIL OF THE STORM

Rauschenbusch devoted the first section of his second major book, *Christianizing the Social Order*, published in 1912, to documenting the extent to which "[the social interest] has been admitted within the organizations of the Church." Many of the changes were subtle. "Formerly some determined spirit would force his ideas on a ministers' conference and be treated with good-humored condescension as a rider of hobbies," he remembered. He continued,

> To-day the concerted study of social problems has become a common thing in ministerial clubs and conferences. Adult Bible classes and study groups turn by preference to books on the social teachings of Jesus. A valuable literature is being created to supply the need for cheap teaching material. Men's clubs, social unions, Chautauquas,

---

[27] Rev. A. A. Little to Walter Rauschenbusch, 29 March 1909 (Box 25, Folder 4, Rauschenbusch Family Collections, American Baptist Historical Society, Atlanta, Georgia).

[28] Walter Rauschenbusch, *Christianizing the Social Order* (New York: Macmillan Co., 1912):

> and church conventions have created an active demand for competent speakers on topics of social Christianity.

He went on, "But the most astonishing change is in the temper of church audiences. Formerly speakers compelled the people to take their medicine whether they liked it or not, and became adepts in sugar-coating their pills. To-day speakers have to be on their guard lest they be swept along by their hearers. Utterances that would have seemed shockingly radical ten years ago are now applauded."[29]

No less astonishing was the fact that large and lumbering religious institutions were responding with alacrity to Social Christian prodding. Rauschenbusch sought to steer clear of "organization work" himself. "I feel that what time and energy I have at my disposal, can be used most effectively in teaching and writing," he explained at one point to his fellow Social Gospeler, the Reverend W. D. P. Bliss.[30] But the changing shape of Christian institutional life was nonetheless an important bellwether. Typically conservative agencies such as the YMCA and YWCA were becoming active on social questions, even going so far as to take progressive stands on questions about wages and the length of the workday. Meanwhile, nearly every denomination was establishing new departments and commissions dedicated to social service. The 1908 founding of the Federal Council of Churches and that organization's rapid adoption of a Social Creed, which represented, in Rauschenbusch's view, "the common sense of the Protestant churches of America," underscored just how heady the times were for reform-minded believers.[31]

They were, in fact, even headier than Rauschenbusch apprehended. While he made every effort to be comprehensive in his survey of recent developments, it nevertheless reflected the sharp limits of his own knowledge and networks. In 1911, as he was preparing to write this section of the book, he sent out letters across the country, many of which went to white Protestant clergymen. This was the world Rauschenbusch knew best. Consider his familiarity with the reform efforts of the Reverend Charles Stelzle, superintendent of the Presbyterian Department of Church and Labor. In a

---

[29] Ibid., 11–12.

[30] Walter Rauschenbusch to the Reverend W. D. P. Bliss, 9 December 1913 (Box 28, Folder 2, Rauschenbusch Family Collections, American Baptist Historical Society, Atlanta, Georgia).

[31] Rauschenbusch, *Christianizing the Social Order*, 14.

letter to Stelzle, Rauschenbusch requested "the exact figure of your letters sent to the labor papers" and "the exact number of fraternal delegates that are now sent to the central Labor Council."[32] Compare the specificity of those requests with his almost sheepish note to his fellow Rochester clergyman, Father A. M. O'Neill. Rauschenbusch knew enough to know that he could not afford to omit the Catholic Church from his account of the fledgling Social Christian movement, and he knew just about nothing more. As he straightforwardly admitted in his letter, "I am sorry to say that I have very little contact with the Roman Catholic church in this country."[33] As it turned out, O'Neill harbored grave concerns about the growing "enthusiasm for social improvement," but he nevertheless referred Rauschenbusch to a number of invaluable sources, including Father John Ryan, whose 1906 book, *A Living Wage*, had begun as a dissertation under Richard Ely. Ely wrote a foreword to the first edition, which gained widespread notice and landed Ryan on the map of American social reform.[34] He was a key leader of a Social Catholic movement that was gaining steam and influence in the early twentieth-century United States—a movement that barely registered on Rauschenbusch's radar.

But at least it did register. Rauschenbusch would go on to declare in *Christianizing the Social Order*, "One of the most important practical questions is the attitude of the Roman Catholic Church to the social movements." He called particular attention to John Ryan's 1909 "Programme of Social Reform by Legislation."[35] The tireless work of another devout Catholic, Agnes Nestor, in building the women's labor movement went unnoticed, but that was hardly surprising given that none of Rauschenbusch's informants—all priests—had referenced her. In the scheme of things, it was but a small omission. There were entire Social Christian worlds that went altogether unaccounted for in his survey. He included a cursory discussion

---

[32] Walter Rauschenbusch to the Reverend Charles Stelzle, 17 May 1911 (Box 92, Rauschenbusch Family Collections, American Baptist Historical Society, Atlanta, Georgia).

[33] Walter Rauschenbusch to the Reverend A. M. O'Neill (Box 92, Rauschenbusch papers, Box 92, American Baptist Historical Society, Atlanta, Georgia).

[34] Rev. A. M. O'Neill to Professor Walter Rauschenbusch, 25 May 1911 (Box 92, Rauschenbusch Family Collections, American Baptist Historical Society, Atlanta, Georgia).

[35] Walter Rauschenbusch, *Christianizing the Social Order* (New York: Macmillan Co., 1912), 25, 27.

of foreign missions but overlooked the American West, where Social Christian reformers were on the move. During the very same spring of 1911 in which Rauschenbusch had sent out his letters of inquiry, the citizens of Berkeley, California, had elected as their mayor J. Stitt Wilson, an erstwhile Methodist minister and avowed Christian Socialist deeply influenced by the likes of Henry George and Eugene Debs. Rauschenbusch made only the briefest of allusions to the settlement-house movement. He cited the writings of Vida Dutton Scudder, Jane Addams, and Graham Taylor, but for whatever reason, made nary a reference to their vital work in founding and administering Denison House, Hull House, and Chicago Commons, respectively. There is no indication that he was even aware of Mary McDowell, whose "enthusiasm for righteousness," as Addams would later say, led her to take up residence in the squalid environs of Chicago's Back of the Yards neighborhood.[36] The University of Chicago Settlement House that McDowell so ably led was a frequent stop for other leading Social Christians, including Ida B. Wells. Rauschenbusch did not mention Wells, though it is hard to imagine he was not aware of her courageous, peripatetic campaign against lynching. In fact, he did not refer to any of the nation's leading Black Social Christians despite the fact that Booker T. Washington, Nannie Helen Burroughs, Reverdy Ransom, W. E. B. DuBois, and many more were even then in the midst of building the kinds of institutions that would have further reinforced his argument in this opening section of the book.[37]

I highlight these omissions not by way of criticizing Rauschenbusch. Far from it. We are all limited by who and what we know, and, to his credit, he seems to have recognized that the social awakening was much more expansive than the Social Gospel movement he had helped to galvanize. Surely that is the implication of his inclusion of John Ryan, whom he had just come to *know of* and in no meaningful sense knew. Rauschenbusch and Ryan were not part of a common "movement" insofar as that term connotes relationship, intentionality, and coordination. But there is no doubt that, within their largely separate spheres of influence, they both capitalized on a historical moment in which churchly institutions were unusually receptive

---

[36] Howard E. Wilson, *Mary McDowell: Neighbor* (Chicago, IL: University of Chicago Press, 1928), xi.

[37] See Gary Dorrien, *The New Abolition: W. E. B. DuBois and the Black Social Gospel* (New Haven, CT: Yale University Press, 2015).

to Social Christian ideas and practices. In retrospect, we can see that even if Rauschenbusch and Ryan were not co-laborers in one movement, they were both key players in the early twentieth-century institutionalization of Social Christianity. The Protestant and Catholic threads of this tradition developed separately but for all intents and purposes simultaneously; and though they remained always distinct, they would in the coming decades be woven together through ecumenical collaboration and joint activism. But as I indicate above, there were still other threads that Rauschenbusch either did not see or saw but did not count.

A century on, we do see them and we should count them. I see no reason why, in the wake of a generation of scholarship that has unearthed these other threads—black and Latino, female and working class, evangelical and Pentecostal, Southern and Western—we would not seek to incorporate them into a *fundamentally* reconceived grand narrative of Social Christianity. We should not ignore the very real differences and sometimes even outright tensions between these different veins, of course, but nor should we any longer presume that Social Christianity was, at its core, an elite, white, Northern Protestant theological project. Rauschenbusch would retain a starring role in any retelling, as his influence was by so many measures—book sales, speaking invitations, scholarly and popular impact, etc.—profound. But if, as I've argued above, the Social Gospel (capital S, capital G) movement that he championed must be viewed in the wider context of activity at the grassroots, which both preceded and outlasted it, then it must also be seen as one subplot in the larger Social Christian story, not as the latter's true center. When we write about these early twentieth-century decades, a period of middle-class expansion and institutionalization, developments within and around both black and Catholic communities especially deserve just as much ink. In years to come, figures such as Ida B. Wells and John Ryan should be no less synonymous with Social Christianity than Rauschenbusch. Notably, if we understand him as one particularly key player in a much wider tradition, his legacy, far from diminished, appears only more significant and more enduring.

A GRANDER LEGACY

The onset of the First World War devastated Walter Rauschenbusch. In the early going he worried primarily about the fate of Germany, though soon enough the anxiety and sorrow he felt became all-encompassing. The hopeful energy that coursed through the pages of *Christianizing the Social Order* was a distant memory by 1916, though even at that point he insisted in a letter to a friend, "I am not curling up. Not yet."[38] By the following year his spirit was more subdued. In August 1917, he revealed in correspondence with another friend, "I am living somewhat apart from the world at present, and see few people. I am writing a book; that is one excuse. But the truth is that I feel somewhat like a stranger in my own world at present."[39] The feeling would not pass. At the end of March 1918, sick and aware that his life might be drawing to a close, Rauschenbusch reflected, "I have long prayed God not to let me be stranded in a lonesome and useless old age, and if this is the meaning of my present illness, I shall take it as a loving mercy of God toward his servant. Since 1914 the world is full of hate, and I cannot expect to be happy again in my life-time."[40] Less than four months later, he passed away.

Historians long took a similarly dismal view of Social Christianity's prospects, citing World War I as a key inflection point marking the beginning of its demise. In more recent years, however, a number of scholars have begun to make the case for a "long Social Gospel movement," one that links the world of early twentieth-century Christian reform to the struggle for black civil rights.[41] There are excellent evidentiary grounds to justify this interpretive move, not least of which is the fact that people like Howard Thurman and Martin Luther King Jr. were trained in seminary environments steeped in the thought of Rauschenbusch, among many others. Building on the work of these colleagues, I want to argue that the connections between Social Christianity and later twentieth-century developments are, if anything, even more dense than this "long movement" paradigm has to this point suggested. Social Christians were intricately involved with

---

[38] Walter Rauschenbusch to the Reverend G. Herbert Ekins, 20 January 1916 (Box 30, Folder 1, Rauschenbusch Family Collections, American Baptist Historical Society, Atlanta, Georgia).

[39] Walter Rauschenbusch to the Reverend Levi M. Powers, 3 August 1917 (Box 99, Folder 15, Rauschenbusch Family Collections, American Baptist Historical Society, Atlanta, Georgia).

[40] Untitled document, 31 March 1918 (Box 39, Folder 2, Rauschenbusch Family Collections, American Baptist Historical Society, Atlanta, Georgia).

[41] See Evans, *The Social Gospel in American Religion*; Dorrien, *The New Abolition*; and Vaneesa Cook, "Martin Luther King, Jr., and the Long Social Gospel Movement," *Religion and American Culture: A Journal of Interpretation* 26/1 (Winter 2016): 74–100.

nearly every major reform movement and initiative of the middle twentieth century.

Take, for example, the New Deal. The unprecedented avalanche of legislation signed by President Franklin D. Roosevelt in his first hundred days alone created a larger and more interventionist federal government than the nation had ever known. In the most immediate sense, it was the economic emergency of the Great Depression that catalyzed these developments, but the spread of Social Christianity in the decades prior was another significant condition of possibility. Perhaps never before had the immorality of economic inequality seemed so intuitive to so many people. More than just shaping the context into which the New Deal emerged, Social Christians had a direct hand in creating it. Many in FDR's cabinet were steeped in Social Gospel ideas, including Frances Perkins, who as secretary of labor from 1933 to 1945 was one of the welfare state's foremost architects. As her biographer, George Martin, writes, "What Perkins chose to do was determined by her religion. Many Democrats supported the Social Security Act because it attracted votes; others, for humanitarian reasons; Perkins, 'for Jesus' sake,' because it brought the City of God closer to the cities of toil and industry."[42] Her colleague Harold Ickes, the secretary of the interior and the only other member of the cabinet to serve through the entirety of FDR's administration, explicitly framed the New Deal as the realization of Christian ideals. When he addressed the leaders of the Presbyterian Church USA in the spring of 1934, he drove home this point. "Christ wanted men and women to live upright lives," Ickes acknowledged, "but he also wanted them to have for each other understanding and good will and mutual helpfulness. He wished them to be good neighbors. He hated injustice with a righteous hatred. His whole life was a fight against oppression." In Ickes's estimation, the New Deal reflected Christ's values. "[It] is grounded on the theory that one should do unto others what he would that others should do unto him," he insisted.[43]

Of course, while the New Deal was constructed in Washington DC, it was truly made, as Liz Cohen and others have shown, at the grassroots. At nearly every level American Catholics threw their collective weight behind

---

[42] George Martin, *Madam Secretary, Frances Perkins* (Boston, MA: Houghton Mifflin Co., 1976), vii.

[43] "Ickes Exhorts Presbyterians to Aid New Deal," *New York Herald Tribune*, 24 May 1934.

it. Working-class believers poured into the ranks of the Congress of Industrial Organizations upon its founding in 1935.[44] While they had embraced a pro-labor Gospel for generations, they were now joined not only by the Vatican—which in 1931 promulgated *Quadragesimo Anno*, an even bolder reworking of a Social Christian program first outlined in the Gilded Age encyclical *Rerum Novarum*—but also a vast array of labor priests, nuns, and bishops. Many of these participated actively in the work of the National Catholic Welfare Conference's Social Action Department and especially its Catholic Conference on Industrial Problems (CCIP). Throughout the 1930s and 1940s the leaders of the CCIP held conferences across the country. Regulars on the speaker circuit included not only the likes of John Ryan—known in many circles as the "Right Reverend New Dealer" after his endorsement of FDR's 1936 reelection bid—but also Vincent Ferrer, a Dominican sister and professor at Rosary College whose expertise on economic and political questions regularly took the men she encountered at such conferences aback.[45]

Protestants also cheered the emerging welfare state. In 1932 the Federal Council of Churches endorsed an updated and more progressive Social Creed, one which united its member denominations in support of collective bargaining and other policies that would become law under FDR. High-ups in the FCC hailed the New Deal as a "Third American Revolution" and one which was consonant with Christianity's highest ideals.[46] These sentiments were widely shared. When Roosevelt solicited clergy feedback regarding his programs, he was soon buried under a deluge of 30,000 letters, many of which were unremittingly positive. Even in the more conservative South, both white and black clergy returned glowing reviews of the 1935 Social Security Act, though in many cases the latter harbored deep reservations about the New Deal state's surrender to Jim Crow.[47] The mainline

---

[44] Lizabeth Cohen, *Making a New Deal: Industrial Workers in Chicago, 1919–1939* (New York: Cambridge University Press, 1990).

[45] Heath W. Carter, "Preaching with Their Lives: Dominican Sisters and the Struggle for Economic Justice."

[46] Paul A. Carter, *The Decline and Revival of the Social Gospel: Social and Political Liberalism in American Protestant Churches, 1920–1940* (Ithaca, NY: Cornell University Press, 1954).

[47] Alison Greene, *No Depression in Heaven: The Great Depression, the New Deal, and the Transformation of Religion in the Delta* (New York: Oxford University Press, 2015).

clergy hardly had a monopoly on the Social Gospel. In Missouri's impoverished Bootheel, it was spirit-filled Pentecostal tenant farmers who galvanized interracial organizing drives for economic justice.[48] Such instances of collaboration across racial lines remained few and far between, however. Even as black Christians in a variety of denominations struggled against the withering reign of Jim Crow, many of their White Social Gospel counterparts continued to prioritize economic over racial justice, while many more remained straightforwardly racist. The failure of Christianity to address social wrongs and especially pervasive racism prompted Howard University theologian Howard Thurman to write *Jesus and the Disinherited* (1949), in which he probed the meanings of the Gospel for those "with their backs against the wall." The book encouraged an emerging generation of civil rights activists whose collective sacrifice would bring Social Christianity to its apex.

While I do not have time to make all the connections in this essay, suffice it to say that elite support for the New Deal ended up triggering a significant backlash against Social Christian leadership within many church bodies. Before long the FCC and its denominational affiliates found themselves swimming in angry correspondence. As institutional momentum slowed, the action moved back to the grassroots, where in the wake of the Second World War faith-infused labor and civil rights movements gained steam. Before all was said and done, what began in Detroit and Montgomery would reverberate all the way to California, where in the 1960s and 1970s Dolores Huerta and Cesar Chavez, drawing explicitly on longstanding Social Christian tradition, mobilized a social movement of Latino and Filipino workers that brought the state's mightiest growers to the bargaining table. It would be wrong to draw a straight line from Rauschenbusch to Huerta and Chavez, who were more directly influenced by the Catholic encyclical tradition and the likes of Dorothy Day. But it would also be wrong not to see them all as part of a larger Social Christian tradition, one which did not expire in the wake of two devastating and disenchanting world wars, but rather decisively shaped the postwar order.

The ordinary believers on the march in Selma, Alabama, and on *peregrinación* (pilgrimage) in Delano, California, inhabited worlds apart from one another, and a different universe in many ways than that of Rochester

---

[48] Jarod Roll, *Spirit of Rebellion: Labor and Religion in the New Cotton South* (Urbana, IL: University of Illinois Press, 2010).

Theological Seminary in the Progressive Era. But pervading them all was a common intuition that to be a faithful Christian was to join the fight against structural inequality—a conviction that separated them from many of their fellow believers, both before and since. The justice movements of the middle twentieth century fundamentally changed not just the churches but the nation as a whole, extending the legacy of earlier Social Christians in ways that Rauschenbusch, for one, could never have anticipated. The world had seemed to him in his dying days so full of hate. Little did he imagine it would be so transformed by Christian love. His own failure to see what might be possible should come as some encouragement to us as we make our way through our own era of historic inequality, more than a generation removed from the height of Social Christianity's public witness. Hope is in understandably short supply at the moment, but we can certainly pray that God will multiply the fruits of our labors as God so clearly did those of Walter Rauschenbusch.

Chapter 12

The Power and Limits of Rauschenbusch's "Kingdom Ethic"

David P. Gushee

WHEN CHILDREN ARE DYING, PIOUS CONSERVATIVE RELIGION IS NOT ENOUGH

Many of us who have spent considerable time in pious evangelical families and churches can easily understand Rauschenbusch's starting point. These are atmospheres of fervent personal and family religious devotion, centered around the Bible and a very high view of biblical authority; a life given to the church and constantly spent within its walls; a strong emphasis on stern personal morality; a religious vision emphasizing evangelism and global missions to save the lost; and a general disengagement from broader social problems in favor of an otherworldly religious vision.

Many fine human beings have lived their lives within this kind of religious framework. But in its narrowness, it can pinch, and it can ultimately pinch so much that young adults graduate out of it either into a wider Christian vision or even an abandonment of Christianity. Walter Rauschenbusch was one such graduate.

This might have happened for Rauschenbusch under any historical circumstances. But Rauschenbusch was transformed by his heartbreaking personal experiences as a pastor in New York's Hell's Kitchen neighborhood. Here, Rauschenbusch could not help but engage what became known as "the social problem" of the late nineteenth and early twentieth centuries.

The "social problem" was created by unfettered industrialization and urbanization. The industrial revolution enabled dramatic advances in all manner of technology and consumer products. But industry was privately controlled by a relatively few "captains of industry" making stupendous profits. Labor was provided by a massive pool of largely powerless workers, many of whom went to the cities from the farms to chase the new jobs that became available. Housing for these millions was grossly inadequate. Sanitary and health conditions were grotesque. Working conditions were just as bad. Laborers sought to organize to secure minimal rights; these efforts were smashed by factory owners wherever possible. Walter Rauschenbusch was especially affected by the most traumatic evidence of the dystopia in which he lived—the frequent deaths of small children.[1]

Walter Rauschenbusch was one of many pious Christian pastors who found the privatized and otherworldly religiosity of most Christians around him grossly inadequate for the situation he was discovering in his pastoral ministry.[2] The new pastor at Second German Baptist Church saw that people needed more than another reminder to look off to heaven for a better future. They needed a church that would advocate for them—for their basic human needs; today we would say basic human rights.

The inadequacy of Rauschenbusch's inherited evangelical religion, as it intersected with his experience in Hell's Kitchen, provoked a religious crisis for him. He could not live based on the "faith of his fathers," nor could he offer it to his impoverished parishioners. He needed something different. He found it in his retrieval of the kingdom of God from the ministry and message of Jesus.

RAUSCHENBUSCH DISCOVERS THAT THE BIBLE IS "ABOUT" THE KINGDOM OF GOD

Walter Rauschenbusch was a deeply biblical thinker. But he was exposed to historical-critical study of the Christian Bible in the early stages of this revolutionary new approach to sacred Scripture. This opened the door to a more flexible reading of Scripture based on what were for his context certain unusual (some would say unorthodox) assumptions about its composition and interpretation.

The most important move Rauschenbusch was willing to make based on historical-critical assumptions was to treat Scripture as a human product, with varied and diverse strands of tradition, *some of which were more morally profound and important than others*. His "hermeneutic," or interpretive framework, for assessing higher and lower, more and less profound, eventually was provided by (his reading of) the message of Jesus himself.

The way Rauschenbusch read the Bible, at least after Hell's Kitchen, was with what can best be described as a *Hebraic-prophetic-kingdom of God*

---

[1] William H. Brackney, "Historical Introduction," in *Walter Rauschenbusch: Published Works and Selected Writings, Volume I* (Macon, GA: Mercer University Press, 2018), 14.

[2] See Brackney, "Historical Introduction," for more detail.

hermeneutic (henceforth, "kingdom hermeneutic").[3] He came to believe that Jesus was a thoroughly Jewish figure, steeped in the Hebrew prophets. Jesus offered a message of God's reign, or kingdom, that dawning reality in which God reclaims divine rule over Israel and the world. Jesus must be read as Jewish—not Greek, not ahistorical. He must be read as prophetic—not priestly or kingly or cultic. He must be read as kingdom-focused, aiming at the reign of God—not at personal salvation or eternal bliss.

It is hard to overstate the significance of Rauschenbusch's retrieval and restatement of this thickly Jewish, prophetic, messianic Jesus. Here is one typical statement of his view:

> That prophetic type of religion...which constituted the chief religious heritage of his nation, had laid hold on Jesus and he had laid hold of it and appropriated its essential spirit. In the poise and calm of his mind and manner, and in the love of his heart, he was infinitely above them all. But the greatest of all prophets was still one of the prophets, and that large interest in the national and social life which had been inseparable from the religion of the prophets was part of his life too.[4]

For Rauschenbusch, Jesus was a Jewish prophet. He was more than this, but he was this. He reflected the themes, priorities, and passions of the prophets. For Rauschenbusch, the link between the Hebrew prophets and Jesus stretches tautly across Scripture. and ought to govern how all the rest of Scripture is read. The Bible has a center and a circumference. Believers should read it all, but focus on what is central. "Modern study has shown that [the prophets] were the real makers of the unique religious life of Israel. If all that proceeded from them...were eliminated from the Old Testament, there would be little left to appeal to the moral and religious judgment of the modern world."[5]

Jesus did not emerge from nowhere. He was Jewish. He was prophetic. He took existing Jewish ideas of the kingdom of God while reworking them in his own distinctive way. Stripping the ancient hope of its violence, na-

---

[3] Brackney, "Theological Introduction," *Walter Rauschenbusch: Published Works and Selected Writings, Volume III* (Macon, GA: Mercer University Press, 2019), 52–55.

[4] Walter Rauschenbusch, *Christianity and the Social Crisis* (New York: Macmillan Co., 1907; cited from Westminster John Knox Press edition, 1991), 53.

[5] Ibid., 3.

tionalism, and catastrophism, Jesus yet offered a vision thoroughly rooted in ancient Jewish soil:

> It was...a national and collective idea. It involved the restoration of Israel as a nation to outward independence, security, and power, such as it had under the Davidic kings. It involved that social justice, prosperity, and happiness for which the Law and the prophets called, and for which the common people always long. It involved that religious purity and holiness of which the nation had always fallen short. And all this was to come in an ideal degree, such as God alone by direct intervention could bestow.[6]

Jesus was not merely a social reformer. He called people to God. But in calling them to God he called them to social reform; that is, to the creation of a new kind of social order, a new kind of community, a/the kingdom of God:

> No comprehension of Jesus is even approximately true which fails to understand that the heart of his heart was religion. No man is a follower of Jesus in the full sense who has not through him entered into the same life with God. But on the other hand no man shares his life with God whose religion does not flow out, naturally and without effort, into all relations of his life and reconstructs everything that it touches. Whoever uncouples the religious and social life has not understood Jesus.[7]

Rauschenbusch's understanding of what he thought Jesus meant by the kingdom of God became the narrative frame for his social ethics. He believed that this story about what God is doing in history is what entirely grounded Jesus's ministry, teaching, and ethics:

> All the teachings of Jesus and all his thinking centred about the hope of the Kingdom of God. His moral teachings get their real meaning only when viewed from that centre. He was not a Greek philosopher or Hindu pundit teaching the individual the way of emancipation from the world and its passions, but a Hebrew prophet preparing men for the righteous social order. The goodness which he sought to

---

[6] Ibid., 56–57, 64.
[7] Ibid., 48.

> create in men was always the goodness that would enable them to live rightly with their fellow-men and to constitute a true social life.[8]

For Rauschenbusch, it is self-evident that Christians should make Jesus's central aim their own, Jesus's central narrative the story in which they situate themselves. Jesus came to bring the kingdom of God. It comes from God, progresses by God's power, and will be consummated by God's will. But human beings have a key role to play in developing it to fulfillment. The kingdom of God looks like love, justice, and social salvation, equality, dignity, and brotherhood.[9]

CHURCH HISTORY BECOMES A TRAGIC SERIES OF WRONG TURNS

For Rauschenbusch, the kingdom of God was the religion of Jesus. But the church instead turned him into the basis of a "system of speculative thought" and "the founder and organizer of a great ecclesiastical machine."[10] Something must have gone terribly wrong. What happened? Why were "the religious and moral thoughts and aims of Jesus...paralyzed and distorted from the outset"? Why did "his social aims and ideas suffe[r] a similar diminution in scope, force, and purity"?[11]

After all, for fifteen centuries the church was the most powerful institution in much of the world. Yet it never really "directed its full available force against any social wrong.... Here, then, is a vast force which by all the tradition of its origins and by its very essence is committed to the moral reconstruction of human society. It has had time and opportunity. Why, then, has it not reconstituted the social life of Christendom?"[12]

Walter Rauschenbusch's massive plunge into the study of church history seems to have been especially motivated by these questions, which had become very urgent for him. The result, as can be seen especially in chapter 4 of *Christianity and the Social Crisis*, became a nearly complete takedown of the entirety of Christian tradition. Rauschenbusch offers an immensely in-

---

[8] Ibid., 67.

[9] The most mature distilled version of his theology of the kingdom is found in Rauschenbusch, *A Theology for the Social Gospel* (New York: Macmillan Co., 1917), ch. 13.

[10] Rauschenbusch, *Christianity and the Social Crisis*, 91–92.

[11] Ibid., 94.

[12] Ibid., 144.

teresting analysis of the ways in which the intrinsically Social Gospel of Jesus was sublimated and redirected by the church he founded.

Rauschenbusch starts with the partial eclipse of kingdom-focused Jewish Christianity by the idiosyncratic Apostle Paul. Note Rauschenbusch's freedom in at least implicitly critiquing Paul: "Paul immensely preponderates in the bulk of our [New Testament] material, and so we get the impression that his ideas and points of view were those generally prevailing in the apostolic age. That is probably far from true. In many respects Paul was a free lance, the propagandist of a new theology, a great dissenter and nonconformist...a radical in theology, but a social conservative."[13]

With Paul and his successors, the social-transformationist kingdom hope transmuted rather quickly into a hope for Christ's return. Then, views on what would happen after Christ returned gradually shifted from social justice to the conquest of death and the glorification of nature.

The only society the early Christians could make was their own internal communal life. And so they focused with great intensity on creating counter-communities in which the Way of Jesus was taught and practiced. These house churches often made impressive strides in humanizing life amid the cruelties of the Roman Empire. Still, rather than a kingdom of God in practice, even the early church at its best offered little more than "the germ of a new social life for humanity, the conception of a social morality based on love and world-wide in its obligation."[14]

The very hostility to the Roman Empire that helped clarify Christian identity and motivate counter-cultural community had a negative effect, says Rauschenbusch. It embedded into early Christianity a germ of otherworldliness, hopelessness, and demonization of this world that sapped moral energy for social change.

The move into Christendom after the fourth century, simultaneously involving the collapse of the Roman Empire and the rise of official Christian states, slowed the germination of the new social order that was intrinsic to Jesus's message and mission. As the centuries went by, the church's otherworldliness and privatized spirituality deepened. To these the church added a mordant asceticism and monasticism. This pulled some of the church's best and most devoted believers further away from concern with family, community, and society.

---

[13] Ibid., 102.

[14] Ibid., 142.

Sacramentalism rose and Christian authorities became fixated on dogma. Everything focused on the church—building great buildings, outfitting these buildings, providing for the many layers of clergy, and always protecting the church's power, privileges, and prerogatives. This was disastrous in every way, says Rauschenbusch. It drained off all the moral energy that should have been devoted to the kingdom, drew the attention of the best people away to ecclesial trivialities, and excused every wrong as long as it benefited the institutional church.

The overall indictment is clear: "The failure of the Church to undertake the work of a Christian reconstruction of social life has not been caused by its close adherence to the spirit of Christ and to the essence of its religious task, but to the deflecting influence of alien forces penetrating Christianity from without and clogging the revolutionary moral power inherent in it."[15]

If there is good news, however, it is that this *old churchy Christianity* is collapsing or already has collapsed. This opens the possibility for a revolutionary sweeping away of the vestiges of morally unproductive Christendom. The church has enough power to change the world but now must engage as a moral force—just like Jesus did. The church must retrieve Jesus's message of the kingdom of God.

It is easy to see how exhilarated Walter Rauschenbusch was by the project that he saw in front of himself, his fellow Christians, his fellow Americans, and the world: "For the first time in religious history we have the possibility of so directing religious energy by scientific knowledge that a comprehensive and continuous reconstruction of social life in the name of God is within the bounds of human possibility."[16]

It was a big project. Sweeping away what was left of misdirected Christianity, Christians could now develop a relevant modern religion in which the social problems of the day could be addressed with vigor and passion. The church could become the strike force for the kingdom of God that it should have been all along.

---

[15] Ibid., 198.

[16] Ibid., 209.

THE KINGDOM OF GOD THEN SETS THE PRINCIPLES AND PROGRAM FOR CHRISTIAN ETHICS

In an important but overlooked 1916 book, Rauschenbusch offered a popular account of what he called "the social principles of Jesus."[17] These principles he grounds in Jesus's teaching, above all in his overarching narrative of the kingdom of God.

These principles, many of which remain central in Christian ethics today, include:

* The Value of Life: Human Life and Personality Are Sacred (ch. 1)
* The Solidarity of the Human Family: Men Belong Together (ch. 2)
* Standing with the People: The Strong Must Stand Up for the Weak (ch. 3)
* The Kingdom of God: Its Values: The Right Social Order Is the Highest Good for All (ch. 4)
* The Kingdom of God: Its Tasks: The Right Social Order Is the Supreme Task of Each (ch. 5)
* A New Age and New Standards: As the Kingdom Comes Ethical Standards Must Advance (ch. 6)
* Leadership for Service: Ambition Must Get Its Satisfaction by Serving Humanity (ch. 7)
* Private Property and the Common Good: Private Property Must Serve Social Welfare (ch. 8)
* The Social Test of Religion: Religion Must Be Socially Efficient (ch. 9)
* The Conflict with Evil: The Kingdom of God Will Have to Fight for Its Advance (ch. 10)
* The Cross as a Social Principle: Social Redemption Is Wrought by Vicarious Suffering (ch. 11)
* Review and Challenge: The Social Principles of Jesus Demand Personal Allegiance and Social Action (ch. 12)

Rauschenbusch did not hesitate to operationalize his principles through detailed moral and policy prescriptions, primarily in what would today be called economic ethics. He sometimes described his approach as a "practical [Christian] socialism." He was sure it was fully consistent with Jesus's teaching of the kingdom of God.

---

[17] Walter Rauschenbusch, *The Social Principles of Jesus* (New York: Grosset & Dunlap, 1916).

Overall, Rauschenbusch's normative program included a comprehensive challenge to the ideology of laissez-faire capitalism and an effort to ameliorate its disastrous effects. This would include developing, improving, or enhancing union rights, employment and worker protections, social insurance, consumer health and safety protections, housing quality, environmental protections, urban living conditions, health care and medicines for workers and their families, and regulation of the liquor trade. It also included taking steps to reduce the power of money in US politics, protect a free press, and punish political corruption.

At its most daring, Rauschenbusch's program struck more clearly Socialist notes such as enshrining a right to work, a living wage (and eventually even abolition of wage labor), price controls, employee shared ownership, and public ownership of public goods such as utilities, water, transit, and land.

Rauschenbusch was sure that these political and economic reforms were fundamentally moral issues. And he believed that the right stance to take on these moral issues should have been obvious from a fair-minded reading of the Bible, notably the prophets and Jesus. He did not need to create a new religion to address "the social problem." The religion was already there. It was the religion of Jesus, the message of the kingdom of God. It just needed to be mobilized.

THE INDISPENSABLE KINGDOM OF GOD

Let us pause for a moment and summarize what the concept of the kingdom of God ended up doing for Rauschenbusch. Whether I am correct about Rauschenbusch is a matter of debate based on the evidence. Personally, I will certainly admit that the kingdom concept has accomplished these things in my own life and work, allowing for differences in context:

> 1) It resolved a personal religious and spiritual crisis caused by the clash between his inherited faith and what he needed for ministry in Hell's Kitchen.

Rauschenbusch found that he did not need to abandon either his faith or the evidence before his eyes; but he did need to retrieve a lost dimension of his faith, the message of the kingdom of God.

> 2) It helped him make sense of the evil he witnessed, and therefore it helped resolve his own theodicy questions.

The problem of evil is one of the greatest challenges to Christian faith. The theology of the kingdom offered his answer, elaborated most fully in his last book, *A Theology for the Social Gospel.* There is a kingdom of God on its way, but it is resisted strenuously by a kingdom of evil, which protects privilege and injustice through myriad strategies, including the use of force against agents of God's reign.

> 3) It gave him a clearly biblical hermeneutic for tackling social problems, centering on Jesus's actual message.

This shielded Rauschenbusch from the charge that he did not take Scripture seriously, but it allowed him to do so while employing a modern methodology and addressing modern problems.

> 4) It gave him a critical lens through which to interpret church history.

The kingdom message gave Rauschenbusch the authority, in Jesus's own message, to dismiss much of the majority Catholic, Orthodox, and Protestant traditions as largely fateful wrong turns, which helped defang traditionalist critics, or at least allow him to dismiss the meaningfulness of their criticisms.

> 5) It gave him a new ecclesiology and mission for the church, also at the same time grounds for political engagement, partnership with government, and support for nonprofit agencies aiming for the common good.

Rauschenbusch had reason to remain engaged in church life, but with a new sense of mission while also offering justification for political work and church cooperation with "worldly" agencies and government.

> 6) It gave him a basis for articulating powerful core principles of a working social ethic.

These principles did not need to be borrowed from secular moral or political philosophers, nor did the unsatisfactory account offered by most Christian ethicists at the time need to limit Rauschenbusch's own ethic, as Rauschenbusch could trump them all with claims to the social ethics of Jesus himself.

> 7) It gave him a sense of heroic mission and reachable hope.

We can and must participate in the advance of the reign of God—nothing could be more exciting, or heroic, than that. We will be bloodied and face obstacles—but nothing could be more worthy of our suffering. We will take losses and see great disappointments, but we can be sure that one day the kingdom will come—and nothing could be more empowering and hopeful than that.

One hundred years later, a central legacy of Walter Rauschenbusch is this—many in global Christianity also have adopted this very same kingdom vision, in part because it has done these very same things for us. I am one of those for whom the kingdom Christianity that Rauschenbusch articulated has become my version of the Christian Gospel. I have staked my career on it, and not just my career but my entire worldview.

MIGUEL DE LA TORRE'S CHALLENGE TO KINGDOM ETHICS

This is one reason why I was very much brought up short when I read recent work by my Baptist ethicist friend Miguel De La Torre suggesting that the entire trajectory of "Kingdom Ethics" is based on a modernist illusion.

In his 2015 book, *The Politics of Jesús*, De La Torre explicitly abandons "hope that all things will work out for the best."[18] Speaking first of disappointed individual hopes in justice, De La Torre moves on to reject any "eventual hope of the triumph of justice" in broader theological or historical narratives like that of the kingdom of God. He argues: "There is nothing inevitable about the passage of time, no teleology to history, nothing but a game of random chance. What we call history is chaos, with no rhyme or reason, mainly because the events are as unpredictable and contradictive as humans. One is hard pressed to notice any type of progressive dialectical march toward a better human existence."[19]

Working from a postcolonial hermeneutic of suspicion, De La Torre rejects the trustworthiness of *any* narrative about the purported direction in which human history is surely moving. He argues that most of the European-developed narratives about history's direction, such as that offered by G. W. F. Hegel, clearly reflect European racist biases.[20] Other modern European-derived hopes, such as in reason, capitalism, communism, science, humanity (we could add democracy, liberalism, etc.), are also false versions of

---

[18] Miguel A. De La Torre, *The Politics of Jesús: A Hispanic Political Theology* (Lanham, MD: Rowman & Littlefield, 2015), 133.

[19] Ibid., 134.

[20] Ibid., 134–35.

"salvation history."[21] Whether premodern or modern, all such hopes are illusory:

But what if there is no salvation history? What if the premodern (history made by God) and modern (history made by the human subject) views are both wrong? What if the historical dialectic that moves history in an upward spiral is but an optimistic construct forced on a very select history?[22]

Explicitly rejecting the oft-expressed hopes of American hero Dr. Martin Luther King Jr., De La Torre says: "Hope, as a product of salvation history...can be optimistically believed if we accept that the arch [*sic*] of history does bend toward justice. But if the past and present are any guides, the existence of such an arch [*sic*] is a faith statement assumed without proof. But...[it] serves an important middle-class purpose...[becoming] an excuse not to deal with the reality of injustice."[23]

This is a truly fascinating rejection of one of the central claims of the iconic figure whom many consider the founder of modern American liberation theology. But perhaps King himself, at least at this point, proved to be captive to the modern, liberal, white, middle-class theology in which he was trained. That, at least, is an implication of De La Torre's claims.

Referring to the wretched experience of hopelessness experienced by the world's poorest and most oppressed people, De La Torre rejects "the virtue and/or audacity of hope,"[24] which he identifies as "a class privilege experienced by those protected" from life's most brutal realities.[25]

Instead, De La Torre argues for a "theology of hopelessness, where meaning and purpose is given to life in the struggle of implementing justice-based praxis" even without a narrative horizon to give it sense.[26] He rejects any mythic hopeful future, calling for "hope against all hope," while we attend today to "messianic solidarity with the oppressed in the midst of hopelessness."[27] He concludes: "Perhaps this is the sad paradox: that hope might

---

[21] Ibid., 135.

[22] Ibid., 136.

[23] Ibid., 136–37.

[24] Ibid., 138; "Audacity of hope" was language used by former US President Barack Obama; clearly an allusion here by De La Torre, reflecting apparent disillusionment.

[25] Ibid., 138.

[26] Ibid., 139.

[27] Ibid., 139.

be found after it is crucified and then may be resurrected in the shards of life."[28]

Here we have witnessed the shattering of kingdom hope. Instead, De La Torre comes to a theology of the cross with glimpses of pieces of shards of resurrection. That's it.

But for De La Torre, this embrace of hopelessness does not cut the foundation from under Christian moral practice.[29] For the work of justice continues just the same. If Christian moral practice was previously motivated by some illusory hope that in the end everything will work out in a certainly on-its-way kingdom of God, that hope is now gone. But this only heightens the significance of doing the ethics anyway. We have no deliverer to wait for. We are the ones we are waiting for.

An interesting question to consider is whether De La Torre's rejection of kingdom hope should also be seen as a rejection of Jesus's own hope. That would be the most natural reading—if we accept that the hope of Jesus in a dawning reign of God is accurately captured in accounts like the one offered by Rauschenbusch. But what if those accounts were all wrong? What if we take up De La Torre's suggestion that this reading of Jesus was and is all too hopeful due to our privileged social location? What if we Rauschenbuschian Social Christianity types are missing the hoping-against-hope spirit of the Galilean peasant whose ministry was snuffed out all too quickly on a Roman cross, and who knew that this was exactly what would happen from day one of his public career? What would Jesus's proclamation of a kingdom of God mean in that context? Would it look more like De La Torre's ethical praxis in the face of hopelessness?

NEW DIRECTIONS IN ESCHATOLOGY FOR "KINGDOM ETHICISTS"?

Christian theologies, and ethics, are products of history. Christians can heighten their claims about the authority and truthfulness of their theological and ethical formulations and their revelatory sources as much as they might want, but whatever a human being or human community produces, including an intellectual product of a religious community or individual, is a product of history.

---

[28] Ibid., 139.

[29] De La Torre's newest book examines this theme at length. See *Embracing Hopelessness* (Minneapolis, MN: Fortress Press, 2017).

I see more clearly now than in earlier years that my own literary output—as an American Christian ethicist trained in the 1980s at the "moderate" version of Southern Baptist Theological Seminary and the liberal/radical Union Theological Seminary in New York—is historically situated. One stream of history that affected my education is a 140-year heritage of Social (Gospel) Christianity. Within Social Christianity, a particular account of the kingdom of God was disseminated.

Social Christianity, with its kingdom-of-God and social-transformation message, remained deeply influential in American Christian ethics at the time of my training. It has experienced a surprising spike of interest among politically progressive evangelical Protestants. One can even find a fairly strong Catholic version of it, though never in quite the same form as on the Protestant side.

Liberation theology emerged in the 1960s and 1970s, beginning in the western hemisphere and among some of our region's most impoverished and mistreated human beings. Liberation theology was also a form of kingdom-of-God Christianity. It shared the this-worldly, participative, social-transformation eschatology of Social Gospel Christianity. It shared the redefining of the "Gospel" as a social and political Gospel. It shared some traces of Marxist influence, in some cases more than traces, both in the content of the envisioned world and perhaps also in the certainty that this world is on its way. It differed from Social Gospel Christianity in being written by people of color (and later by other persons on the margins) rather than the heretofore ubiquitous European and American white men. It differed also, and perhaps consequently, in the political radicalism of its demands, the focus on the needs of the oppressed, and the anger naturally on offer from people whose very existence had been invisible to the previous definers of Christian ethics and theology.

At this moment, it seems to me that "kingdom ethics" is in trouble, in both its social-Christianity liberal and liberationist forms.

Kingdom-of-God ethics was always problematic if the primary confessional traditions of the church were taken seriously. Nothing like the claims of either Social Christianity or liberation theology appear in historic Catholic or Protestant creeds and confessions. Of course, this could mean that the historic creeds and confessions were misguided, a claim often made by Social Gospel and liberationist Christians, including Rauschenbusch, as we have seen.

It is certainly the case that liberal and liberationist kingdom-of-God theology and ethics produces a certain energy—sometimes great passion—

for moral effort toward social transformation. God is changing the world through us! What could be a more inspiring message?

But this message may also subtly create inordinate hopes about the transformability of human nature and human history through human effort. Such hope is theologically questionable and empirically problematic. When those "seeking the kingdom" read history as offering hopeful victories, kingdom ethicists can become triumphalistic; when kingdom hopes are being disappointed, they can become despairing or even slide out of Christian faith altogether.

The gravity of the threats to human survival that are posed today by contemporary ecological problems, ongoing global security problems, and the rise of revanchist political movements raise stringent challenges to any hopeful kingdom ethic. Empirically, given the flaws of human nature and society, the carnage human beings have produced, and the imbalance between human technological power and moral performance, it appears more likely than not that the relatively brief run of human beings as lords of our ancient planet will end in disaster. If Christian eschatological hope is fixed on a happy outcome to human history, it looks like a losing bet—and a sure ticket to the kind of despair that appears to be seeping into the recent work of Miguel De La Torre.

The challenge for Christian theology and ethics is acute. What is the motivation for ethical praxis if we abandon an immanentist kingdom-of-God theology? If we lose hope that the kingdom will ever be "built" by human effort (even with God's "help"), then what is our hope and what motivates our ethics? What has become of our "Gospel"?

Perhaps we need to return to the idea that the effort to fulfill Christian moral obligations and to embody Christian moral virtues is not contingent upon any particular outcome to human history. Perhaps Christians are those who have pledged to serve Jesus Christ as Lord, together in covenantal Christian community, in the time we are given—whatever time that is, however long it lasts, and no matter how it "ends." Some of us confess weekly that "He will come again in glory to judge the living and the dead, and his kingdom will have no end," suggesting that there will be a kingdom of God, but its arrival will be under God's power, in God's timing, and somehow discontinuous with human history and human effort.

Perhaps it is time for our disillusioned selves to revisit some of the riches of the Christian theological tradition that Rauschenbusch dismissed. Much of it was written during days in which despair made an awful lot of sense, in which worlds, or "the world," seemed to be ending but despair was not the path taken. Perhaps we move forward by looking further back in the history of Christian thought and ecclesial practice, to contexts in which people cared deeply about this world, but their theological hope did not ultimately depend on the visible progress of human history.

Perhaps we might also look to strands of the Christian tradition in which the kingdom of God was still what Christians longed for, but it was more of a dream and less of a program, more of a hoping against hope and less of a confident certainty. I think this is what we really see in much of the black church tradition in the United States. African American religion has most often sounded less like confidence in the certain march of history and more a defiant moral commitment in the teeth of history.

This, at least, is where my reflection on the kingdom ethic of Walter Rauschenbusch is taking me, in a far less hopeful age than the one in which he offered his own beautiful and inspiring work.

Chapter 13

Walter Rauschenbusch's Contribution to Baptist Life and Thought

William H. Brackney

Much has been written about Walter Rauschenbusch from a variety of perspectives since his death in 1918. His working bibliography, to be included in volume III of the "Works of Walter Rauschenbusch Publication Project," reveals many denominations and kinds of disciplines. Dores R. Sharpe's major biography in 1942, followed by Winthrop S. Hudson and Robert Handy, were written from a Baptistic perspective, but as Rauschenbusch has become an enlarged figure among Protestants and Christians, his contribution to the Baptist tradition has often been overshadowed.[1]

In this essay, I shall look at seven facets in the context of his home denominational orientation, the Baptists: his genetic Baptist identity, his use of a "basileic" theology, an evolving theology of the Social Gospel, a unique interpretation of the Reformation, his spirituality, his ecumenism, and his iconic profile. I do not mean to diminish the various orientations to Rauschenbusch, but unless one understands his Baptistic perspectives, one does not fully engage Rauschenbusch's thought and his basic contributions to his own tradition.[2]

BACKGROUND ON RAUSCHENBUSCH AS A BAPTIST

As all of his biographers have pointed out, Walter was shaped by the perspectives of his father, August, an heir to several generations of Lutheran orthodoxy and Pietism in Germany. The conversion of August Rauschenbusch to Baptist principles in his work as a domestic missionary was profound. We first must acknowledge that Walter's young impressions of being

---

[1] Doubtless this has also been attributed to the theologically conservative tendency among North American Baptists in the last half century.

[2] In a series of essays entitled "Why I am a Baptist" published in 1905, Rauschenbusch underscored four reasons: experiential Christianity, a non-creedalist interpretation, democratic organization, and the authority of the Bible.

a Baptist were mediated through his father's blend of Lutheran Pietism, American frontier revivalism, and the congregational family at Andrews Street Baptist Church in Rochester, New York.

A second Baptist influence was his education in two denominational schools: the University of Rochester (UR) and Rochester Theological Seminary (RTS). Theoretically, theologically, and practically, these institutions were of highest importance to Walter. A significant percentage of the faculty at UR was Baptist, and the entire faculty at RTS was Baptist.[3]

Walter deeply imbibed Baptist principles and he gave back in kind. In 1905, he said he was a Baptist by birth, inertia, and conviction.[4] Two examples are worthy of note. Rauschenbusch was a devoted student of scriptural Christianity. His was not a dogmatic predisposition to Scripture as inspired according to a theory, but a gradual adoption of the contemporary biblical criticism:

> All the biblical sciences are now using the historical method and striving to put us in the position of the original readers of each biblical book. But as the Bible becomes more lifelike, it becomes more social. We used to see the sacred landscape through allegorical interpretation as through a piece of yellow bottle-glass. It was very golden and wonderful, but very much apart from our everyday modern life. The Bible hereafter will be the people's book in a new sense. For the first time in religious history, we have the possibility of so directing religious energy by scientific knowledge that a comprehensive and continuous reconstruction of social life in the name of God is within the bounds of human possibility.[5]

Unlike other ivory-tower biblical scholars, Rauschenbusch sought to blend democratic principles with the message of the Bible. He was one of the leading storytellers in his denomination: "Why not tell the Bible stories

---

[3] Those in the RTS German Department were affiliated with German Conference congregations.

[4] Walter Rauschenbusch, "Why I am a Baptist," *Rochester Baptist Monthly* (November 1905): prelude. These lectures were published widely in various newspapers and are still available at present.

[5] Walter Rauschenbusch, *Christianity and the Social Crisis* (New York: Harper Torchbooks Edition, 1964), 209.

as if nobody had ever heard them?," he asked.[6] So effective was he as a Bible teacher that secular magazine editors sought him out to write a series for the religious readership.[7]

What he meant by taking the Bible as a Baptist seriously contrasted with other groups:

> The Bible is totally different from a creed. A creed contains sharply defined and abstract theology; the Bible contains a record of concrete and glowing religious life. A creed addresses itself to the intellect; the Bible appeals to the whole soul and edifies it. A creed tells you what you must believe; the Bible tells you what holy men have believed. A creed is religious philosophy, the Bible is religious history. A creed gives the truth as it looked to one set of clever men at one particular stage of human history; the Bible gives the truth as it looked to a great number of God-filled men running through many hundreds of years. The strength of a creed is in its uniformity and its tight fit; the beauty of the Bible is in its marvelous variety and richness. A creed imposes a law and binds thought; the Bible imparts a spirit and awakens thought.[8]

A second instance of applied Baptist principles pertained to church-state relations. In his "big book" he surveyed the history of church-state relations from the early church through the nineteenth century and concluded, "The State is the representative of things as they are; the Church is the representative of things as they ought to be." In a prescient Baptistic conclusion, he said, "The separation of Church and State has the double advantage of removing the clerical influence from political life, and the political influence from church life. It leaves the Church unmuzzled to speak out, if it has anything to say. It does its best work when it is the party in opposition, poor but vociferous."[9]

Neither Isaac Backus nor John Leland, let alone E. Y. Mullins, could have said it better. In fact, no writer before Rauschenbusch had so astutely analyzed church history to arrive at an appreciation of Baptist principles.

---

[6] Walter Rauschenbusch, "The Value and Use of History." Address Delivered at the Special Session of Rochester-Colgate Theological Seminaries, May 1914.

[7] Notably, Theodore Dreiser, editor of *The Delineator*, a leading contemporary women's magazine.

[8] Walter Rauschenbusch, "Why I am a Baptist—My Fourth Reason."

[9] Rauschenbusch, *Christianity and the Social Crisis*, 186; 188.

BASILEIC THEOLOGY

"Basileic" or kingdom theology derives from the Greek term *basilieou tou theou* or "kingdom [reign] of God." Walter Rauschenbusch used the term and it is a major underused descriptor of his thought. Essentially understanding the church as a local congregation, for Rauschenbusch the kingdom was an expansive theological necessity that broadened the immanence of God in all of creation. In order to appreciate fully Rauschenbusch's contribution to Baptist thinking about the kingdom, one has first to have a contextual understanding of contemporary Baptist theologians.

In the far reaches of Baptist kingdom thought was the venerable eighteenth-century English Baptist theologian John Gill. Gill ventured into the meaning of the kingdom under the heading of Christology, or the kingly office of Christ. He defined the kingdom as God's overall dominion over his creation in every aspect. Seen in light of his messianic offices, Gill noted the evolution of the kingdom to be synonymous with the church: ministry of the Word, ordinances, discipline, etc. being present aspects of the kingdom. It is a spiritual kingdom, not carnal, worldly, or earthly. When the mediatorial kingdom is delivered up to God, according to Gill, Christ will reign a thousand years, and then forever.[10]

Similar to Gill, less stridently Calvinistic, was Andrew Fuller. Fuller was an English Baptist pastor-theologian who was influential in launching the world missionary advance and shaping American Baptist evangelical thought as well. In a tract in which he interacted with a leading sacramentarian, "Strictures on Sandemanianism," he characterized the kingdom of God (or Christ) as a "moral and spiritual army going forth to battle...men who conscientiously attend to the positive nature of Christ."[11] He was not prepared to equate the kingdom with a form of the church, including his own denomination. Fuller was pragmatic enough to see the flaws in the life of the visible churches and sufficiently Christological to hear Jesus's words

---

[10] John Gill, *A Complete Body of Divinity: A System of Evangelical Truths, Deduced from the Sacred Scriptures* (London: John Gill, 1769), 439–48.

[11] Andrew Fuller, "Strictures on Sandemanianism," in Andrew Gunton Fuller, *The Complete Works of the Rev. Andrew Fuller, with a Memoir of His Life* (London: Henry G. Bohn, 1859), 288, 290.

that the kingdom was "not meat nor drink." His works paved the way for a generic understanding of the term "evangelical" in the nineteenth century.[12]

Rauschenbusch was thoroughly indebted to his Rochester teachers Ezekiel G. Robinson and Augustus H. Strong. But in neither did he find any foundation for his basileic theology. Strong was virtually silent on the kingdom, preferring to define the church as a voluntary society, in Lockean terms. Robinson, whom Dr. Strong described as still hewing out his theology, was no friend to the emerging eschatology of the Darbyites and equated the kingdom of Christ with the church: "The church of Christ is to us the only visible exhibition of this kingdom. Christ is the head of the church and the king in Zion."[13]

The most extensive, relatively concurrent explication of the kingdom among Baptist theologians was found in John L. Dagg's *Manual of Theology* (1871). Dagg was the leading nineteenth-century theologian associated with Baptists in the southern United States. He was influenced by a personal reading of Andrew Fuller and John Gill, himself an evangelical Calvinist.[14] Dagg spoke of the kingdom as God's dominion, including those who willingly and voluntarily give themselves up to God's authority. Dagg associated the kingdom with the reign of Messiah, especially those who are the "good seed," culminating in the judgment of Christ. The kingdom will be fully realized, he believed, when all enemies have been subdued and all things restored.[15] It was both an inner spiritual submission and a coming literal kingdom.

At mid-nineteenth century, there was a strong hint of basileic theology noticed in Francis Wayland, the prominent Baptist moralist and president of Brown University. He concluded from a reading of the Lord's Prayer that the kingdom of God (also known to him as Christ's kingdom) was attainable through sacrificial giving and witness to its reality. "If we really pray,"

---

[12] A. Fuller, *The Gospel Worthy of All Acceptation; or, The Duty of Sinners to Believe in Jesus Christ*, Third Edition. (Philadelphia, PA: Charles Cist, 1805), 148–49; 202.

[13] Ezekiel Gilman Robinson, *Christian Theology* (Rochester, NY: E. R. Andrews, 1894), 342.

[14] William H. Brackney, *A Genetic History of Baptist Thought, with Special Reference to Baptists in Britain and North America* (Macon, GA: Mercer University Press, 2004), 391–93.

[15] J. L. Dagg, *Manual of Theology: A Treatise on Christian Doctrine* (Philadelphia, PA: American Baptist Publication Society, 1871), 225–29; esp. 229.

Wayland said, "for the extension of Christ's kingdom, we must live like men who make the extension of that kingdom the great business of our lives." Further, he reasoned, "If we pray, Thy kingdom come, can we do less than live so that the kingdom of God may come?"[16]

Another interesting foray into basileic theology was noticed in William Newton Clarke's 1894 *Outline of Christian Theology*. Clarke much anticipated Rauschenbusch and it is highly likely that Rauschenbusch read Clarke and interacted with him.[17] Clarke was biblically founded:

> When Jesus entered upon his ministry, he took up John's word, and declared that the kingdom of God was at hand. The proclamation of this kingdom was not confined to the beginning of his ministry; it was a constant element.... The idea of a kingdom of God was no new idea: it came over from the prophets, and formed an element in the Hebrew hope. To Jesus, however, the kingdom was no national organization, no political institution: it was the spiritual reign of God in the actual life of men.... The peculiarity of Jesus with respect to the kingdom of God was that he recognized the king as Father and the Father as king. To him the spirit of the kingdom was no other than the filial spirit, and the reign of God is simply God's rule over his family.... This is the purpose that is expressed by the mention of the kingdom of God.[18]

Contemporary Baptist relative theological silence on the kingdom led Rauschenbusch far beyond his North American contemporaries. He was particularly enamored of German and English theologians like Albrecht Ritschl, Adolf von Harnack, and F. D. Maurice, who saw the kingdom as a continuous growth in history of the ideals of Jesus where Christian action and a Christian way of life would reflect God's kingdom.[19] Von Harnack

---

[16] Francis Wayland, *Notes on the Principles and Practices of Baptist Churches* (New York: Sheldon, Blakeman & Co., 1857), 223.

[17] A considerable correspondence survives between the two in the ABHS Rauschenbusch collections. Clarke was a frequent attender of the Brotherhood of the Kingdom.

[18] William Newton Clarke, *An Outline of Christian Theology*, 4th Edition (New York: Scribner's Sons, 1894; repr. 1899), 276–77.

[19] As early as 1892 Rauschenbusch recognized Ritschl's contribution to "basileic" theology in bringing it forward into his own thinking. Maurice, an advocate

had written about the kingdom being aligned with practical godliness. Ritschl's words were especially penetrating: "The Kingdom of God is the divinely ordained end of the preaching of Christ including the demand for change of heart."[20] Rauschenbusch's definition of the kingdom of God was "humanity organized according to the will of God...a progressive reign of love in human affairs. It is divine in its origin, progress and consummation. It embraces the whole of life."[21]

One of Rauschenbusch's published prayers was relative to the kingdom of God:

> Help us, O Lord, in the courage of faith to seize what has now come so near, that the glad day of God may dawn at last. As we have mastered nature that we might gain wealth, help us now to master the social relations of mankind that we may gain justice and a world of brothers. For what shall it profit our nation if it gain numbers and riches, and lose the sense of the living God and the joy of human brotherhood?[22]

THE SOCIAL GOSPEL

All interpreters recognize that Rauschenbusch was not the first among Baptists to espouse ideas about the Social Gospel, nor perhaps the most articulate. His contribution lies in the proliferation of his work and the power and influence of his principal books, both positive and negative.

Rauschenbusch's "baptism" in Social Gospel thought among Baptists may be dated to his pastoral work in New York City. It was as the minister of Second German Baptist in New York City that he observed and experi-

---

of "Social Christianity," an English idiom, believed that with the Incarnation, Jesus had ushered in the "Kingdom of Christ."

[20] Albrecht Ritschl, *Instruction in the Christian Religion*, trans. Alice Mead Swing, in Albert Temple Swing, *The Theology of Albrecht Ritschl* (New York: Longmans, Green, and Co., 1901), 174. Further, "The kingdom of God is the divinely vouchsafed for highest good of the community founded through his revelation in Christ, but it is the highest good only in the sense that it forms at the same time the ethical ideal, for whose attainment the members of the community bind themselves together through their definite reciprocal action."

[21] Rauschenbusch, *A Theology for the Social Gospel*, 139–45.

[22] Walter Rauschenbusch, "For the Kingdom of God," in *Prayers of the Social Awakening* (Boston, MA: Pilgrim Press, 1909), 107.

enced the issues that helped him to search for new ideas and solutions. His definition of the Social Gospel remains classic:

> The Social Gospel registers the fact that for the first time in history the spirit of Christianity has had a chance to form a working partnership with real social and psychological science. It is the religious reaction on the historic advent of democracy. It seeks to put the democratic spirit, which the church inherited from Jesus and the prophets, once more in control of the institutions and teachings of the Church.... The Social Gospel seeks to bring men under repentance for their collective sins and to create a more sensitive and more modern conscience. It calls on us for the faith of the old prophets who believed in the salvation of nations.[23]

In formally engaging Social Christianity, Rauschenbusch joined forces with an unusual coterie of Baptists: Leighton and Mornay Williams at Amity Baptist, Nathaniel Schmidt at First Swedish Baptist, Edward Judson at Judson Memorial, and from time to time, William Newton Clarke at Colgate, Samuel Zane Batten at Manayunk in Philadelphia, and George Dana Boardman Jr. at First Baptist, Philadelphia.

Among those in the Baptist community who applauded Rauschenbusch's 1907 book were William Newton Clarke, Brown University president William H. P. Faunce, Augustus Strong, and John D. Rockefeller.[24]

Regional and national Baptist recognition of Rauschenbusch's Social Gospel emphases came along three lines. First were his students who carried the Social Gospel into their ministries. Foremost among them were Dores R. Sharpe and Edwin Dahlberg. Sharpe moved among Baptists in Chicago; Saskatchewan; Cleveland, Ohio; and Rochester. As an executive minister or city missionary society director, he formulated policies and executed strategies according to his mentor's writings. Dahlberg became a regional and national leader in the advance of home missions and interdenominational work. In later years, he fully credited his mentor with launching his vision.[25]

A second line of recognition for Rauschenbusch in the Baptist family came with his "literary baptism." In the first full-scale history of the Baptists since Henry Vedder (1927), Robert G. Torbet wrote in 1950: "Unrest was

---

[23] Rauschenbusch, *A Theology for the Social Gospel*, 5–6.

[24] Cited in Evans, *The Kingdom Is Always but Coming*, 191–92.

[25] Edwin Dahlberg and John Skoglund, *Reminiscences of Walter Rauschenbush*, n.p., 1973.

being aroused by the spread of theological liberalism, and by the preaching of those who were seeking the salvation of society through the Social Gospel, which had sprung into prominence through the writings of Walter Rauschenbusch, church historian and professor at Rochester Theological Seminary."[26]

This was the first overall denominational historical acknowledgement of the place of Rauschenbusch and the Social Gospel.

Additional heavyweight support was given to Rauschenbusch's place in Baptist history by Robert T. Handy and Winthrop S. Hudson. These two high-ranking Baptist historians deliberately connected Rauschenbusch with the Liberal Baptist position, as incarnated in Colgate-Rochester Divinity School.

There was also a negative response in the Baptist family to Rauschenbusch's Social Gospel. Upon attending the Baptist Congress in 1898, E. Y. Mullins at Southern Baptist Seminary quipped that he had been to hear Rauschenbusch but found "more social than gospel in the Social Gospel." Clergy who identified with the Evangelical Alliance could be very critical of Social Gospelism.

One of the major catalysts for the distancing and eventual separation of the German Baptist Conference from the Northern (American) Baptist Convention was the powerful influence of the Social Gospel. Walter Rauschenbusch and the "social question" were at the core of this coming separation. Beginning in 1890, a literary debate on the social question commenced in the editions of *Der Sendbote* that brought Rauschenbusch fully into focus. Given his family's reputation in the conference, Rauschenbusch was taken very seriously. He debated various aspects of Christian responsibility with E. Anschuetz of West Hoboken, New Jersey, that gave great exposure to his new interest in the social implications of Christianity. A large segment of the German Baptist Conference was apathetic, some were offended at Rauschenbusch's interpretation of the Bible, and a very few became converts. Klaus Juergen Jaehn observed, "The German Baptists were those who heeded him least. For the most part, they steadfastly refused to listen to his message of the social responsibility of the church. The discussion of the social question in *Der Sendbote* was soon forgotten. Later ar-

[26] Robert G. Torbet, *A History of the Baptists* (Philadelphia, PA: Judson Press, 1950), 425.

ticles in *Der Sendbote* indicate that the original conservatism withstood the discussion unscathed."[27]

Other Baptist groups slowly responded to the Social Gospel. In the South, Wake Forest College became a kind of developing epicenter of Social Gospelism under the presidency of William L. Poteat. Poteat led North Carolina Baptists and later the national denomination in recognition of social values inherent in the Christian witness.[28] Southern Baptist Theological Seminary appointed an ethicist, Henlee Barnette, who was much enamored of Rauschenbusch's ideas. Southeastern and Golden Gate Baptist Seminaries (SBC) displayed quiet interest in the Social Gospel as well. In the Southern Baptist Convention, the creation of a Social Service Commission in 1913, later to become the Christian Life Commission, brought the largest Baptist group into an awareness of Rauschenbusch's programs.

On the resistant side, entire Baptist come-outer groups aligned against the Social Gospel. First was the Baptist Bible Union of America, later to evolve as the General Association of Regular Baptist Churches (GARBC). Among the hundreds of Baptist congregations in New York State, the GARBC had a profound impact, drawing numerous churches from the Broome-Tioga Association, and in the Southwest, the Allegheny, Cattaraugus, and Genesee Associations out of the state convention. By 1960, Baptist life in New York State was divided between two schools and epicenters: Colgate-Rochester in Rochester and the Rauschenbusch influence, and Practical Bible Training School in Binghamton, New York, an anti-Rochester and anti-Rauschenbusch coalition. The formation of the national Conservative Baptist Association in 1943 took yet another group of Northern Baptists out, opposed to Social Gospelism.[29]

---

[27] Klaus Juergen Jaehn, "The Formation of Walter Rauschenbusch's Social Consciousness as Reflected in His Early Life and Writings, Part II," *Foundations* (March 1974): 73. The 1890s debates are exhaustively treated in Frank H. Woyke, *Heritage and Ministry of the North America Baptist Conference* (Oakbrook Terrace, IL: North American Baptist Conference, 1979), 273–81.

[28] William L. Poteat and his son Edwin McNeill Poteat were catalysts in social awakening in the denomination. Edwin McNeill Poteat went on to become president of Colgate Rochester Divinity School in the 1940s. See H. Leon McBeth, *The Baptist Heritage: Four Centuries of Baptist Witness* (Nashville, TN: Broadman Press, 1987), 656.

[29] An interesting conglomeration of pro- and anti-Social Gospel identities was found in the District of Columbia Baptist Convention (Washington, DC). An

By the 1970s the tide had turned in a more positive direction for Rauschenbusch and the Social Gospel. Colgate-Rochester had regular courses devoted to the implications of the Social Gospel, in the 1940s to the 1960s mostly under the guiding hand of Conrad H. Moehlman and later Winthrop Hudson. At Crozer Seminary, Kenneth L. Smith openly identified Martin Luther King Jr. with Walter Rauschenbusch, and the University of Chicago Divinity School produced several doctoral dissertations focussed on Rauschenbusch or the Social Gospel. Berkeley Baptist Divinity School in California acknowledged Rauschenbusch through its church historian, Eldon Ernst,[30] and Eastern Baptist Theological Seminary required Rauschenbusch's 1907 book, *Christianity and the Social Crisis,* in its Christian Social Ethics course. Social Gospel enthusiasts, mostly CRDS alums, founded the Roger Williams Fellowship as an activist enclave in the national convention.[31]

Rauschenbusch and the Social Gospel were regularly recurring features in *Foundations: A Baptist Journal of History, Theology, and Ministry*, the official intellectual outlet of the American Baptist Convention. Under the editorial direction of George D. Younger, a committed social activist with a degree from Yale, eight major articles appeared from 1958 to 1981.[32]

---

amalgam of Northern and Southern Convention-related congregations in the same association, the churches were willing to work through their respective theological affiliations. Those affiliating with Crozer and Colgate Rochester were strong in advocacy.

[30] Ernst was a distinguished student of Winthrop S. Hudson and married the daughter of John Skoglund, a later disciple of Rauschenbusch.

[31] Among the RWF members were Wilbur Eddy Saunders, Oren H. Baker, Glenn B. Ewell, Winthrop S. Hudson, Gordon Torgerson, Andrew and James Davison, James Ashbrook, Robert Newell, Gene E. Bartlett, Roger Sharpe, and Hugh Q. Morton. The RWF met at the time of the Rauschenbusch Lectures at CRDS.

[32] They were: Donovan Smucker, "The Rauschenbusch Story"; Carlyle Marney, "The Spirit of Walter Rauschenbusch for Today"; Sherman Barnes, "Walter Rauschenbusch as Historian"; Henry Warner Bowden, "Walter Rauschenbusch and American Church History"; Klaus Jurgen-Jaehn, "The Foundations of Walter Rauschenbusch's Social Consciousness as Reflected in His Early Life and Writings, Part I"; "Part II"; Dennis R. Davis, "The Impact of Evolutionary Thought on Walter Rauschenbusch"; Glenn C. Altschuler, "Walter Rauschenbusch, Theology, the Church, and the Social Gospel."

INTERPRETATION OF THE REFORMATION

Theologically, Rauschenbusch approached church history and Baptist history from an historicist/immantest point of view. A powerful critic of oppressive religious institutions, he believed that God thinks in action and speaks in events. God's historical realities are a surer word of God than any prophecy. Human history was thus a revelation of God's will, Rauschenbusch wrote. His interpretation of the Anabaptists well illustrates his theological interpretation of history.

For Rauschenbusch, the Anabaptists were the truest of Reformers, contrasting sharply with what he called the "Reformatory Protestants" (another term for the Magisterial Reformers). Relying heavily upon Josef von Beck's *Geschicbucher der Wiedertaufer* (1883), Henry Clay Vedder's *Short History of the Baptists* (1907), Champlin Burrage on the Swiss Anabaptists (1912, A. H. Newman's *Antipaedobaptism* [1897]), Rufus Jones's *Studies in Mystical Religion* (1909), and especially Richard Heath's *Anabaptism* and *The Captive City of God* (resp. 1895; 1904), Rauschenbusch assembled the known data and reached seven points affirming the value of the Anabaptists.

Rauschenbusch first noted the widespread influence of the Anabaptists in central Europe, a fact not much realized until the late nineteenth century. He linked the Anabaptists with the Waldensians, Lollards, and Taborites in a stream of the initial stirrings of Christian democracy, expressions of lay religion, and working-class ethics. Here he reflected a common Baptist interpretive scheme known as "successionism," or an attempt to connect modern Baptists with an unbroken line of Baptistic groups from the New Testament to the nineteenth century.[33] When he visited Munster in 1891, Rauschenbusch heard the German historian Ludwig Keller declare that "Anabaptists contained more of the future than the Reformers."[34]

Next Rauschenbusch noted the inadequate historical treatment of the Anabaptists in the standard church histories. He found them mostly a caricature of a fanatical sect. He turned to the historical predominance of infant

---

[33] On successionism, see J. R. Graves, *Old Landmarkism: What Is It?* (Texarkana, TX: Baptist Sunday School Committee, 1880), 166–82, and W. Morgan Patterson, *Baptist Successionism: A Critical View* (Valley Forge, PA: Judson Press, 1969), and James E. Tull, *High-Church Baptists in the South: The Origin, Nature, and Influence of Landmarkism* (Macon, GA: Mercer University Press, 2000), 220–22.

[34] Quoted in Minus, *American Reformer*, 82.

baptism from the third and fourth centuries and observed that it was inevitable that the practice should be called into question: in this regard, he believed the Anabaptists were ahead of their age.

As Rauschenbusch saw it, across several types and regions, the Anabaptists held common convictions that produced a group life and a "true" church. The Anabaptists alone held a commitment to the restoration of the Apostolic life, regardless of the circumstances. He agreed with the Anabaptists that society had become corrupt and all true Christians should lead a sanctified life.[35] He went so far as to compare the courage of the Anabaptists to the Donatist sect of the third and fourth centuries.

As an American of German descent, for Rauschenbusch this connection with the Radical Reformation was of the essence. The sixteenth-century Reformers had bequeathed the ideals of individual freedom, personal religious experience, and opposition to ritualistic religion. Joining American nationalists like Josiah Strong, Rauschenbusch believed the fulfillment of the Anabaptist vision was in the American democratic nationalist movement, of which the Baptists were the leading expression.

Amidst the ever-present debate among Baptists over their typological origins, Rauschenbusch helped to establish an early version of the Anabaptist Kinship Theory, popularized among sectarian Baptists of the twentieth century.[36] His words in an editorial ring true: "By being a Baptist I am a Radical Protestant."[37]

History was always a corrective and broadening influence for the professor. "For the wider wisdom needed for large leadership," he wrote, "there is nothing like the study of history."[38]

SPIRITUALITY

Walter Rauschenbusch was known to his students as a deeply pietistic, spiritual man. His three books, *Prayers for the Social Awakening*, *Dare We Be*

---

[35] Franklin H. Littell later referred to this as the "fall of the Church," in his *The Anabaptist View of the Church: A Study in the Origin of Sectarian Protestantism* (Boston, MA: Starr King Press, 1958; 1984), 57–61.

[36] This in contrast with the Successionists/Trail of Blood theory, advocates of the Puritan-Separatist theory, and the pluralist position of multiple points of origin.

[37] Walter Rauschenbusch, "Why I Am A Baptist—My Third Reason."

[38] Rauschenbusch, "The Value and Use of History."

Christians?, and *Unto Me*, reflect his literary spirituality. One of his early editorials was devoted to prayer:

> The main thing is to have God; to live in Him; to have Him live in us; to think His thoughts; to love what He loves and hate what He hates; to realize His presence; to feel his holiness and be holy because He is holy; to feel His goodness in every blessing of our life and even its tribulations; to be happy and trustful; to join in the great purposes of God and to be lifted to greatness of vision and faith and hope with Him—that is the blessed life.[39]

J. W. A. Stewart, Rauschenbusch's dean at Rochester Seminary, said of his colleague, "He walked with God.... He sought to bring his daily life, the inward life as well as the outward, constantly under the eye of God, our heavenly Father."[40]

Rauschenbusch was raised in a home that valued the authority of Scripture. However, when the emerging fundamentalists overemphasized the infallibility of Scripture or ancient dogmatic articles over Christ, he moved in another direction. For him, the key to spirituality was inspiration. He saw inspiration as "the spirit of Christ bearing up the flutterings of the human mind with the sweep of mightier wings."[41] Surely, he knew that Scripture was inspired, but his emphasis went beyond. Men and women like him, as artists, craftsmen, and writers, were equally inspired. In the contemporary debate over extraordinary spiritual gifts, Rauschenbusch preferred prophesying over tongue-speaking because spiritually, it involved the human element of reason. Prophesying took into account the social dimension of things, not merely the personal aspects of religion.

Dare We Be Christians? exhibited Rauschenbusch's priority on love. He pointed out that Jesus set love into the center of religion. Jesus spoke words of love and embodied the principle of love in the charm and youthful strength that touched many lives. He taught his friends to think of God as a loving, unselfish father. Ultimately the cross depicted the redemptive love of

---

[39] Walter Rauschenbusch, "Thoughts on Prayer," *Baptist Monthly* (January 1901).

[40] J. W. A. Stewart, "The Record," *Rochester Theological Seminary* (November 1918): 25.

[41] Walter Rauschenbusch, *Dare We Be Christians?* (New York: Pilgrim Press, 1914), 11.

God. In its most emphatic theological statement, Rauschenbusch said, "Christianity stands for the belief that God is love."[42]

Rauschenbusch found love at the heart of Paul's spirituality. He was drawn to the Apostle's angelic poem in I Corinthians and even rewrote it to fit modern circumstances. He wrote that Paul asserted that love is the last and best word of life and the indispensable ingredient of all that claims to be Christian. Typical of his contemporary contextualization of biblical teaching, Rauschenbusch urged his readers, "Have we faith enough to believe that the Christian doctrine of love is the solution of our big modern questions? Do we dare to asset the futility of everything in our great world of commerce and industry that leaves love out? Do we dare to undertake the readjustment of all social life to bring it into obedience to the law of love?"[43]

Rauschenbusch the pastor was a man of prayer. He prayed publicly, and often his phraseology was to a degree captured in his *Prayers for the Social Awakening*. In that second of his "little volumes," he penned prayers for morning, noon, and night, thanksgiving, social groups and classes, wrath, and the progress of humanity. In the preface, he wrote, "Whenever a great movement stirs the deeper passions of men, a common soul is born, and all those who feel the throb of a new age have such unity of thought and aim and feeling, that the utterance of one man may in a measure be the voice of all."[44] Theologically, Rauschenbusch reasoned, "If we had more prayer in common on the sins of modern society, there would be more social repentance and less angry resistance to the demands of justice and mercy."[45]

Reading through Rauschenbusch's prayers, one has the impression of a high priest in ancient Israel who brought the sins of his people before Yahweh. "When we work with others, help us to regard them not as servants to our will but as brothers equal to us in human dignity, and equally worthy of their full reward."[46] "Bless with a sevenfold blessing the young lives whose slender shoulders are already bowed beneath the yoke of toil and whose glad growth is being stunted forever."[47] For women who toil, he prayed, "Save them from the terrors of utter want. Teach them to stand loyally by their

---

[42] Rauschenbusch, *Dare We Be Christians?*, 57.

[43] Ibid., 24.

[44] Rauschenbusch, *Prayers for the Social Awakening*, 11.

[45] Ibid., 12.

[46] "Morning Prayers," 27.

[47] "For Children Who Work," 51.

sisters, that by united action they may better their common lot."[48] Of immigrants, "We mourn for dark sins of past and present, wherein who are held in honor among us made spoil of the ignorance and helplessness of the strangers and sent them to an early death."[49] Rauschenbusch had strong words for the promoters of war: "Ever the songs of the past and the pomp of armies have been used to inflame the passions of the people. Our spirit cries out to thee in revolt against it, and we know that our righteous anger is answered by thy holy wrath."[50] Plaintively, he exclaimed in confession: "O God, we know that all our prayers can never bring back the past, and no tears can wash out the red marks with which we have scarred some life that stands before our memory with accusing eyes."[51]

One of his most memorable contributions was his commentary on the Lord's Prayer. Critiquing its contemporary use, he said, "The churches have employed it for their ecclesiastical ritual. Yet it is not ecclesiastical. There is no hint in it of the Church, the ministry, the doctrines of theology, or the sacraments."

Instead, "The Lord's Prayer is the great prayer of Social Christianity. It is charged with what we call "social consciousness." It assumes the social solidarity of men as a matter of course. It recognizes the social basis of all moral and religious life even in the most intimate personal relations to God."[52]

Clearly Walter Rauschenbusch was among the outstanding mystics in the Baptist family of his era.

BAPTIST ECUMENICAL LEADER

From his pastoral experience in New York, Rauschenbusch learned and practiced the values of ecumenicity. In his urban context, he worked with Protestants of various stripes, Jewish leaders, and persons known to be agnostic. This was to be of high significance for the Baptist community.

In his early travels in Europe, Walter visited and interacted with leaders of many denominations. Through his father's connections, he met most of the leading German Lutherans of his era. His study at Gütersloh gave

---

[48] "For Women Who Toil,"55.

[49] "For Immigrants," 60.

[50] "Against War," 97.

[51] "On the Harm We Have Done," 111–12.

[52] "Introductory: The Social Meaning of the Lord's Prayer," 16; 23.

him a firsthand critical understanding of Lutheranism, both the Orthodox and Pietist traditions. He built working friendships with Anglicans, Catholics, Fabian Socialists, and freethinker social theorists during his travels.

The formation of the Brotherhood of the Kingdom was an ecumenical venture. Eleven men at first formed the group, fostered by Leighton Williams, most ecumenical of the Brothers. It soon came to include Richard Ely (Episcopalian), Josiah Strong (Evangelical Alliance), Washington Gladden (Congregationalist), Jacob Riis (Lutheran), Joseph Alling (Presbyterian) of Rochester, and Mornay Williams (Baptist-become-Episcopalian). The original vision for the Brotherhood was the Society of Jesus, founded by Ignatius Loyola.

Early in his ministerial career, he branched out into Baptist associational life, most importantly by participating in the German Baptist Conference, the Baptist Congress, and the Baptist World Alliance.

When the Federal Council of Churches of Christ in the USA was founded in 1908, Rauschenbusch was one of its principal promoters within the Northern Baptist Convention.[53] In an era when the Southern Baptists turned aside an invitation to join, Rauschenbusch led the forces in the Northern states to become charter members representing the Baptists. Within his own denomination, he was a continual resource to the Social Service Commission, one of the major national agencies of the new Northern Baptist Convention.

Rauschenbusch's writing and thinking circle was an ecumenical potpourri. He exchanged opinions with Shailer Mathews, a Chicago Baptist, Francis Peabody, a Unitarian, Vida Scudder, a Congregationalist, Henry C. King, a Congregationalist, Paul M. Strayer, a Presbyterian, and Archbishop Ed Hanna, a Roman Catholic. He read Giuseppe Mazzini, F. W. Robertson, F. D. Maurice, and Charles Kingsley, and he coauthored hymns with Ida Sankey, a Methodist. He was reviewed favorably in the denominational papers of Congregationalists, Presbyterians, Disciples of Christ, and Methodists.

The ecumenical posture of Rauschenbusch cut two ways. He brought acclaim for his theology and literary achievements to the Baptists, and Baptists through him found new comrades in arms.

---

[53] One of his student secretaries, Edwin Dahlberg, became long-time executive of the council.

ICONOGRAPHIC IMAGES

One of the leading images that endures of Walter Rauschenbusch was that of an urban Baptist minister. Thousands of Baptist ministers before him, contemporary with him, and afterwards have been defined in city work. Rauschenbusch was different. Cast in a difficult setting in New York's Hell's Kitchen, he was defined by environmental blight, abuse within families, and circumstances beyond his individual transformation. In a real sense, the Baptist ecclesiology of an autonomous local church was inadequate to the situation. What Rauschenbusch gave to Baptists was a reflective element upon one's ministry (he wrote hundreds of essays and treatises while a city pastor) in which he called attention to urban issues and potential solutions. Further, he affirmed the need to consult broadly and ecumenically and build a collective response to his situation. The formation of the Brotherhood of the Kingdom was a result, as were two periodicals that brought a variety of writers together. His two big books, *Christianity and the Social Crisis* (1907) and *Christianizing the Social Order* (1912), were gifts from his own ministry. Both have endured over time.

Another of Rauschenbusch's iconic images was that of a prophet. The Baptist community was transfixed on the New Testament era, building faith and practice largely upon the apostolic churches.[54] In contrast, Rauschenbusch was early interested in the Old Testament ideal of the prophet who connected with real issues and called Israel to account. Gradually, he began to see himself in the role of a prophet. Rauschenbusch called the prophets the beating heart of the Old Testament. He concluded that the prophets were an indispensable tool for understanding the social influence exerted by historic Christianity but also for comprehending the mind of Christ.[55] Christ, he taught, was the very embodiment of the prophetic tradition. Crossing to his own time, he asked of the prophets, "If they lived today, would they place the chief blame for poverty on the poor and give their

---

[54] The theologically liberal wing of the Northern Baptist Convention in 1922 voted 1,264–637 to have the New Testament as "the all-sufficient ground of faith and practice." See *Baptist Life and Thought: A Sourcebook*, Revised Edition, ed. William H. Brackney (Valley Forge, PA: 1998), 358.

[55] Walter Rauschenbusch, *Christianity and the Social Crisis* (New York: Macmillan Co., 1907), 3; Rauschenbusch, *Christianizing the Social Order* (New York: Macmillan Co., 1912), 50–53.

admiration to the strong?"[56] Among Baptists he revitalized interest in the history of Israel, the Hebrew language, and the living dynamic of the prophetic office for ministry.[57]

Part of Rauschenbusch's emphasis as a prophet led to the unintended consequence of his being considered a martyr for his theology. This had roots in the traditional evangelical community's vicious rejection of his writings.[58] In the days leading to the First World War, Rauschenbusch suffered at the hands of the Anglo-Saxon communities because of his attempt to be balanced in understanding Germany's posture.[59] When he was stricken with fatal illness, seemingly at the peak of his literary career, it was as though he had made the ultimate sacrifice. The myth of a martyrdom was greatly enhanced by his students in the Colgate-Rochester tradition.[60] The memorial window in the Samuel Colgate Chapel is the ultimate statement: a modern-day prophet-martyr. It stands next to windows dedicated to Roger Williams, William Newton Clarke, and Adoniram Judson. Hundreds of students and wedding and funeral guests have pondered that unusual select company of Baptist icons.

In Baptist geography, Rochester, New York, became synonymous with Walter Rauschenbusch and the Social Gospel. From the days of the Removalist Controversy in the 1850s, the Baptist urban community in Rochester became synonymous with a progressive, liberal tradition. As a Baptist theologian and professor, Rauschenbusch had an unusual impact upon his home city, able to speak to power about its economic, social, and environmental darker sides.[61] Rochester was not New England, or the Middle States, or the

---

[56] Rauschenbusch, *Christianity and the Social Crisis*, 41.

[57] Rauschenbusch was much influenced in his appreciation for the prophets by the Scottish theologian George Adam Smith (1856–1942) and the Swedish-American Old Testament scholar Nathaniel Schmidt.

[58] See for instance, William S. McBirnie's books, *The Social Gospel: A Perversion of the Christian Gospel* and *Walter Rauschenbusch: Apostle of the Social Gospel*, and the critiques of I. M. Haldeman, and William Bell Riley.

[59] He received a good deal of antagonistic mail and his Ontario, Canada, cottage was burned by neighbors.

[60] The major mentees were Dores R. Sharpe, Edwin Dahlberg, and Conrad H. Moehlman.

[61] In April 1904 Rauschenbusch gave a much-publicized address to the Rochester Labor Lyceum, "What's the Matter with Rochester," in which he called attention to numerous issues crying out for reform. The address is summarized in *The*

Midwest, in Baptist terms. It was upstate New York, not New York City. Rochester was a successful urban center with a diverse immigrant population, a literate and literary culture with a science and industrial orientation. In fact, the German community was definitive.

The Baptist churches in Rochester spawned a university and a theological school that within four decades of their establishment were on the cutting edges of intellectual, social, and religious culture. In doing so, they outdistanced the Presbyterians and the Methodists. Rochester Seminary and the University of Rochester won the regional "competition" with the Colgate schools, largely because of the generous Baptist philanthropy in Monroe County.[62] In Baptist terms, they far exceeded the contributions of Colgate in leather-stocking culture.[63]

Augustus H. Strong was administratively the solid helmsman of the seminary, but the unique theological tradition that dominated the city after 1907 was clearly and singularly focussed in Walter Rauschenbusch.[64] While he lived, people came to study and observe him; after he passed away, they came to study in the environment where he had lived and taught. Like no other Baptist seminary/church relationship in the Progressive Era, the Monroe Baptist Association (forty to sixty congregations) and the Rochester Baptist City Mission Society[65] "owned" and nurtured Rochester Seminary and later Colgate-Rochester Divinity School as a gathering place for intellectual inquiry, the practice of experimental urban theology, and profession-

---

Rochester Democrat and Chronicle, 4 April 1904. I am grateful to Prof. Stephen Shapiro at the University of Warwick, and a Rochester native, for calling this to my attention.

[62] These included lawyers, brewers, industrialists, and book publishers.

[63] Hamilton Literary and Theological Institution (1819), later Madison University (1836), still later Colgate University (1888), was a small New England Baptist college located in a small rural village, several miles from the railroad connections. It was founded to provide missionaries for upstate New York and to educate local pastors.

[64] Strong attracted the Rockefeller family and introduced the Rockefellers and the Rauschenbuschs. A voluminous correspondence opened over several years. See the correspondence files in the Rockefeller Archive as listed in *Rauschenbusch: Published Works* (2018), vol. III.

[65] Since 1973 combined as The American Baptist Churches of Monroe Association (TABCOMA).

al fellowship and celebration. The Rauschenbusch lectures and the fellowship in his name attest to this remarkable synergy.

CONCLUSION

Walter Rauschenbusch made a significant, far-reaching contribution to Baptist life and thought. Being Baptist was fundamental to his character and outlook. He exhibited democratic nationalist and revivalistic traits, as did most Baptists in the United States of his generation. He incarnated experiential Christianity and espoused local church governance and polity. His name was table talk in the German and North American Baptist communities for a generation and more. He was among the best educated Baptist ministers in North America of the later nineteenth century.

In some ways, as we have seen, Rauschenbusch's work and advocacy powerfully enabled Baptist Christianity to enlarge its mission horizons, theological inquiry, and social ideals. The application of his ideas by his sister, Emma, and her husband, John E. Clough, in India, internationalized the Social Gospel in American Baptist overseas missions. But in other ways, Rauschenbusch created a permanent fissure within his denomination. During and after his life, the debate over individual or social salvation raged. Was he a true American evangelical or the transitioning leader of a "new theology"? Baptist evangelicals were admonished by their confessions and validation agencies not to venture close to Social Gospelism. Liberal Baptist thinkers saw the Social Gospel as the sole, positive, enduring thrust of the program that came unglued in the post-World War I era.

The rediscovery of Rauschenbusch by evangelicals and social activists has redoubled Walter's Baptist reputation at both extremes. Following the ultimate North American Baptist icon, the evangelist Billy Graham, most evangelicals now acknowledge something called the "whole gospel." Many now speak of the "social implications of the Gospel" as they wrestle with human rights, race, gender, and the issues raised by alternative lifestyles, etc. At the other end of the perspective, there is a resurgence of progressive thinking and activism among Baptists in North America energized by Rauschenbusch's exemplification of the role of a prophet. Both Cooperative Baptist Fellowship leaders and those associated with the Alliance of Baptists have lionized Rauschenbusch.

Identification of the "Black Social Gospel" attests to the ongoing influence of Rauschenbusch among liberal and social-activist thinkers.[66] Few characters have occupied the space in the entirety of Baptist life that Walter Rauschenbusch has enjoyed—after a century. Reinhold Niebuhr's assessment remains valid: "Rauschenbusch is the real founder of social Christianity in this country, and its most brilliant and generally satisfying exponent."[67] Canadian Baptists would agree as well.

[66] See the essays above by Dorrien, Trimiew, and Bond, especially emphasizing the work of Adam Clayton Powell, Sr. and Jr., J. M. Ellison, Richard McKinney, J. Pius Barbour, Mordecai Johnson, Nannie Helen Burroughs, Benjamin Mays, Samuel Proctor, and, of course, Martin Luther King Jr.

[67] Quoted in Robert D. Cross's "Introduction to the Torchbook Edition" in *Christianity and the Social Crisis* (New York: Harper Torchbooks, 1964), xx.

About the Authors

William H. Brackney is the Millard R. Cherry Distinguished Professor Emeritus at Acadia University, where he also directed the Acadia Centre for Baptist and Anabaptist Studies. More recently, he is the Pioneer MacDonald Professor of Baptist Theology and Ethics and director of the William Carey Centre for Excellence in Ministry at Carey Theological College in Vancouver, British Columbia. The author of more than fifty works, he has published widely on Walter Rauschenbusch. He is the general editor of *Walter Rauschenbusch: Published Works and Selected Writings, Three Volumes* (Mercer: 2018) and general editor of the *Baptists in Early North America Series* for Mercer University Press. Previously he was curator of the Rauschenbusch Family Papers at the Samuel Colgate Baptist Historical Library of the American Baptist Historical Society. In 2018, he was co-convener of "The Legacy of Walter Rauschenbusch," an international conference at Mercer University.

Heath Carter is associate professor of History at Valparaiso University, specializing in American Religious History. He is the author of *Union Made: Working People and the Rise of Social Christianity in Chicago* (2015), *Turning Points in the History of American Evangelicalism* (2017), and *Social Christians and the Fight to End American Inequality* (forthcoming). Presently, he is coeditor of the Library of Religious Biography Series for Eerdmans Publishing.

Wendy J. Deichman is professor of Church History and Theology at United Theological Seminary in Dayton, Ohio. Previously she taught at Ashland Theological Seminary and Colgate Rochester Crozer Divinity Schools. She is coeditor of *Gender and the Social Gospel* (2003). Currently, she is working on a biography of Josiah Strong.

Gary Dorrien teaches at Union Theological Seminary and Columbia University, where at Union he is the Reinhold Niebuhr Professor of Social Ethics. His many books include *Kantian Reason and Hegelian Spirit*, which won the Association of American Publishers' PROSE Award in 2013, *The New Abolition: W. E. B. Du Bois and the Black Social Gospel*, which won the Grawemeyer Award in 2017, and *Imagining Democratic Socialism: Political Theology, Marxism, and the Making of Social Democracy*, forthcoming in 2019 from Yale University Press.

Christopher Evans is professor of the History of Christianity at Boston University School of Theology. Previously he taught at Colgate Rochester Crozer Divinity Schools. He is the author of *The Kingdom Is Always but Coming: A Life of Walter Rauschenbusch* (2004) and *The Social Gospel in American Religion* (2017). He convened a national Social Gospel conference in 1999 and edited *The Social Gospel Today* (2001). He is currently working on a biography of Francis Willard.

Dominik Gautier is a lecturer in systematic theology at the Carl von Ossietzky University of Oldenburg, Germany. In 2011, he studied at Union Theological Seminary in New York. Currently he is pursuing a PhD in systematic theology. Both his research and teaching focus on the intersection of identity, race, and theological ethics in the work of Reinhold Niebuhr.

David P. Gushee is Distinguished University Professor of Christian Ethics and director of the Center for Religion and Public Life at Mercer University. He is author of *Righteous Gentiles of the Holocaust* (2003), *Kingdom Ethics* (2012), *Changing Our Mind* (2015), and *Moral Leadership for a Divided Age* (forthcoming), among numerous other titles. He is president of the American Academy of Religion and immediate past president of the Society of Christian Ethics. In 2018, he was co-convener of "The Legacy of Walter Rauschenbusch," an international conference at Mercer University.

Christina Littlefield is assistant professor of Religion and Journalism at Pepperdine University. She is the author of *Chosen Nations: Pursuit of the Kingdom of God and Its Influence on Democratic Values in Late Nineteenth-Century Britain and the United States* (2013).

Roger Prentice is university chaplain, retired, at Acadia University. He is the author of works on the military chaplaincy, the Social Gospel in Canada, and the volume on Wolfville Baptist Church in *Baptists in Early North America Series* (forthcoming). He has also published a series of popular works of fiction and directed various dramatic performances.

Paul B. Raushenbush is senior vice president and editor of "Voices of Auburn Seminary." Previously he was associate dean of Religious Life and the Chapel at Princeton University. He is an ordained American Baptist minister who has served the Riverside Church and Madison Avenue Baptist Church in New York City, and First Baptist Church, Seattle, Washington.

Andrea Strübind is professor of church history at the Institute of Protestant Theology and Religious Education in Carl von Ossietzky University of Oldenburg, Germany. She is a member of the German Ecumenical Study Committee, a Fellow of the Acadia Centre for Baptist and Anabaptist Studies, and executive editor of the international journal *Kirchliche Zeitgeschicte.*

Darryl Trimiew is visiting professor of Christian Ethics and interim director of the Black Church Studies Program at Candler School of Theology, Emory University. He is also director of the Disciples Divinity Center of the Christian College of Georgia. Previously he has taught at Brite Divinity School, Texas Christian University, Medgar Evers College of City University of New York, Colgate Rochester Crozer Divinity Schools (where he was holder of the John P. Crozer and Martin Luther King Professorships and director of Black Church Studies), and the Interdenominational Theological Center in Atlanta.

Chakravarthy Zadda is the associate regional minister of the American Baptist Churches of Metro Chicago and senior minister of First Baptist Church, Waukesha, Wisconsin. He has taught missiology at Northern Baptist Seminary and several Lutheran seminaries. He has served with the Baptist Peace Fellowship of North America and the Theologians Commission of the American Baptist Churches USA.

Index